THE TUTTLE TWINS
—— and the little ——
Pink House

CONNOR BOYACK

ILLUSTRATIONS BY ELIJAH STANFIELD

Libertas Press
2183 W Main Street, A102
Lehi, UT 84043

The Tuttle Twins and the Little Pink House

Edited by Chris Jones

ISBN-13 978-1-943521-40-1 (paperback)

10 9 8 7 6 5 4 3 2

For bulk orders, send inquires to info@libertasutah.org.

Other titles by the author:

Skip College: Launch Your Career Without
Debt, Distractions, or a Degree

Lessons from a Lemonade Stand: An Unconventional
Guide to Government

Feardom: How Politicians Exploit Your Emotions
and What You Can Do to Stop Them

The Tuttle Twins children's book series

Ethan lifted a spoonful of sludgy cereal to his mouth. He savored the slightly crunchy, just-starting-to-get-soggy goodness of his Admiral's Avalanche cereal and pretended that if he didn't open his eyes, what Mom had just said would float away and disappear. It would never have existed.

"Did you hear me?" Mom said. "Your grandmother called. She wants you and Emily to spend the Fourth of July holiday at her house."

Clearly it wasn't going to work, but Ethan kept his eyes closed all the same. "Mo wa oh," Ethan said.

"Don't talk with your mouth full," Emily said

Ethan swallowed. "I don't want to go," he said.

Mom dropped butter into a pan, and the sizzle filled the kitchen. "I knew what you said. One of the skills you have to have as a mother is understanding your children when they talk with their mouths full of food."

Since he couldn't change the future by keeping his eyes closed, perhaps his debate skills would do the trick. "Why do we have to go to Grandma's?" Ethan said. "I was going to light sparklers and shoot off bottle rockets with my friends."

"Partly *because* you were going to shoot off bottle rockets with your friends," Mom said, arching an eyebrow. "Actually, your grandmother is having kind of a hard time, and she is hoping that having the two of you around will allow her to get some things fixed up around the house."

"Terrific," Ethan said. "A working vacation. That's what every kid wants on the Fourth of July."

"Oh, settle down," Emily said, although the idea was making her somewhat testy herself. "You know she'll feed us a ton. You always love that."

"Food is, indeed, one of the best things in the world," Ethan said. "But so are bottle rockets. And I'm still taking them. At least I can shoot them off over the river."

"And don't forget the parade," Emily said. "That parade gives out more candy per float than any place we've ever been."

Ethan had forgotten about the candy thing, but he wasn't ready to give in. "I still think we could go for a day and maybe still come back for the Fourth of July fireworks here," he said.

"That won't work," Mom said. "In fact, we thought we'd take you up a bit early. The Fourth is on a Friday, so we're going to take you up the Tuesday before, drop you off, and head upstate."

"'We' being you and Dad?" Emily said.

"That's right," Mom said. "With the two of you out of the way, we can finally put our plans for world domination into effect."

"How long do you think it will take you to accomplish your evil designs?" Ethan said, picking up his bowl and carrying it to the sink. He swished water into it and racked it on the drying board.

"Ten days to two weeks," Mom said. She cracked a couple of eggs. Salt, pepper, and garlic followed them into the pan. She stirred and the smell was heavenly. "Things are fluid in the Sudan."

Ethan hugged her, a quick one as she stood at the stove. "You're nuts, Ma," he said.

"That's what teenagers are good for—keeping me humble."

Ethan laughed and headed outside to shoot some hoops.

The truth of it was—especially since he didn't have much choice—Ethan didn't really mind spending time at his grandmother's house. She wasn't the kind that nagged, and his twin sister Emily loved being there and hearing Grandma's stories of growing up. There was the river and the dock, swimming and fishing. And Grandma's cooking, that was something that *any* guy could get excited about. So the prospect of spending a Fourth of July weekend—or even a couple of weeks—at her house just on the Pennsylvania side of the border with West Virginia, didn't make him nearly as sad as he had made it sound. But sometimes a teenager's job is to make sure his parents really mean it when they tell him to do something.

The two weeks leading up to the holiday went by in a flash, and there they were in the back of the family car on the way to Grandma's house.

"We're lucky to be able to come and visit Grandma at this house," Mom said. "Who knows how long we'll be able to do that?"

"Grandma's going to live forever," Ethan said.

"Probably," Dad said. "But her house may not. There's been some trouble with the city and some developers who are interested in her land even though she doesn't want to sell it. There are complications. We don't know how long she'll be able to keep the old place."

"Hasn't Uncle Ben tried to help her?" Ethan said. That man could do anything.

"He has, but he's awfully busy these days. The price of fame. His media work is going so well he's off chasing stories around the country," Dad said. "We hope he'll be able to do something to help, if we can find out something important."

"Grandma's house is in such a great spot there by the river," Mom said. "I hope she'll always live there."

Yes, Ethan thought. The beautiful Monongahela, that river named after a tribe of Native Americans the locals had long since forgotten, and now just a big challenge for people to try to spell.

Ethan hoped the rope swing was still there, hanging from the wide old oak on the riverbank. He wasn't entirely sure that swimming in the Monongahela would be endorsed by the health department, but it was better than sweltering in the summer sun, wishing he had a pool to swim in. Grandma certainly didn't have the kind of house that would have a pool. It was almost the kind of house that didn't even have a bathtub.

Emily turned a little green in the seat next to him and rolled down the window to get some air.

It's a good thing I don't get carsick, Ethan thought. Having to ride in the backseat of a car going up, down, right, and left seemingly every few yards, made the road an absolute nightmare for anyone who got any kind of motion sickness. Which his sister Emily absolutely did. Ethan always spent the first few minutes of the trip feeling superior, and the next few minutes being disgusted, and all the rest of the time feeling miserable for her.

Every half hour to forty-five minutes, they would need to get out of the car for a few minutes to let Emily stretch her legs, or to vomit in the bushes, depending on the level of sickness. Long before they reached Grandma's house, Emily had thrown up everything that she had eaten in the past several months and vowed that she would never ride in another car again. Medicine just didn't seem to do any good. They had tried practically everything in the pharmacy.

"Some people are just lucky," Mom said.

"I'll take *my* kind of luck, any day," Ethan said.

Turn to page 131.

The four teens arranged to meet at Thusnelda's Burger Shack the following Monday morning. Xavier was already there when the twins walked in. He had a corner booth, and he was slumped over and leaning on the table. He didn't look up as the twins approached.

"I have to work later," he said, his voice muffled by his arm and shirtsleeve.

Emily slid into the booth on the right, and Ethan on the left.

"No Shannon?" Ethan said, halfway as if he hoped the answer would be no. Xavier sighed, but made no more response than that.

It was only about 11 o'clock in the morning, and the lunch rush had yet to begin. There was one couple wolfing down fries in the other corner of the restaurant, but other than that, they were alone.

"Things really didn't go well last week, did they?" Emily said.

"Depends," Xavier said, lifting his head and giving her a bright smile.

"On spreading the word about the referendum," she said, punching his arm.

Xavier rallied enough to push his head up off the table and slump backwards against the bench. "I guess you could say that," he said, his voice thick with sarcasm.

"So, honestly, how do you think this referendum is going to go tomorrow?" Emily said.

Xavier rubbed his face, as if trying to wake himself up. Maybe he was. "I think we're going to lose."

Ethan studied him for a moment. "Are you saying that because you actually think we will, or because it's Monday and you have to go to work in a little bit?"

"Probably a little bit of both. Understand guys, I'm not experienced at this kind of thing. I got involved because I love my town, but even if they bulldoze your grandmother's house, I'm still going to live here. Thusnelda's might even get more business. I just think it's horrible what they're doing, and especially how they're doing it. I don't have any way to read the mood of the town, really."

"Do people talk about it a lot when they come in here?" Emily said. She leaned in a little closer to him, offering sympathy.

"If they do, I don't hear them. The only thing I ever hear anybody talk about in this place is football. I take it the Steelers are supposed to be pretty good this year."

"Is there any chatter about a golf course?" Ethan said. It was worth asking. "There's those construction guys from the north of town. They come here a lot, don't they?"

Xavier squinted as if trying to remember. "Yeah, I see them in here sometimes. Is that what they're building, a golf course? That would make sense. They do talk about having a timetable, and being behind schedule, and how they really need to get moving on the other half of the project. I just figured they were talking about some kind of a housing subdivision or something."

Ethan and Emily exchanged a glance.

"It all makes a kind of sense," Ethan said. "It's all linked together. They need the zoning to change so they can bulldoze the houses and build the chemical factory along the river. Once they've done that, they will have a brand spanking new golf course in the north part of town for all of their people to play on."

Xavier looked like he was alive for the first time that morning. "How do you know this?"

At that moment the door jingled and Shannon came stalking in. There were bags under her eyes and tear stains on her cheek. She marched directly over to the corner booth and, without sitting down, said, "If anybody says one word about giving up, I'm out of here."

Xavier barked a cynical laugh. "That'd be a terrible loss, but I'm sure we would bear up." Shannon recoiled as if she had been struck.

Xavier waved his hands at her both palms out. "Sorry, sorry. I'm not feeling myself today. It was a crappy weekend, and I fear that tomorrow will be crappy too, but I don't mean it has anything to do with you. You've done everything you can do," he said.

Shannon looked a little bit placated. She tried to figure out which side of the table she wanted to sit on.

Eventually, to Ethan's surprise, she sat on his side, sliding along the bench until they were a foot or so apart. He could feel the heat coming off of her. He wondered if she had run all the way.

"Ethan was just about to tell us how this all fits together," Xavier said.

Shannon made a face. Or maybe it was just Ethan's imagination. "Go ahead, genius, tell us all about it."

Ethan decided it would be a terrible time to get offended, as they were close enough to completely breaking up the partnership anyway. "I'm no genius, but I have gotten lucky a couple of times, and, uhh... 'somebody' did a little low-level snooping the other night and brought to light some new information, which has helped me put a theory together."

Emily said, "If this is going to take a minute, I'm going to get onion rings."

This reminded everyone that they were in a fast food place, and that there were probably decent eats to be had. Everyone piled out of the booth and went up to the front, where Xavier rounded the counter and rang everyone in with his employee discount.

"It only gets you a free shake, but that's not nothing," he said, "Especially because if I make the shakes, they'll be the best you ever had."

Shannon puffed out her cheeks. "He's not kidding. They really will be the best we ever had, but I think we need him in the corner booth more than back here at the shake machine."

9

When the food was rung up and Ethan had grabbed the plastic card that told the server where to deliver it when it was ready, they all traipsed back to the table and sat back down in the same positions they were in before.

Ethan felt a little self-conscious but cleared his throat and began. "It all started when we were here the first time. My dad overheard some workers talking about building a golf course in the north part of town. That didn't really matter to us, because our grandmother lived along the river—" here Shannon snorted and rolled her eyes— "But we went out and took a look anyway. That land isn't empty up there. There are people living on it. There's a house back in the bushes, and a whole lot of people nearby, like some kind of village living in RVs. It's not a case of bulldozing a bunch of scrub land and putting something green and beautiful on it. It's going to affect people's lives over there."

"Everything they're going to do is going to affect people's lives," Shannon said. The heat had gone out of her, and she was now back to just being depressed.

"I understand that," Ethan said. When Shannon looked sceptical, he said, "No, I really do. It's not just my grandmother, it's the whole character of the town. There are four other houses on that street they'll have to bulldoze, and they're all lived in by people who have been in this town a long time. Building that factory will change a lot more than those people's lives. It will change the whole town, and knocking down the wilderness at the north end of town will do it just as much." The food arrived, a kid named Pablito bringing it on two huge trays that he balanced expertly.

For a moment, everyone was busy arranging sauces and unwrapping their food. Once they were settled, Ethan went on. "At first, I thought the golf course and the chemical factory had nothing to do with each other. But then I got to thinking, what if they did? What if the two things were connected?"

"Connected how?" Shannon said through a mouthful of fries.

Emily dunked her onion rings in ketchup and made smacking noises with her lips. "These are awesome," she said. "We didn't know how connected, but we figured if anybody did know, it would be the people at city hall."

"That's what I thought," Shannon said, "I was going to break into city hall last night."

Xavier goggled at Shannon. "You were really going to break into city hall?" He pitched his voice very low so that it wouldn't carry beyond a couple of feet.

"It was just an idea," she said.

"It's a terrible idea," Xavier said.

Shannon frowned but then said, "I didn't do it."

"Anyway," Ethan said, "breaking into city hall would certainly have been a bridge too far, but there is another place to find information that would help us put the pieces together. So, last night our Uncle Brock helped us out... on the river."

Xavier took a massive bite of his burger and was barely able to say the word, "River?" Actually, Ethan wasn't entirely sure what he said, his voice was so muffled by bits of burger and bun. But he figured that must have been it.

"Yeah, the river. Our Uncle Brock, he's a researcher, and he's looking for the monster they call the Monongy on the river. He has all sorts of interesting equipment that you can use for surveillance. And he captured recordings of a conversation at Jaxton Chemical."

Shannon let a touch of a smile onto her face. "Really? You won't break into city hall, but you're okay with using space age equipment to spy on Jaxton Chemical?"

He thought she was actually kind of pleased, and a little bit impressed. All of a sudden, he wanted to fan that into a flame. "Yeah. He used his special observation gear to eavesdrop, and look in some of the office windows."

This time it was Xavier's turn to look impressed. Apparently city hall was a problem, but no one liked Jaxton Chemical enough to even care whether laws were being broken. "That's very James Bond. I like it," he said, sending a wink in Emily's direction.

She blushed, covering it up with a bite of her fish sandwich.

"*Anyway*," Ethan said, a little testily. "There really wasn't much said that was recorded that made any difference. All they were doing was talking about things that seemed like they didn't have any importance, stuff like golf games and recreational activities, things like that. But from what was said, there's no doubt the people pushing for the building of the golf course are the same people who were pushing for building the chemical factory."

"That does fit together," Xavier said. He punctuated his sentence by stabbing a fry in Ethan's direction. "But I don't see how that helps us much. The referendum is tomorrow. Can anybody at this table tell whether it's going to pass or not?"

Everyone shook their head. "If I asked you to bet, which way would you bet?"

Shannon said, "I would bet yes. We lose."

Emily said, "I'm afraid of yes."

Then Ethan said, "If I asked you to tell me whether it would be close or not, what would you say?"

Shannon thought for a moment. "I think it's going to be very close," she said. "It's even possible, I guess, that we could win. But I couldn't bet on it. I think there's too many people who work for the city, and too many people who worked for the chemical corporation, and they both seem to want this to happen. I think they'll overwhelm us."

"How many people voted in the last election like this?" Emily said to Xavier.

"About 1100," he said. "That's not very many, but of that 1100, probably half of them, maybe a little less, work for or have friends or family that work for either the government or the corporation."

"And even so, we all think this referendum is going to be pretty close. Most of the town seems like they are against it, except for the parts that worked for the companies that will benefit," Ethan said. "That's what I was counting on. If it's going to be close, I think I know what might tip the balance in our favor. It wouldn't have mattered if the two things hadn't been connected. But I think they are. And I think that gives us an advantage we didn't know we had."

"Like?" Xavier said, spooning up some shake.

"I think I know where we can maybe get another hundred votes."

Shannon stopped, her spoon halfway to her mouth. "A *hundred* votes?" she said. "That's an awful lot."

"It might not be a hundred," he said, a little sheepishly. "It might only be sixty or seventy. But I'm pretty sure we can get those sixty or seventy, if the law really says that people can register to vote the same day that they cast a vote."

"That's what the law says," Xavier said. "That's why signing people up at the park would have been a great idea—those people's votes count."

Emily whacked her hand on the table. "I get it," she said. "You really are a genius."

Ethan looked a little embarrassed, but he was glad to have somebody call him a genius in front of Shannon. He explained. "Remember I told you about the area they're going to bulldoze for the golf course? Well, one day when we were kicking around with nothing to do, we did some investigating. There's a whole group of people living back there. I didn't count or anything, but it sounded like there were a lot. I guarantee you none of them are going to vote, because I think they hardly ever come out of that area at all. But if they knew that their secluded camp was going to disappear because some people wanted to build a golf course on it, and that those people might back off the golf course if they couldn't build their factory, they would come out in droves and all of them would vote against the referendum."

Shannon finished her bite of shake and set her spoon carefully down on the table, as if she were afraid to disturb the flow. "You're telling me you know where we can get seventy votes against the referendum tomorrow?" She turned those blue eyes on Ethan as if to make absolutely sure there was no joke and no kidding around.

He stared right back. "I can't guarantee it, but I really think those people will vote no. They just have to be told that unless they do, they could lose their families' camp."

Shannon crumpled up the remains of her burger and started shoveling empty containers and wrappers onto the tray. She stood up and grabbed her shake. "I can eat this on the way." There was a gleam in her eye. "You pull this off," she said to Ethan, "And I'm going to totally revise my opinion of you as a selfish, stuck up, out-of-town jerk who just happens to have the most adorable face in town."

Ethan shoveled what seemed like half his shake into his mouth at once. He swallowed, and said, "Which part of that will you be revising?"

Turn to page 460.

Every library in the world, from the modern glass-and-steel ones to the ancient columnar temples, has a vibe you can feel when you walk past it, a vibe that says "I have all the stories in the world inside me."

This library was neither an ancient temple nor a modern marvel. If it had been either, Ethan could have hardly resisted going there the very first minute he was in town. Rather, it was a red brick, flat-topped, single-story building with dingy casement windows and a plain glass front door that swung inconveniently to block the wheelchair ramp.

Emily tugged it open and saw it cut off the ramp. "That's bad design," she said. "It must be terribly inconvenient for the handicapped patrons."

"Are there any of those in this town?" Ethan said.

"That's beside the point," Emily sniffed. "There could be. And if there were, they'd have to wheel themselves all the way over to the other side of the porch and then get the door open. It's inconsiderate."

The open door let a waft of air roll out to greet them like an unfurling scroll. Whatever the exterior plainness of the building, there was no mistaking the intoxicating smell of books on the air.

Ethan inhaled, his eyes closed. "Aaaaah," he said. "That's the smell of home."

Emily snorted and let the door close in his face. But the truth was, she loved the smell, too.

Inside, dim fluorescents illuminated stacks of books, adult to the right, children's to the left, with a bank of computers pulsing softly like an electric fence. Directly ahead sat the information desk, and behind it was no one at all.

"Welcoming," Ethan said, scooching through the door and coming to a stop next to his sister.

"Oh, come on," Emily said, dragging him by the wrist. "You don't need anyone to show you where stuff is in the library."

"We could just do this on the Internet," Ethan said, dodging a stray book cart.

"You really think the town paper is web-indexed?"

"No, but I also don't think the town paper is likely to have printed any deep dark secrets. Places like this keep a very tight rein on their media outlets."

Emily smiled an indulgent smile at him. "Probably not. But what are the chances they don't *know* any deep dark secrets? And where are we going to find the name and address of the paper? Right here," she said, sweeping her hand over the rack of newspapers, local and national, hung on old-fashioned wooden poles, like laundry laid out to dry.

The *Au Courant* had its own rack with six months of back issues, all easily accessible. "It's a weekly," Ethan said, comparing dates.

"That reduces the number we have to comb through," Emily said, plucking half a dozen papers from the stack. "You start at the beginning of this year, and I'll start from the present and work backward. Flag anything about Jaxton Chemical, and we'll copy it."

Emily carried a small pile over to an empty table. There weren't many people around, just a couple of older ladies tucked back into corners, their noses deep between the covers of novels. It was so quiet she could hear the clock ticking—not a big clock either, just one of those cheap MegaMart versions with the AA battery in the back.

As she suspected, the name of the editor-in-chief was on page two, down at the bottom, tucked into a corner between a short article about the macrame club and an ad for a fireworks stand—a Penelope Burns, lived over on Klickitat Street. Emily didn't know where that was, but she was pretty sure there was a map of town around here someplace. Come to think of it, that might be a good thing to get hold of. Next assignment.

The paper didn't list a website, but that didn't necessarily mean there wasn't one. She'd have Ethan look for it when he got bored, which he would.

The paper laid the town bare, that was for sure, as long as the town consisted mainly of bake sales and gardening. There were hard-hitting exposes on the Japanese beetle invasion, on the kinds of snakes that dominated the Monongahela banks, and how much money was being raised for the local Girl Scout troop through a combination of cookies and Mrs. Walsh's pastries. Emily learned that the school—a combination of elementary and junior high, it appeared—had recently repaved its playground, which some parents weren't terribly happy about (they wanted an upgrade to the jungle-gym equipment instead, but "the budget simply couldn't be found for that").

She learned that the city council was going to hold a special meeting next week to consider "critical town business." She learned that a group of feral cats—the editor called this a "pounce," which was about the cutest collective noun Emily had ever heard of—had taken up residence in the woods south of town. And tucked in the back of the paper, page 8 right at the bottom, were two obscure paragraphs about Jaxton Chemical's plans for a new factory "in the area." According to Gary Aspindall, whoever that was, the factory "would bring several dozen jobs to the area, the first economic expansion in the southwestern Pipaluk County region in several years."

That ended the most recent edition of the paper. Emily folded it carefully and put it to one side for copying.

On to the next, one week before—June 21. Much of the same kind of thing. The town was going crazy for a new kind of candy, said the owners of the Main Street Candy Company; the local police were asking residents to be on the lookout for small predators: foxes, stoats, and the like; the school welcomed its new principal for the upcoming school year. Not a word in the entire edition about Jaxton Chemical or any zoning issues. Each edition of the paper had a report on the city council, though, and that was helpful. Ms. Burns—she appeared to write the majority of the paper's articles—did a fair job of keeping minutes, though there wasn't any way to know whether she was getting it all. If she was, the town was almighty dull, that was for sure. Discussion about whether or not to place a stop sign on Oneonta Drive where it crossed Clay Street, for instance. Nothing about Jaxton, though.

Across the table, Ethan heaved a mighty sigh and slapped a paper down. "This is going to take forever."

"You're a Tuttle. All Tuttles are sworn eternally to the quest of preserving Grandma's home."

"Eternity is long and filled with things I don't want to do."

"Yes. Almost certainly."

He picked up a paper, as if dredging a swamp and coming up with a rotting carcass. Emily smiled. "Never mind. I'll do this. Why don't you go check the Internet over there, and if you can't come up with anything interesting, find us a quality paper map of the town."

Like a prisoner released from jail, Ethan bolted for the bank of computers. Emily turned back and picked up the next paper. Mid-June.

The midsummer water quality survey announced that the Monongahela was filthy. *Shocking*, Emily thought. Hank Barlow struggled to keep some unknown predator from picking off his chickens. The city council wrapped up its final meeting before taking the summer off.

Wait.

The problem was, Emily felt like she was reading the story of the town on rewind, getting the end of the story before the beginning. She wasn't following the story as well as she might have. But wasn't there something before this—or rather, *after* this—about the city council having decided to hold another meeting?

Yes. There it was. Two weeks after deciding the summer doldrums could do without them, the city council reversed itself and called a special session for the day after election day.

Emily sat with the paper open in front of her and thought about what that could mean.

A moment later Ethan came jogging over. "I found out that the city paper has a website," he said.

"Good," Emily said.

"Not good," Ethan said. "The website is just a couple pages about how to subscribe. It doesn't have a digital copy of the paper."

"Crud. I'll have to keep at this, then."

"I did find a map, though. I printed it off the Internet." He handed her a fully-printed piece of paper on which the whole town—what there was of it—was laid out in an approximate grid, like a photograph taken from space, which is what it was.

"We need one that has the names of all the streets on it. And then it would be good to have one zoomed out a little so we can see the forests to the north and south and where the chemical company is located now."

"Back in a second," Ethan said, and turned to go, then stopped. "You making any progress?"

"I think I might be," Emily said. "I won't know until I dig a little more."

"This might take me a minute. How long for you?"

Emily thought a second. "I think I need some help. There are too many things I don't understand because we don't live here. I think I need to visit Ms. Burns."

Turn to page 487.

The humiliation of it was worse than anything else.

Long before they had actually been brought over to the police station, booked at the desk, had their pictures taken, their belongings removed, and been deposited in one of the two tiny cells the little jail kept for the occasional drunk or a shoplifter, Ethan could imagine the look on his grandmother's face as she arrived at the jail to bail them out.

He had imagined that look sometimes in connection with his Uncle Brock. He never thought he would see that look on her face as she stared at him. But it was coming. He knew it was, and there was nothing he could do about it. The intense, almost unbearable stupidity of the whole operation was obvious to him now. He lay face down on the floor of the mayor's office, listening to the night-watchman radioing for backup to take in three criminals for breaking into the city council offices.

Next to him, Shannon's back rose and fell, sometimes accompanied by a little jerk, which he knew meant she was crying. He felt like crying himself, but all that happened was his eyes burned.

Tears would not come.

Uncle Brock, on the other hand, once he got over the pain of the caster underneath his back, began regaling the policeman with an unending stream of profanities.

Apparently, they knew each other. Several times, the policemen made reference to times when they had been like this before. Brock had taken some of his frustrations out when the policeman tried to handcuff him. Brock rolled over and kicked him in the shin.

The cop responded by pulling a stick out of his belt and whacking Brock in the back of the knee with it. Brock screamed but didn't seem to learn his lesson, because when the cop went to put the handcuffs on him again, he did a similar thing and received a similar whack. Ethan resolved to go quietly when it was his turn.

He had broken the law. He was a criminal.

It got worse. The cop only had two sets of handcuffs. Ethan made sure he got the second one, so that Shannon wouldn't have to suffer the indignity of it. But all of them were frog marched out the front door, around the back of the building, and back up the front stairs of the police station. By then, two other cops had shown up, one of them in plain clothes, and together the three officers went about the process of booking them into the jail.

They confiscated his thumb drive, Brock's lockpick set, and Shannon's backpack.

"What do you think you found here?" one of the cops said.

"Evidence to incriminate the city in a bribery scandal that would make your hair curl," Brock said.

Ethan didn't think that would be helpful, and as it turned out, he was right.

One policeman immediately dropped the thumb drive to the tile floor and put his boot on it.

With a crunch, all that evidence disappeared. Shannon's backpack, no doubt, would suffer a similar fate. There went all the evidence.

Ethan was quite confident that by the middle of the next morning, all existing copies of the evidence they had found would disappear. He could still tell his story, of course, but the story would now be coming from a criminal, and no one would believe it. Ethan knew he wouldn't believe it himself, if he was told.

When they had booked Uncle Brock, they found a small pouch in his pocket, in which were a few pills, some kind of prescription drugs, it appeared.

"Ho, ho, ho," one of them and said, "what have we here? Back to our old habits, Brock?"

Brock scowled and, for once, didn't say anything.

Bail was rather light, Ethan thought, considering that they had broken into the major city building in town. A few hundred dollars was sufficient, and Grandma ponied it up without a whimper, but with a tired, defeated look that was worse than the jail cell. Emily had come down with her, as well, and stood there with wide, sad eyes.

The sun had not even begun to light up the eastern sky when they reached home, and without any conversation whatsoever, they went to bed. Ethan, lying down, staring at the ceiling, heard Emily trying desperately to find a way to get back to sleep. Ethan thought he might not sleep again for days.

Finally, Emily said, "Tell me that at least you found something."

"That's the worst of it. We found something, all right. We found evidence that the city is accepting bribes from the chemical company to pay off the people that live here on this street so that they will leave town and the city can take the land and give it to the chemical company so they can build their factory."

"You know they took these bribes?"

Ethan thought about it. "Well, there was an email... It said...they were talking about it. Thinking about it. I'm sure they did it."

Emily made her saddest face yet. "You didn't find anything, did you? All that, and you got an email that they were *thinking about it*?"

"We also found something else, something about a golf course in the north part of town. Somehow Jaxton is mixed up in that as well. But we'll never know, because the evidence of it was in Shannon's backpack. Which is now gone."

All of a sudden, Ethan remembered that Shannon had still been lying there on her concrete slab when they had been bailed out. Her phone call had not gone as well, from what Ethan had heard.

"It doesn't matter," Emily said. "We've ruined any chance we had of winning the referendum. The 'evidence' you got wouldn't have been admissible in court, and now won't even be believed. And you have a court date."

"I always swore I wouldn't turn out like Uncle Brock. I promised Dad I would never do anything like this. When they find out, I think I'll die."

"That sounds like a very wise course of action," Emily said.

It was bad enough to have to go back for a meeting with the city's attorney. But the worst part was that Mom and Dad had to cut short their vacation to come back and sit in on it. When they arrived, they had very little to say. Ethan didn't want them to say anything, either, because realistically, what was there to talk about? What he had done was wrong and stupid. He knew it, and he knew that they knew it. They had obliged him by saying very little, mostly talking quietly with Grandma about what was likely to happen now that the referendum had passed.

The attorney agreed to move things along expeditiously, seeing that Ethan was from out of town and that he was a minor. The biggest difficulty was with Uncle Brock. He had not been allowed to come home with Ethan, this being a second offense on drug charges. Now they were meeting in one of the police station's conference rooms, and the city attorney went over their options.

Dad made sure that his own attorney was present, although it was a long drive for him, and that made Ethan feel even worse.

"The trouble here," the city attorney said, "is that there are multiple charges being contemplated. There's the breaking and entering charge, but also a drug charge."

"But I didn't do any drugs," Ethan said. "They found them on Uncle Brock."

"That's very true," the attorney said, "But that doesn't actually make much difference. Because the drugs were involved in the incident, everyone who is a party to it is also under the same indictment. More, we're pretty confident that we can get a conviction for any or all three of you."

"My client is a minor," the Tuttles' attorney said.

"We are aware of that, but given that this was a serious crime on a city property we are strongly considering charging him as an adult."

"Whoa," Dad said. "That's not—"

"We're aware that that would cause certain complications. But there are additional things that you need to be aware of, as well. In addition to trying Ethan as an adult, we also have the situation that because your uncle was involved in the drug trade and living at the house, the house is therefore involved in the illegal trafficking of drugs and is subject to seizure under civil asset forfeiture because of the drug crimes."

The Tuttles leapt to their feet. "What?" Dad said. "You can't seize that house. The owner of that house has done nothing wrong."

Ethan was similarly incensed. "That's crazy," he said. "My grandmother has nothing to do with any of this."

The city attorney was unmoved. The Tuttles' attorney also remained in his seat, as if he knew it was futile.

Unperturbed, the city attorney went on. "I'm afraid that's how things work. If we have a suspicion that any property at all was used in the commission of a crime involving drugs, we can seize it in the name of the state."

The Tuttles looked over at their attorney, who motioned for them to sit down. "I'm afraid he is right," their attorney said. "There are a number of cases like this where police suspect certain assets were involved in the drug trade, and in order to prevent criminals from being able to keep the proceeds of their crimes in assets rather than in cash, the police are allowed to seize any property that they think might have been involved."

"Can they actually take my grandmother's house?" Ethan said.

"I'm afraid they can. They could take a lot more than that, if they wanted to."

The Tuttles, ashen-faced, sank slowly into their seats. This nightmare just got worse and worse. The city attorney shuffled some papers, stacked them neatly, and ran a manicured fingernail over the front cover of the folder.

"However," he said, "there are certain things that don't necessarily have to be done in this case. There are, ah, certain concessions we are prepared to make, depending on how cooperative you are."

Ethan got a wary look in his eye and saw that his father did the same.

"Go on," Ethan's father said.

"The state is perfectly within its rights in charging Ethan with breaking and entering as an adult. I'm sure you know, that's a severe, serious crime and that he could be facing as much as seven to ten years in jail." This came as no surprise. "I'm sure you are also aware, that if the police were to seize your grandmother's house," he said, speaking to Ethan, "that she would be entitled to no compensation whatever."

"But she didn't do anything wrong," Ethan said.

"She harbored a drug criminal. That's enough. She would receive no compensation," he repeated. "We are perfectly within our rights to do these things. But they involve certain complications that we would rather avoid. Therefore, I'm prepared to offer on behalf of the city, a lesser charge of trespassing, and to charge Ethan as a minor. I'm also prepared to waive the forfeiture of the house, instead allowing your grandmother to sell the house to the city for what I understand is a very generous offer."

Ethan's father closed his eyes and blew out a long breath. "This is really cute," he said. Even the Tuttles' attorney had to shake his head.

Ethan tried to follow what was happening. "So," he said, "What's the jail time for trespassing?"

"There's no jail time," the attorney said. "Customarily, for the first offense, a trespassing charge would only carry a sentence of community service that would not be entered on your record, because you would be charged as a minor. After your community service was completed, there would be no further consequences."

That sounded pretty good to Ethan, a lot better than spending time in prison in the adult population. Dad, however, remained still as a statue in his chair. "This is all part of a ploy to get hold of that house. This is extortion."

The attorney took visible offense. "That is absolutely not what we are talking about here," he said. "This is a very serious crime. Although we understand that your son and his grandmother are significantly less guilty, it nevertheless remains the case that they have broken the law, and there have to be consequences for this. We have to stamp out the drug trade up and down the river."

"It's a few pills," Dad said. "You have no evidence that it even came via the river. He could have bought them anywhere."

The attorney looked down at his folder. "That is irrelevant," he said. "The deal on the table is that if

Patricia Tuttle will sell her house to the city, removing that particular avenue for drug trafficking, and if Ethan Tuttle will plead guilty to trespassing, the city is prepared to take those avenues rather than going for harsher measures. We don't wish to cause any more hardship to the Tuttle family, but these are the things that have to be dealt with if civilization is to continue. I'll give you a couple of minutes to talk it over."

But there wasn't anything to talk over. The four of them sat in the antiseptic, white room and repeated back to each other the state's offer. It was generous, the attorney said. In their place, he would take it for certain. "You cannot risk having your son with a police record," he said. "He would be unlikely to win the case, and he would have adult charges on his record. At fifteen, that's not a situation you can entertain. Also, the offer from the city allows Patricia to at least recoup some money and get her personal effects from the house. If they seize it, she won't even get her pictures off the wall."

A few minutes later the city attorney returned and had the Tuttles sign several documents. "That should wrap things up," he said. "Thank you for your cooperation. Ethan is free to go. We will naturally have some more paperwork to do with Mrs. Tuttle, but as far as we are concerned, our business is concluded."

He stood, a signal that the meeting was over. The Tuttles and their attorney exited the building. Ethan was surprised to find the sun shining and the town still decked in Independence Day finery. To him, the whole world was gray.

They spent the final day of their vacation at the little pink house. Mom and Dad insisted on gardening, mowing, and painting the places that were peeling. Emily saw no sense in it.

"They're taking the house," she said, bitterly. "Why do we care if the porch boards are nailed down tight? Let them deal with it."

Mom kept right on nailing. "That's not who we are," she said. "When people lost their houses in the Great Depression, most of them made sure they were tidy, swept and clean, before they got in their cars and headed west. We can do no less."

Emily wanted to go inside and draw nasty pictures on the walls, but thought it was probably not a good idea to say so.

Grandma said she'd get some neighbors to help her pack, and maybe Mom and Dad could come back out for the last couple of days or so. The city said it would probably not be before the end of July that they would be taking possession, so they had some time. Grandma did not suggest that the twins come back and help, and Ethan totally understood why. He'd tried to help. He'd ended up destroying any chance they had to save the house.

Mom and Dad still didn't talk to him very much about it. Ethan dreaded the day they would.

Grandma kissed them all goodbye, even Ethan. When she came to him, she hugged him tightly, and held his face between her hands, searching his eyes. "I forgive you," she said.

"Don't... don't do that, Grandma," Ethan said, tears burning behind his eyes.

"You meant well. It will all come right," she said.

But it wouldn't. Ethan watched out the back window as they drove away. Grandma waved cheerfully enough for a long while, but just before the car got out of sight, he saw her slump against the post of her porch, her shoulders shaking. He knew she was weeping.

He wished he could join her.

THE END

When they reached the city hall, the illusion of the sleepy town exploded into fragments.

People milled about on the street, drifting their way toward the town center, and there was a mighty noise, as if dozens of voices were chanting something.

"Remind you of anything?" Emily said.

Ethan grinned. "It sure does," he said. "It sounds a lot like the protest we engineered for the taco truck fiasco."

"It's not taco trucks this time, but I bet it's something similar," Emily said.

When they reached the main square there were indeed a couple of hundred people, waving signs and marching back and forth between city hall and the library. The signs said things like "no chemicals in our backyard" and "our houses, not your factory."

"They sure seem to be angry about something," Ethan said. "This is more than just being annoyed that a factory wants to get built. This has to be something to do with how the land is being acquired."

A moment later, Emily saw her chance. "I know how to get some answers," she said. She took off into the crowd. Ethan craned his neck, trying to see over the waving signs and heads of the people. A moment later, Emily returned, dragging by the hand the young man from the malt shop. "Xavier here appears to be one of the ringleaders," she said. "Can you tell us what the issue is here?"

Xavier said, "I'm *dying* to tell you. But let's get inside for a second so I don't have to yell."

He held open the library door, accompanying it with a sweeping bow. The twins exchanged a glance and went through ahead of him. He let the door shut and led the twins over to a small alcove where a copy machine sat humming, out of the way of the front door.

"Okay," he said. "That's better. We're protesting because the chemical company is coercing the city council into changing the zoning so they can build a factory in a residential area."

"Zoning again, I know about that, where the city uses specific restrictions in an effort to control what gets built where," Emily said.

Xavier shook his head sadly. "I used to think it was a good thing, the kind of thing that would protect our families and keep our town from being destroyed. But the truth is, zoning is a weapon that can be used for good or bad. If the city council likes what the people like, then the zoning works to protect the people. If not, it works to protect someone else, in this case Jaxton Chemical Corporation."

"Down by the river," Ethan said, "I'll bet the zoning says that you can only build a certain kind of house."

"That's right," Xavier said. "Up until fairly recently, the only thing you could build by the river was a house like your grandmother's. Now, though, the city council has decided to amend the general plan to allow an industrial building to be built there."

Emily said, "Something as important as this should be a referendum."

"Wow, you guys really do know your political stuff. Yes, a referendum would be better. And in fact, we have a referendum—it's on the ballot for next week. But that's not likely to make much difference either, unless we are able to raise some significant awareness."

It appeared that he was about to go on, but just at that moment, the front door of the library opened and a girl about their age poked her head in.

"I don't want to break up your confab here," she said, "But the protest outside is getting kind of ugly. I think you might want to be there."

"Thanks, Shannon," he said. "You sure you won't get in trouble for being outside when you're on the clock?"

Shannon snorted. "Look around. See anyone here? All the action is outside." She looked askance at Ethan and Emily, as if she was trying to determine whether or not she could trust them. "Who are they?" she said.

"This is Emily," he said, indicating to his right. He started to introduce Ethan, then had to stop. "I'm sorry, I don't think I ever asked you what your name was."

Ethan stood up very straight. "My name is Ethan Tuttle," he said, extending his hand to the girl in the doorway. She had very long auburn hair and crystal blue eyes. Her head was at least even with Ethan's, and she might even have been an inch taller.

She took his hand limply, gave it one shake, and let go. "Charmed, I'm sure." She turned back to Xavier. "Anyway, you should probably get out there. I'm not off for another half an hour to an hour, depending on how many books have to be put back on the shelves."

She hurried off toward the reference desk.

"She's one of the ones that got me involved in this," Xavier said. "Shannon's family has lived in town for a long time. She takes this stuff pretty personally."

Ethan said, "My family has lived in this town for a long time, too. I take this stuff pretty personally as well. Her name is Shannon, you said?" His eyes followed her back to her post.

"She says it's Irish," Xavier said.

"I think it's awesome," Ethan said. Behind the reference desk, an auburn head bobbed up and down behind the stacks of encyclopedias.

Outside, the sun had practically set. Thin rays still shot through the scattered clouds in the west, down over the mountains, and into the central square, but for the most part, it was bathed in gloom except for the lights around the exterior, which were just coming on. In the center, the group of protesters were shouting rather more stridently than before and hurling invectives at a couple of uniformed policemen. Someone was standing in front of the city hall, hands outstretched and lifted, as if trying to calm the crowd down.

Xavier charged directly into the fray, leaving the twins standing on the porch of the library.

Emily kept her gaze on the crowd and said, "We don't really know anything about this. I mean, they could be right, or this could just be another example of people peacefully trying to make sure that they get theirs, even though the market is telling them to do something else."

"Does that look like peaceful protest to you?" Ethan said. His eyes were also locked on the melee in the middle of the square. It had not come to blows yet, just a bunch of people shouting in each other's faces, but it looked like it could boil over at any moment.

"Is this something we really ought to get involved in?" Emily said.

If you think they should get involved, turn to page 491.

If you think they should go home to Grandma's, turn to page 158.

Ethan raced Emily down the block and beat her by a mile. Of course, he had taken off before he'd even said go, so the head start might have been the reason. Still, it's always nice to beat your sister.

From behind him, Emily's voice floated out. "Where are we going? What is this thing you're going to look for?"

Ethan slowed down and let her catch up. It was fun to beat her, but it was awfully hard to have a conversation from half a block away.

"I'm going to look at the north part of town. That's where the guys said the golf course was going to be built. Or at least," Ethan said, thinking about it, "maybe they didn't say that, maybe that's just the only place anybody can think of that it might be."

The road eventually swung east and connected to Main Street at about the point it became State Route 41. Nothing remarkable here. It must be farther on.

A hundred yards farther along, a kind of wide path led off to the left, through some nasty thorn bushes.

"I bet that's where we want to go," Ethan said. "But we can't take our bikes; those briars will go right through the tires."

They parked their bikes in some gentler-looking bushes. Then they walked down the road—really more of a track made up of two ruts with a grassy line between them, all the way back as far as they could see.

It was a kind of a forest, but it consisted mostly of saplings and not the enormous, spreading oaks of most of the local forests. Dogwoods sprouted in and around the bracken, making it nearly a kind of tunnel. But there was no real structure, no old growth that would have made it a beast to knock down and break up for firewood.

Ethan found the remains of a toaster. He prodded it with a stick, as if it might come alive. He stood up and wiped his hands on his jeans. Looking around, he had the sense that they were being watched—not that he was in danger, or that anyone or anything out there might mean them harm, but simply that someone might be looking at them, measuring their progress, and deciding what sort of action to take. Looking at the bracken and underbrush, Ethan was certain that a couple of bulldozers could wipe out the entire area in just a few days.

"If they're going to build a golf course, this looks like a pretty good area to start doing it. The hills aren't too bad. The terrain is not very steep. And these bushes," he said, giving one of them a whack with his stick, "these you could knock over with a couple of machines in no time at all."

And then they heard it—the hum of large machines. Far off to the left, so far they couldn't see them, some large engines were doing work. Ethan shot Emily a glance. "You want to try working our way that direction?"

"There's a path here," she said, moving down it.

It took a bit of careful negotiating, but they made it far enough down the path to be able to see the bright yellow sides of large earthmoving equipment. "Bingo," Emily said.

They weren't far along with the work, still scratching their way through the initial clearing, but there were enough dozers there for a major project. "That's all I need to know," Ethan said. "Let's get back before someone sees us."

They returned to the initial road and kept going in the direction they'd been moving.

"Come on," Emily said, "I think I can hear the river."

They entered a stand of elm trees, standing almost like the walls of a castle, and the moment they did, it was like entering another place and time. A moment before they had been on a single-lane rutted road with grass growing down the middle. The next moment, the grass had fallen away, and the road was level and well-packed. On either side of them, the woods disappeared, and ahead of them was a clearing and a lawn. It was scraggly and weed-strewn, but obviously lawn, not meadow.

Down a little way, another fifty yards or so, stood a house. Not a small cottage, either, but an actual house, with a porch that wrapped around to the north and windows winking out of gables on the second floor. It looked like a scene out of a Brothers Grimm fairy tale. If an old woman in a tall pointed black hat had come out the front door and begun sweeping the porch, Ethan wouldn't have been even a little bit surprised.

"What on earth? Emily said.

"I have no idea," Ethan said, "But I'm not getting in her oven, no matter what she tells me."

Emily would have laughed, but the strangeness of it made laughing difficult.

It was only as they got closer that they could see the house was not in very good repair. From a distance, the white and gray siding and fine red trim had looked rustic, but well maintained. In the moving, dappling sunlight, it had looked like any other house in town. But as they approached, they could see the paint was

peeling. The porch sagged a little bit on one side. There were cobwebs in one corner and the remains of some kind of animal decomposing on the porch in the extreme north corner, almost like a sentinel that had stood its post too long.

The road, however, was fairly well maintained and led directly to the front door. They stopped about ten yards from the front steps, not trusting that those steps would hold them if they decided to climb up and knock on the front door. Even so, Ethan was almost ready to do it, had even taken a step forward, when a voice from behind them said, "I wouldn't do that if I were you."

They whirled around and behind them stood a man, slightly shorter than they were, but extremely old, with great chasms of wrinkles running up and down his face. His floppy hat and stained overalls might have given them pause, but what really got their attention was the double-barreled shotgun pointed in their direction. Ethan's hands came up.

"There's no need for the gun," he said. "We're not dangerous." Emily shook her head but didn't trust herself to speak. The great open mouths of the barrels remained pointed firmly in their direction. At this distance either one of those barrels would cut them both in half. How had he managed to sneak up behind them? They hadn't been making a lot of noise, hadn't been talking. But there he was, as if he had sprung from the ground.

He spoke again. "That may be so, but I don't know it for a fact. I think it might be best if the two of you turned right around and walked back up the road, back out where you came from." He spoke with a thick bland accent, like somebody's parody of a southern Pennsylvania farmer. It was hard, at first, to even understand what he said.

From over the trees came the unmistakable sound of children playing. It sounded like a barbecue, and smelled like one, too. Somewhere close were a lot of people. This man seemed to be the one who stopped intruders from meeting them.

"We'd be only too happy to just turn around and go," Ethan said. "We didn't mean to trespass."

"Is this your house?" Emily said. She would never know what possessed her to ask that question.

The man's floppy hat swung from side to side. "Not my house, never will be. Them as used to live there have been gone awhile, as no doubt you can see from the state of the place."

"It doesn't look like a lot of people come here," Ethan said, "And if you'll let us by, we'll go on our way and never bother you again. "

"That's good," the man said. He pronounced 'good' with such long vowels it seemed to take him three seconds to say the word. "We've been left alone here for some time, and we aim to keep it that way. And if you ever decide to come back, I'd be singing a tune or making some kind of a racket such that folks with itchy trigger fingers don't think you're sneaking around. Ask for Zoltan."

The shotgun wavered a fraction, and then drifted downward. As soon as it was no longer pointed directly at them, the twins dropped their hands and began to walk very slowly back in the direction they had come. They twisted a little, making sure they kept sight of the old man as they did so.

Emily said, "We might leave this guy behind, but you can bet the city won't. If they really want this land for that golf course, there will be a lot of people in here bothering him in no time. Maybe we should tell him."

"The guy has a gun. You really think we ought to stick around for a chitchat?" Ethan said.

If you think they should stick around, turn to page 383.

If you think they should leave, turn to page 397.

"I take it you're some sort of Native American expert," Ethan said.

"Some sort," St. Lawrence said, rumbling in his chest, which Ethan thought probably meant a different kind of laughter. "I've done a fair amount of work on the subject, yes."

"That's just what we need," Ethan said.

St. Lawrence sat expectantly, motionless, waiting for them to go on. He didn't fidget, didn't seem to be trying to hurry them up or encourage them to speak more quickly. He seemed content to wait forever, until they came to the point, which, Ethan thought, might be a little tricky. How does one go about saying, "What we really want is for you to produce a bunch of Indian artifacts that we can claim came from my grandmother's property, so that we can use one branch of the government that's interested in preserving Native American relics against another one that wants to hand over a bunch of property to a chemical corporation"?

Ethan couldn't, off the top of his head, come up with any particular way of going about saying that. Or even circumlocuting it. This was going to be interesting. And for once, he was grateful that his partner seemed only too willing to take over the conversation.

Shannon took it up again. "What we want is for you to give us some Native American artifacts that we can bury on his grandmother's property in such a way that the authorities at the State of Pennsylvania will think that it is a Native American site and forbid any excavation or construction work to be done on it."

Ethan's mouth dropped all the way to his chest. Apparently, Shannon couldn't think of any other way to say it either, and in her own inimitable style, decided to just go ahead and say it.

Shannon slowly turned her head to look directly at Ethan's face. "You didn't really think I was going to come here and lie to this man, did you?" she said. "I could never lie to him. First off, he would see right through it. Second, once he did, he would never agree to help us."

Ethan tried to muster up the breath to say something sharp but he felt as if he had been punched in the solar plexus.

Once again, St. Lawrence's guffaw broke out and rolled across the lawn. "I take it Mr. Tuttle here does not have a relationship such as ours." Shrug. "That's not surprising. Practically no one does. But you must understand, Mr. Tuttle, this young lady and I have a relationship that goes back quite a ways. I've known her since before she could hold her bladder, and she has never had any particular reason to lie to me."

"That's not entirely true," Shannon said, clearly enjoying Ethan's continuing discomfort. "I've had many reasons to lie to him. He has both beaten them out of me and convinced me with his constricting logic that it would be smarter just to tell him the truth. Especially, that is, because on almost every one of my mad escapades, he has not only been interested in assisting me, but likely to join in.

"As I always say," St. Lawrence said, laying an affectionate glance on Shannon, "If you're going to do something stupid, before you do it, call me, and see if I want a cut." He cleared his throat a little, shifted in the sagging chair, which gave a groan as if it might at any moment collapse, and said, "This is, to be sure, an exceedingly stupid idea. I can tell that neither of you are experienced in Native American lore, nor are either of you particularly interested in actual history, archaeology, or anthropology. Hardly surprising for a young American teenager, but disappointing all the same. That said, the truth is, even were I disposed to help you, which in this instance I am decidedly not, I would not be able to. It is theoretically possible that you could deposit some artifacts from this area in such a way that it would convince the so-called experts at Pennsylvania State that you had indeed uncovered a previously unknown set of Native artifacts. However, when the fraud was discovered—and I assure you, the fraud would be discovered, sooner rather than later—you would make your cause far less supportable, not to mention getting yourselves into a world of hurt in the process.

"No, as sympathetic as I am to your cause, as much as I want to see your aims achieved, I cannot assist you in this particular bit of madness."

He saw the disappointment on their faces. "Can't you see how it would be?" St. Lawrence said. "I know most of the guys they have in the state office. They're pretty good. Not enterprising sorts, of course, but good. Professional. Lots of people are looking to get rich by capitalizing on finding cool Native American artifacts, and you wouldn't be the first one to try to pull the wool over their eyes. They're pretty vigilant about that kind of thing."

"Wouldn't that at least slow them down a little bit?" Ethan said. With the obviousness of the failure of this plan, the impending disaster with his grandmother's property was coming home to roost.

"No," St. Lawrence said, slowly shaking his head. "Understand, they don't have a whole lot of power unless they can mobilize the state government to back them. That's only going to happen if they're certain that what they're looking at is a truly important set of artifacts. Anything I have, of course, they already know about. Some of them will have helped me in that site across the street where we dug a few of them up. As far as I know, that site across the street is the only Native American village site in this part of the country. Oh, there might be some others, hidden here and there, but I doubt it. And they doubt it too. That would make them especially suspicious. No, I think there is practically nothing that you could do on that angle to even slow down the march of the chemical company."

At this, he turned his eyes on Shannon as well. "I'm sorry for you, too," he said. "It's a hard thing to watch this happen to this town. But understand, this kind of thing happens all the time, everywhere. It happens in most of the towns in the country, and it's happened almost everywhere in the nation. You're not special. The universe is not picking on you."

Shannon gave up sitting on her haunches and flopped down on her bottom on the grass. She sat cross-legged, underneath the gaze of St Lawrence, and put her head in her hands. "I don't care if it's not personal to the universe. It's personal to me."

It was personal to Ethan, too. His grandmother was one of those people who was an irreplaceable piece of his life. He didn't know what he would do if she moved off to a rest home someplace. He suddenly realized that coming to this town for the Fourth of July, or even for just a couple of weeks during the summer, was one of the things he most looked forward to every summer. No matter how much he complained, the truth was, he loved it. And now he had friends here, and coming here was even more important. That would all be gone. And in its place, there would be another chemical factory, an entirely unnecessary one, as far as he could tell.

Still. Although all of this flashed through his mind, he felt like it would be ungentlemanly to show it to this apparently very nice man who, although he had not been able to help, or even shown any inclination to help, at least had been kind and not told them they were stupid and sent for the cops. "Thank you anyway," Ethan said. "Shannon, I guess I better be getting home."

St. Lawrence stirred himself from his lawn chair. "Listen, as long as you've come this far, and done this much very creative thinking—I don't want you to think that I don't appreciate what kind of creative solution you've tried to invent here—I'd like to show you a couple of things that I have found in this local area."

He lifted the flap of the tent behind him, and beckoned for Ethan to go inside. Ethan was a bit dubious, and he was aware that Shannon had not stirred herself from her spot on the ground, but it did look like an extremely cool tent, and Ethan had been wanting to see inside it ever since he saw the poles jutting up above the roofline of the house. He nodded to St. Lawrence, crouched over, and floated his way through the door.

St. Lawrence, moving deftly for a man his size, pirouetted through the hole and let the flap drop behind him. The interior of the tent was about ten feet across, and the edges were lined with tables, on which were placed a number of artifacts: arrowheads, bits of pottery, lumps of charcoal carved into totemic images. St. Lawrence took a moment to handle each before letting Ethan pick it up, heft it, and take a close look at it. He explained where he had found each piece and what it meant. Ethan marveled. The man's knowledge was encyclopedic. If the guys at the state were anything like this good, there's no way he could fabricate anything that would even slow them down for a minute. All they would do is get annoyed and call for the police.

When he reached the final table, there were a number of small pots and a plastic bucket filled to overflowing with additional pieces of pottery. "We do a pretty good job of restoration here, as good as we can do, anyway, but the truth is, we've dug up so much stuff now, so many pieces of pottery, that we can't possibly put them all back together again. If you want, you can take a few of these home. Kind of as a memento of your trip, although I'm sure it hasn't turned out the way that you wanted."

It certainly hadn't, yet Ethan felt the kindness of the gesture, and took a few moments to run his hands through the bits of pottery in the plastic bucket. Toward the bottom, there was a wide piece about four inches long, and two inches wide, with an intricately-painted fish on it.

"Can I really have this?" Ethan said.

St. Lawrence chuckled a little. "Sure," he said. "Anything in the bucket. Here, take a couple more pieces as well." He handed Ethan a couple of additional pieces, about the same size, painted with lines that meant nothing to Ethan, but probably had some great mystic significance.

He handed Ethan a small plastic sack. Ethan placed the pieces of pottery in the sack, shook St. Lawrence's hand, and went back out the tent flap Shannon had disappeared. Ethan stopped for a moment, scanning the area to see if she was around somewhere.

"Don't mind her," St. Lawrence said. "She gets in moods and there's no getting her out of them. But she likes you. That's clear enough. She would never have invited you to come and meet me if she didn't think you were OK. That's a rare thing. She doesn't like people very much."

Ethan could well believe that. He thanked St. Lawrence again, and mounted his bicycle, heading back toward the waterfront. It seemed this was another dead end.

Turn to page 401.

The only thing that marred the perfection of the quiet street on which Grandma lived was the number of empty houses. Always before at this point in the middle of summer, nearly every house on the block was decked with flowers. Every tree would be budding or laden with fruit, and from every porch would fly bunting or an American flag. It was like walking into a small town from the 1940s, driving down Grandma's street.

But now, house after house had weedy front gardens, trees that were untended and unpruned, fruit falling on the ground. Emily saw a couple of scrawny cats dive behind a house as their car passed.

The quickest route to her brother's heart may have been Grandma's chocolate chip cookies, but the fastest route to Emily's heart was the beautiful view from Grandma's house across the river to the rolling hills beyond. Not every year, but most years, and as long as she could remember, her family had been coming here for a week or so on summer break, and to be able to spend two weeks here with her brother, just him and her and their grandmother, seemed like a dream come true.

Every night she could sit on the small dock at the edge of the water, dangling her feet in the flowing Monongahela, and watching the sun go down behind the hills. It was heaven on earth. And if perhaps one of those nights a certain young man from the local burger joint happened to have a night free, well that might just be OK as well.

Grandma couldn't possibly have known exactly when they were coming, nor did it seem likely that she was standing on her front porch for the last few hours waiting for them to arrive, but before their car had even finished the turn into her driveway, there she was.

Grandma's house looked the same, with the same border of petunias and the same bright pink. The only house like it in the world, Emily was sure. And Grandma seemed the same as well. She had aged a little, and for the first time Emily began to see that she was truly old. But she welcomed them with warmth and brought them all into a house that smelled, as always, of freshly-baked cookies.

Ethan crossed the front room, headed for the kitchen, "Oh boy, Grandma's cookies. It's worth almost any drive for a pile of those."

Emily took a moment in the front room, gazing at the pictures of family that decked the walls. Over here was a picture of Grandma and Grandpa on their wedding day. It was Emily's favorite. If she looked closely at her grandmother, she could still see the woman who had been there on that day. On another part of the wall hung a picture of their whole family, all five kids, with their father the oldest of them all.

"Emily, how you've grown!" Grandma said, throwing her arms around the girl.

Emily hugged her back with enthusiasm. "I have grown some, but not as much as Ethan.'

"Oh, when a boy grows up it's hard to tell, because they always seem so much bigger than life already," she said. "But seeing you grow into a fine young lady is one joy in a million."

Emily gave her another squeeze. "You always say the nicest things," Emily said. "I think I'll go and have a chocolate chip cookie as well. They just came out of the oven, isn't that right?"

"Of course," Grandma said.

"I don't know how you do it," Emily said, "But you always seem to pull a batch out of the oven just as we pull up. You can't possibly be baking cookies all day just in case that happens to be the minute we get here, can you?"

Grandma laughed. "That's a grandma's secret," she said. "When you're a grandma, you'll know how I do it."

"If you're lucky," Mom said. She gave Grandma a ferocious hug. "I always tell my friends that no woman was ever so fortunate in her choice of a mother-in-law."

"And where is that hard-working son of mine?" Grandma said.

Dad burst through the door and wrapped Grandma in a huge hug. "I missed you," he said.

"I'm just glad you're here for however long you're staying," she said.

All at once, practically as if he had materialized there out of thin air, Uncle Brock was sitting in the white leather chair at the edge of the living room.

He did not say a word, just sat there, his legs crossed, bouncing his right leg over his left. His dark eyes kept a steady watch on the twins and their parents. His face was not unpleasant. Emily wasn't sure exactly what it was he did for a living, but he was still living with his mother. Now probably permanently since Grandpa had passed on.

"Hello, Brock," Father said. "You look well."

"One tries," Brock said. "But I look the same as I did the last time you saw me."

"That's not exactly true," Father said. "The last time I saw you, you were cleaning a stain off the front of your shirt where your hot dog had let go its contents."

Emily waited for Brock to rise to the bait—or laugh—the way she would have if her brother had been teasing her like that. But Brock didn't. He just sat there in the chair, bouncing his leg, his dark eyes glittering.

After a moment Father hugged Grandma again, and said, "I'm assuming the cookie jar is full. Judging by the smell, that is."

"Of course it's full," Grandma said. "But you can have one right off the sheet. Still warm."

They went out together, laughing, with Grandma's arm threaded through Dad's.

That left Emily alone in the room with Uncle Brock.

If you think Emily should stay and talk to Uncle Brock, turn to page 435.

If you think she should go and get a cookie, turn to page 433.

The twins played rock-paper-scissors for who got to pigeonhole Uncle Brock. Ethan threw rock, because Emily never threw paper. Except this time she did.

"Ha. You have to ask him. Do it tonight at dinner, before we tell him for sure we're going out on the boat with him."

So Ethan did, in between forkfuls of pot roast.

"Uncle Brock, we don't want to pry—well, okay, Emily does—"

"Hey!"

"But, what is it you do with that boat out on the river?" Ethan said. "We've seen you go out there, sometimes late at night even."

"We know you're not fishing," Emily said. "None of the fishing gear has ever moved."

Uncle Brock put down a fork of mashed potatoes. "You two are proper snoops, aren't you?"

Ethan laughed. "Yeah, that's what mom says."

Emily kicked him under the table. "I don't think he meant that as a compliment," she said.

"A compliment is in the eye of the beholder."

"I think you mean the ear of the beholder. But we really are curious as to what you're doing. The boat isn't new, but it's not cheap, either."

Uncle Brock almost looked embarrassed. "It's... I have a job."

"On the river? That's awesome," Ethan said. "See, Em? It's nothing nefarious."

"It's kind of an odd job." Brock shoveled in a huge forkful of mashed potatoes.

Grandma came in, carrying a bowl of green beans. She set it in the center of the table top and sat down. "Asking about Brock's job?" she said. "It's a fascinating one. He's an oceanographer."

Emily and Ethan looked at each other incredulously. "An oceanographer?" Ethan said. Grandma knew about this?

"You didn't know that I studied marine biology in college," Brock said.

"No, I had no clue," Emily said.

"You probably wouldn't. Your father and I… Well, it's a sibling thing. Don't get crossways, like we did, kids." There was an uncomfortable silence, in which Ethan tried to imagine what it would be like to have a decades-long fight with his sister. He couldn't do it.

"Anyway, I graduated and realized I don't very much want to live by the ocean. There's way too much sand. I much prefer the river, and anyway, I could never leave the green hills here."

He loaded his plate with steaming green beans, slapped on some butter, and went on. "So I thought, what better way to use my time than using my degree on the river? It's right here, I know it. And besides, there's a legend about this river."

"It's more than a legend," Grandma said, waving a knife around to emphasize her point. "Those of us on the river, we know it's no legend."

Uncle Brock made a motion with his hand like he was trying to calm her down. "I'm not saying legend as in it's not true," he said. "I'm saying legend as in it goes back so far in time that nobody is really sure where it got started. You've heard of the Loch Ness Monster?"

Ethan and Emily both said they had. Uncle Brock nodded. "On the Monongahela, ever since the first traders arrived here, they heard from the native tribes that there was a monster in this river. They called it the Monongy. Not real original, I admit."

Ethan's eyes grew very wide. "Wait. You mean to tell me that there is a Loch Ness monster in the Monongahela River? You're hunting *Nessie*?"

Emily's face split in a wide grin. That explained the boat. He wasn't smuggling. He was *monster hunting*.

"Well," Brock said, a bit sheepishly, "obviously not *the* Loch Ness Monster. But something? Yes. Way back in antiquity, the earliest time we have records—I'm talking here about 1600, you understand—there were reports of a large creature in the water. Some of the natives claimed to have seen it; others just said they had heard about it from their ancestors. Whatever the case, the natives were certain that there was something here. Some of the traders claimed to have seen it, but nobody knows if they were simply trying to bring people to their trading post, or whether they really had. Obviously, there are no photographs that far back, so the only documentation we have is old journals. Still the legend was relatively prevalent."

He paused to take a sip of juice and set his glass on the table. Nobody would have dared to interrupt. "Most of the legends talk about a long creature, maybe 100 feet long, something like a catfish."

"OK, so nothing like the plesiosaur everybody says is the Loch Ness Monster," Ethan said.

Emily waved her fork at him. "You see, he's not a believer," she said.

Ethan violently shook his head. "I think the whole thing is nonsense."

Uncle Brock chuckled a little bit under his breath. "I get that a lot. And I can't blame people. These days kids don't believe in anything. Still, there were enough rumors about it to get me interested. I talked to some of the guys at the local university, and they said that once upon a time there had been a project to try and discover the truth about this Monongy. But it closed down when it ran out of dough. I had some time on my hands…" he said, and at this glanced up at the table toward Grandma, whose mouth was set in a hard line.

"But anyway," he went on, "there had been enough interest to mount an expedition. I did some research on the subject down at the library, and then at the University of Pittsburgh. What I found made the legend even more interesting."

By now, the twins had stopped eating and were locked on to every word he said. Brock looked across the table as if he were unsure whether he were being believed, or possibly made fun of, but he could see the twins were truly interested in what he was saying.

He laughed a little and went on. "OK, I can see that at least the story jigs at you a bit. That's more than most. Here's what I found:

"In the 1930s and 1940s, a buncha people say they saw something big in the river. It might have been, I don't know, a catfish or something. The river's pretty deep. My depth finder shows me places where it's as deep as 100 feet. A lot of things can hide in a place like that. There was never any pictures or that kind of evidence, but cameras were pretty sketchy back then, and even in the 1930s and 40s it would've been weird for someone to have been able to take a picture of it. But one day there would be a report, and then another one a few years later, enough to keep people interested. The thing that really got me was what happened in the 1950s." He mopped up the last of the gravy on his plate with a roll and popped it in his mouth.

Emily said, "I wish you'd stop eating so you can tell us this story."

Uncle Brock held up a finger while he chewed. He swallowed and continued. "In the 1950s, they had a training air base in southern Pennsylvania. Just propeller planes and the like for teaching the greenest fliers how to operate their machines. Well, one of them, on a routine training flight, developed a propeller malfunction. The pilot was at least smart enough to know to eject, so he saved his life by bailing out of the plane.

"While he was floating lazily down into the forest, he saw his airplane glow go down in the river. He marked the spot by triangulating it from a couple of the mountains and a stand of large trees. When he was rescued, he told the rescuers where the plane had gone down so they could go and retrieve it."

"Let me guess," Ethan said, rolling his eyes, "when they went to retrieve the plane, they saw a huge monster in the water."

Brock didn't take the bait. He didn't laugh, he didn't even shrug or look embarrassed.

He leaned forward across the table as if telling a great secret, and his eyes never wavered. "No, of course not. What they did find, was nothing."

"What do you mean, nothing?" Emily said. "Nothing besides the plane, you mean."

Uncle Brock shook his head. "No. Nothing as in *nothing*. They found nothing at all. No wreckage, no airplane, nothing in the river whatsoever. They searched for two weeks, dredging the river up and down, and they found nothing. The plane had simply disappeared.

"Now, that can happen. The plane wasn't terribly sturdy. It was an old World War I to World War II model, and maybe it broke up on impact. Lot of things could have happened to it. What gets really interesting is a newspaper report from a couple of weeks later where one of the backpackers in the area told the story of the plane going down into the river."

"Someone saw it!" Emily said.

"Yep. He said that the plane went down and floated on the surface for a few minutes, and then something enormous rose out of the depths, swallowed the plane, and disappeared."

Uncle Brock sat back. Now he shrugged. "That sounds impossible to me, of course, and practically no one believes it. But it was enough for the Pittsburgh Police Department to form a special task force for the next ten years to investigate whether this beast existed. That much is not a matter of speculation. And there is one other thing."

Grandma at some point had gotten up from the table, gone into the kitchen, and returned with a peach pie. Neither of the twins had noticed, which told Uncle Brock all he needed to know about how interested they were in the subject.

"In 2003," he said, "a man actually managed to snap a photograph of something in the waters of the Monongahela. He had several decent photographs, people say, and he took good notes on where he took the pictures and under what circumstances. Now, this is nothing like the faked picture of the Loch Ness monster that everyone's so familiar with."

"Hey!" Emily said. "Those pictures aren't faked."

Uncle Brock waved this away. "Suit yourself. Either way, these pictures were almost certainly not fakes. People that have seen them say they are the real thing."

Ethan said, "What do you mean, the people that have seen them? It was 2003. Wouldn't everybody be able to see them?"

"That's just it," Uncle Brock said. "The photographs were up on the internet for a while, and then they disappeared."

Ethan scoffed. "Nothing disappears from the Internet. Once it's up, it's up there forever."

"That's what they say," Uncle Brock said, "But in this case, they're wrong. The pictures were definitely there. People from the area saw them. People all over the *world* saw them. But then they disappeared. All of them vanished. There are no pictures remaining. What's more, the man who took them has disappeared as well. No one knows what happened to him, either."

"And of course, people say that the government is trying to cover things up, and made the pictures and the man disappear," Ethan said.

Emily said, "As if the government doesn't do things like that."

Uncle Brock laughed. "Now hold on, you two. I'm not accusing anybody of anything. All I can say is that once there were pictures, and now there are not. Once there was a fighter craft, and now there isn't. I don't know what happened, and nobody knows what happened, but part of my job is to find out about all that."

He took the last swallow from his glass. "As you might imagine, it wasn't too complicated to find someone who was willing to pony up some money for an expedition. I have the necessary qualifications, and I have the time. What's more, I'm curious about the story. I've lived on this river all my life, and of course as kids we told ghost stories. But how often do you get to research a true ghost story, right in your own backyard?"

Grandma slid slices of peach pie in front of the twins. They sat there, staring at them, processing what they had heard.

Ethan finally spoke, cutting a forkful of pie and lifting it toward his mouth. "I don't care that I don't believe it. That just might be the coolest story anyone has ever told me."

"Why haven't you told everyone in town about this?" Emily said. "It's just about the coolest thing ever."

Brock looked down at the tablecloth for a second. "Well, you have to understand. I don't have the best reputation in this town. A lot of people don't really like me. Not that I blame them. Things here are complicated. Also, as you can probably imagine, there are a bunch of people who don't really think very much of this legend. They're not really into the idea that we might have a river monster.

"Some of the old timers, the people who've been here for a while, grew up here, they know about the legend, but they think that it's either silly or it hurts tourism, and all that's doing is making everyone poorer. So, I don't really talk about it very much."

Ethan drummed his fingers on the table. "If I were a fisherman, and I wanted to take people out on the river, the last thing I would want is for people to think that there's a monster in there that might swallow their boat."

"Exactly. I find it's just simpler to go out and do my research and not mess with people who might be unhappy with me or think what I'm doing is stupid." He picked up his plate, asked Emily if she was done and retrieved hers as well. He took it into the kitchen.

Ethan spooned out another piece of pie, set it on his plate, and dolloped some whipped cream on it. "I love your peach pie, Grandma. It's one of my favorite things about coming here."

"Why do you think I make it every time you come?" she said. "I'm really very proud of Brock. He's worked hard, and things haven't always gone his way. But this seems to be a really great opportunity, and he seems pleased about it."

"He should be," Emily said. "It's been a long time since something really good happened for him."

"And that's another reason why we can't move from here. Brock's finally found something that makes him happy. He's even making a little bit of money. I don't want to have to pack up and move, even if we could find a piece of property somewhere on the riverfront farther up or down stream. This is my home. Everything I know is here. I won't leave if I have any other choice."

"We're working on some things to help turn the tide in this town. We have some experience with that, you know," Ethan said.

"Yes, I know," Grandma said. "It's nice to have you both here for a little while. Maybe if we all work together, we can come up with something."

Emily shot Ethan an excited smile. They were going to come up with something, all right. That very night.

Ethan stopped at the shed on the way down to the dock. Uncle Brock paused on the path and swiveled back to him. "What do you think you're doing?"

"I'm grabbing some fishing gear," Ethan said. "If I'm going out on the river, I'm taking my pole. You never know. I might not get another chance."

Brock shrugged and continued toward the dock.

Emily paused and waited for Ethan. "Do you think it's normal for oceanographers to fish while they work, or would that be out of the ordinary?" Emily said.

Ethan snapped the lock shut and hefted his tackle box and pole. "One, not ocean, therefore not oceanography. Maybe riverography or something. Forensic rivernautics? Second, why ask me? I don't know where ordinary *is*. I'm not sure you can see it from here."

They trudged down the path, reveling in the descending sun. There was just enough cloud for the sun to cast purples and oranges across the landscape. "I'll say one thing," Emily said, "it's just about as pretty as a place can be."

"And just think," Ethan said, "If we fail in our task, we'll have a lovely chemical factory here to block out the view."

"Yeah," she replied, "But chemical fumes make the best sunsets."

"There is that."

When they reached the end of the dock, Brock was fishing around in the back of the boat. As they came up to the side, he dropped something into the rear cargo space and dropped the hatch over it. There was a click of a lock.

Brock straightened with a smile. "All set?"

Ethan handed over his rod and tackle box. "You bet," Ethan said, "I've been dying to get out on this river since we got here. Thank you for helping us. We're kind of running out of options."

Brock reached out a hand and helped Emily aboard. "I don't think you're going to get very far with this expedition, either, but I'm happy to be of whatever small service I can."

Ethan scrambled his way over the gunwale and stood by the pilot's cabin. "Can I go down below?" he said.

"Knock yourself out," Brock said. "I'm just going to show Emily here how to drive the boat."

"Whoa," Ethan said. "I don't want to miss that."

Brock laughed. "Don't worry, kid. You'll get your chance."

Ethan tugged the handle of the forward cabin door. It wouldn't open. "You push it," Emily said.

Feeling like a fool, Ethan gave it a shove, and the door ground its way inward.

He stepped through the door.

Immediately, he could tell that this part of the boat was not nearly as well maintained as the rest of it. A mildew smell rose up all around him, so thick he felt like he could probably swim in it.

Two small windows, one on each side of the boat, allowed some dim illumination, but they were thickly crusted with grime. The light outside was fading so fast he couldn't see anything by them. He felt his way back to the door. "Hey," he called out, "is there a flashlight or something around?"

Something dropped down the stairwell. It bounced, clattered, and rolled to a stop at his feet. "Isn't that kind of a harsh way to treat a flashlight?" he said.

"Not that flashlight," Brock said. "You could hit that thing with a nuclear bomb and it wouldn't make any difference."

Ethan reached down and picked up the metal cylinder. It lay cool in his hand, but rough and snaggy, as if it had been well battered over the years. He found the button and clicked it, and light sprang out, bright as brand new. He turned back to the cabin.

Inside, along one side—*the portside,* he reminded himself—ran a long, low bench. It was padded in some kind of green vinyl. And it had seen better days. The floor undulated under foot. It was some kind of grimy linoleum with years of accumulated grime on it.

To the right, a narrow bed lay against the starboard side. It was wide enough for one or, at a pinch, two people. No blankets, no sheets, not even a pillow. At the extreme forward end, right up against the bow of the boat, a small cabinet stood closed. Ethan took the two paces to it and tugged on the ring to open it up.

Inside was a thick blanket, the woollen kind that is good forever unless moths get to it. Unfortunately for this one, moths had indeed gotten to it. They sprang to life and fluttered about his head looking for a source of light, before locking in on the flashlight and descending again to flutter about it. Ethan hauled the blanket out and lay it on the bed. Once thick and warm, it was now threadbare with holes in it.

Ethan yelled out, "I don't think you're gonna want to use this blanket anymore."

There was no response from above. They were still there. Ethan could hear their footsteps shuffling back and forth every now and then.

Other than that, the cabin was bare.

Ethan thumped his foot on the floor and was rewarded with a hollow, booming sound.

There was more space underneath this.

He swung the flashlight back and forth along the floor, looking for the access point, but none appeared. However you got into that space, you didn't do it from here. Shrugging, Ethan folded the blanket back up and stuffed it into the cabinet. At least the moths could continue to have a meal. He went back to the stairwell, climbed up, and kicked off the flashlight.

"Once the key is in and turned like this, all you have to do is press this button here." Brock pointed. Emily pushed the button, and instantly the engine roared to life.

"Nicely done," Brock said. "Now remember, when you are backing the boat out from the dock, you have to steer backward, just like a car."

Emily said, "It doesn't steer like a car."

"Remember the river will be pushing against you, and all you have to do is swing the back end of the boat out into the current, and the river will do most of the rest of the work. You use the steering wheel, and it will mostly do what you want to do. Just remember, this isn't driver's ed. Streets don't move underneath you and carry you along even if you don't want to go."

"Going upstream must be pretty complicated," she said.

"We're going to find out right now," Brock said. "Because we're headed upstream toward the chemical plant."

"Why?" Emily said.

"That's the most likely place for the creature to live," Brock said. Emily wasn't convinced.

Still, that was where they were headed, and it was as good a place as any. Besides, it would give her and Ethan an opportunity to do a little scouting about the plant itself.

"Take hold of the throttle here," Brock said, "then you shift into gear, like this."

Emily did and engaged the propeller. The boat slid smoothly back from the dock. As soon as the stern of the boat got out into the main current, the boat began to slew sideways.

Emily fought it with the steering wheel.

"No, don't do that," Brock said. "If you let the river do the work, we'll end up with our bow pointed upstream, which is what we want."

"It's just totally weird," Emily said, relaxing her hands and letting the wheel slide through them. "Rivers just aren't supposed to flow north."

"It does take a little getting used to," Brock said.

Once the boat was headed in the right direction, keeping it aligned between the banks was a cinch. Dusk fell very rapidly in the highlands, and what little light there had been from the sunset when they had boarded the boat disappeared within ten minutes. This section of the river went its way upstream, south, into the mountains of West Virginia. It was so lightly populated that only occasionally was there any light to be seen at all. At least, that was true for about twenty minutes, until the boat came round a slight bend, and there, on the port bank, was Jaxton Chemical Headquarters.

Ethan, seated on the stern, right over the motor, said, "Sticks out a bit, doesn't it?"

"That it does," Brock said. "I remember when they built this thing. It's only been about fifteen years."

Emily turned her head from the wheel. She had discovered that you could do that on the river, where doing it in a car was probably not the smartest thing. They were only moving about five miles an hour, she judged, possibly a little faster. The throttle was only a quarter of the way up, and of course they were working against the current.

"Only fifteen years ago? Why on earth do they need to build another factory then?"

Brock shrugged. "Beats me. That decision's being made at higher levels than I'm invited to meetings about."

Slowly, as if they were watching a slow-motion video, the chemical company slipped by on the left. All three of them kept their eyes glued to the bright lights tipping the spires, smokestacks, and buildings of the complex.

Brock rustled in a pack underneath his feet and came up with a couple of dark packages. There was a ripping sound, like Velcro, and he handed Ethan something heavy and cool. "Try these on," he said.

They were binoculars. Not the cheap kind that you could get from *Boys' Life* magazine, either, but the real article: heavy, metal, with outstanding magnification. Ethan figured they must magnify by at least ten times, maybe more. He swung them up to his eyes and the factory leaped toward him. The lights of the buildings were the old kind, yellowing and not very bright in the dusk. They cast little pools of shadow where their beams didn't reach, which was pretty much everywhere.

Without taking the binoculars from his eyes, Ethan said, "There's a lot of dark over there. I can't see a thing outside those lamps."

"Let me take over, Emily," Brock said. "I've seen it, more times than I care to count."

Emily relinquished the wheel and took the offered binoculars. She said, "Do you have a piece of paper?"

Brock said, "I don't know, probably down in the cabin."

Emily put the strap of the binoculars around her neck and tromped down the stairs. After thirty seconds or so, she said, "Hey, Ethan, come and help me look."

"Little sisters," Ethan said.

She had the flashlight out and was waving it around, but when he arrived, she pointed it down at the floor and said, "Push the door closed." She said it so quietly there was no chance that it would carry over the hum of the engine. He swung his hip and the door clicked closed. "Two things," she said. "One, this boat is hollow underneath us."

"I know that," Ethan said, and thumped his heel on the deck. "I checked when I came down."

Emily nodded, taking her brother's initiative for granted.

"Two, what kind of oceanographer goes out on the water without anything to record his observations by?" As it turned out, there was a small desk tucked away behind the swinging door that Ethan had missed when he came down to investigate earlier. The desk only had a single drawer and was maybe eighteen inches to two feet wide, but in the drawer was a spiral notebook and a couple of decent pens. Emily plucked it from the drawer and leafed through it.

She huffed. "Well, that's something, at least." She pointed. A few of the beginning pages were covered with a dense, almost unreadable scrawl. But what they could make out seemed consistent with somebody who was making observations about depths, water flow patterns, and observed natural phenomena.

"See?" Ethan said. "Nothing sketchy there."

"No, not for this," she said. "But what happens after September 18 of last year?" That was the last day he had written anything in this notebook.

"That's the day he gets a really good observation journal," Ethan said. "How do I know? Did you see all that electronic equipment on the dash? Nobody has that equipment for fun. Some of that stuff is really expensive. Besides, if he's not looking for this monster, what's he doing out on the river in the middle of the night every night?"

"I'd like to know that myself," Emily said. She reached over and flicked the door open.

"You guys get lost down there?" Brock said. "You need to come up here. There's something I want to show you."

Emily took the spiral notebook and both of the pens and went back up the stairs.

The pitch of the boat's engine changed while Ethan was climbing the stairs. The tone dropped, and the boat slowed until it was, for all intents and purposes, not moving at all. In the reflected glare of the lights of the chemical company, Ethan saw Brock point.

"See that building there?" he said. "The long, flat one?" Ethan did. It was the longest building they had yet passed, probably at least a hundred yards long. "That's the administration building. It's the first building they built. I guess you could call it the headquarters of the company."

"Very interesting," he said. "Do you think they'll give us a tour?"

Brock threw him a withering glance. "If that was what I thought, I would have let you linger downstairs in the mildew." He shook his head. "No, what I want you to do is train your binoculars on those windows. Remember, these are the office buildings for the entire chemical complex. Every worker of any stature in the company has an office in that building."

"That means," Emily said, her voice displaying the kind of excitement Ethan had learned to associate with something really fascinating, "that if you pass the right office, and they've left the blinds up—"

"Which they mostly do," Brock cut in.

"Darn straight," Emily said. "With the right kind of binoculars, you can see right in."

Ethan swung up the binoculars. He trained them on the building and screwed them into focus. It was true. You could get significantly closer with the binoculars. Ethan could see right into most of the offices along the way. It was still too far for anything useful, unless you wanted to know how these particular engineers decorated their desks. A hand reached over and tapped a button on his binoculars.

"These are not just optical binocs," Brock said. "They have enhanced zoom. Try this," and Brock clicked a switch.

A high-pitched whine came from the device, and the building seemed to rush toward him. All of a sudden, Ethan went from being able to see how close the chair was to a desk, to being able to tell what was on the tag attached to the back of the chair itself.

"Holy..." he said.

Brock chuckled, low and quiet. "I thought you might say that," he said.

"Emily, are you seeing this?" Ethan said.

"I certainly am."

As beautiful as it was, it wasn't a great deal more informative. The problem was, all the papers on the desks lay flat along them, and they didn't have any height to be able to look down on them and read what they said. The only things they could read were taped to the walls.

"It's not nothing," Ethan said. Emily picked up the pad and began to scribble things. "What are you doing?" Ethan said. "Surely you're not getting any secret information out of those binoculars."

"No," she said, and stuck her tongue out of her mouth a little bit, the way she did when she wrote things. "But I can tell whose offices belong to whom. That could be useful, if we could get closer, or even inside."

Ethan put his binoculars down. "Are you nuts? Get inside? Those people are far more likely to shoot us than to give us a guided tour."

"Of course they are," Emily said, brightly. "But I didn't expect we will ask them. Look at all this lovely section of unpatrolled riverbank."

"Not exactly unpatrolled," Brock said. "They actually patrol it fairly regularly, Although, my suspicion is they aren't particularly vigilant."

Brock threw the boat back into higher throttle and moved up the river. At the far southern end of the building, in the corner office, two men sat by the window, having a conversation. The blinds were partially closed, so it was very difficult to see what was inside the office other than the men, even with the high powered binoculars.

"I wish we could hear what they were saying," Emily said. "Maybe we can sneak over to the building and listen. I don't see any of the guards."

Brock stepped over to the starboard side and drew something out of the water. It dripped on the deck as he brought it up. It was a conical device, black plastic and metal, with a cord that ran to a box on the dashboard. Brock flipped the switch on the box, and they covered their ears as a shrill screech erupted from it. It subsided quickly, however, and Brock did something to the dial. It settled down to produce only a faint hum, interspersed with static.

"What the heck is that?" Ethan said.

"One of the things I thought might be useful for this expedition to find the river monster was a sonar device for listening to sounds underwater. It's kind of an experimental gizmo and listening to sounds in the river isn't terribly interesting. Still, it works pretty well. And here's something else I've discovered."

He hefted the device—it looked like it weighed several pounds—and braced it on the port gunwale,

pointing at the building. A clamp secured it to the gun-wale, so that he could direct it. Loud and clear, through the speakers, came the sound of air conditioning. He moved it a couple of inches, and the sound of a vacuum cleaner came through. And then, with another adjustment, voices.

"Are we seriously hearing—"

"Shhhhh," Ethan said.

"Working on my golf game," one of the men said. "It seems like I never get an opportunity to do that."

"I've noticed that," the other man said. "Here we are still at the office at 9:30pm."

The two of them chuckled slightly. One of them got up to leave.

"So next Tuesday, this referendum thing. How do you think it's going to go?"

"I wouldn't worry too much about the referendum. Oh, I think we're going to win, but even if we don't, that's not going to matter much. It's just a referendum. There's too much momentum behind this project already. Where the money goes, the decisions always follow. And there's a lot of money riding on getting this thing built."

"You're right," the first man said. "Night. See you in the morning."

The three of them on the boat stared at each other with eyes wide.

Ethan whispered, "Did we just hear what I thought we heard?"

"Sounded like it to me," Brock said.

"I wish we had that recorded," Emily said.

"Who says we don't?" Brock said, pointing to a red light on the box on the dash. "I always set it to record whenever I turn it on, just in case. This is the first time I've ever been able to record anything I actually wanted to keep."

"What did he mean when he said there's too much money behind this thing?" Emily said.

"There's not enough context to really know," Brock said. "It could mean anything from paying off the city council to the receipt of federal money for development. You know there's a lot of money flowing out of Washington, D.C., into these rural areas for towns to use to do redevelopment, get rid of blighted areas, and so on. Most of the time they issue these things in block grants where you can buy up a big chunk of property and then either build something on it or sell it to a developer so they can."

"Wait," Emily said. "A memo I saw on the wall had something to do with block grants. I sure wish I could have gotten a better look at it. It's just too fuzzy from this distance."

Ethan said, "Hey, that fellow in the office, he's getting ready to make a phone call."

"Who makes a phone call at ten o'clock at night? I want to hear what he says."

Brock again aimed the device at the building. This time, however, all he got was the occasional vacuum cleaner and some air conditioning noise.

"I can't hold it steady enough," he said. "I can't keep it aimed at the corner."

"I bet you could do it if we tied up on the bank," Ethan said.

"It'll have to be the far side," Brock said. "Even a blind security guy would be able to see us on their side."

"I want to get a closer look at that memo," Emily said. "Can we go over to the chemical side and drop me off?"

Brock said, "We can't do both. It's one or the other."

If you think Emily should explore the building close up, turn to page 255.

If you think they should get a better listen to the conversations, turn to page 320.

"Editor first," Emily said. "I bet the zoning maps for the city are online. The county will surely have the ownership tax records for the properties. We can get the addresses just from riding by and look them up on the computer at Grandma's."

Ethan scowled. "That old thing? I'd rather use the ancient beasts in the library."

"Fine by me. The library is open a lot longer than city hall. If we don't get back in time, you can go use their machines. Either way, I think the editor is the place to go first."

Ethan tugged his bike loose from the rack and slung his leg over the seat. "OK. You're the boss. For now, anyway. Which way are we going?"

"Two blocks south and three blocks east, across Main."

"You have the address?"

Emily tapped her head. "Right here. Let's go. I'm going to beat you this time."

They were evenly matched, as twins should be, but Ethan had better endurance. He began to pull away. Emily let him go and turned behind him while his back was turned. She pulled up in front of the house of the editor, parked her bike, and waited.

A couple of minutes later Ethan cruised up, a smile on his face. "Was it two blocks south and three blocks east, or three blocks south and two blocks east?"

"The former," Emily said. "But I don't blame you for getting it wrong."

"You could have just told me the address."

"But then I wouldn't have beaten you. You owe me a shake at Thusnelda's."

Ethan shrugged. "Suits me. I win that way, too. So what do we know about this person?"

Emily briefed him on what she'd found out from the newspaper on the way to the front door. On the flag bracket to the left of the door fluttered a yellow flag with a severed snake on it.

"Don't Tread On Me," Emily read. "That sounds hopeful."

Before she could ring the bell, the door opened and a thin, weatherbeaten woman came out, holding a can of Pepsi and carrying her purse.

"Saw you ride up," she said. "You got a hot tip?"

"How did you know we were here to talk about the newspaper?" Ethan said.

She snorted. "Two kids on a summer afternoon, ride up and park their bikes in front of my house. There aren't a lot of other possible reasons for them to be here. Simple deduction." She sighed and went back inside. She came out without her purse, and said cryptically, "I guess some things are meant to be."

She took a seat on the porch swing and a swig from her can. "I guess I can spare the time. So you're here about the paper. Question is, what part of the paper are you here about?"

The twins stayed silent—it seemed like she wanted to work this out on her own.

The editor squinted up at them, seeing them against the sunshine. "I don't know you, which means you're definitely from out of town. You're probably visiting for the holiday, but there's a lot of candy in the world, so you didn't come for the parade. That means you have relatives here. But you're not *with* those relatives at the moment, and you're not down at the rope swing by the river, or doing some other sensible summer activity. That means whatever brings you to my door isn't idle curiosity—you didn't come to find out what the holiday festivities are. It must be important. Probably very important, the kind of thing that can't wait. There are two things I can think of that fit in that category. The final question is, which of those two are you interested in finding out about? Well, that and who are you?"

Ethan opened his mouth. Ms. Burns put her finger up and slurped from her soda.

"No, I'm not finished yet. The first possible issue does involve a fair number of children, but you don't look like those children, so you're not here about the golf course. That means you're here about the other thing. You want to know about the new chemical plant. And that means your relatives live on Riverside. And that means you're Patty Tuttle's grandkids, because she's the only one of the right age that still lives there. You are the Tuttle twins, and you're here about saving the Little Pink House."

The twins exchanged a glance. Emily said, "That's pretty good. Even Sherlock Holmes would be impressed."

"Elementary."

Emily said, "Do you actually have a way to save our grandmother's house?"

"Who said I was interested in helping you?"

"Nobody. But I read a few editions of your paper. You don't talk about the city council meetings very much, and when you do, there's not a lot of controversial information. But you make remarks that sound like you're trying to sneak information into the paper that people will understand but the council can't object to. The thing that clinched it for me was when you wrote about the city council knocking off for the summer, then you put in a couple weeks later that they had called a special session. No commentary. But you didn't have to put in the first article that they were taking the summer off, unless you suspected they'd be coming back. Then if people were paying attention the next article would clue them to something going on."

"Which it seems to have done, though I didn't expect the most interested person to be an out-of-town sixteen-year-old."

"Fifteen. How did you know we are the Tuttle twins?" Ethan said.

"Patty Tuttle has twin grandkids. If you've ever met her, you know that. She can't shut up about it. How did you know I would be on your side?"

"*Are* you on our side?" Emily said.

"I am indeed."

"Lucky guess, actually. We needed a break. I figured you were a better bet for one than the city clerk's office."

Ms. Burns broke into laughter and quaffed the last of her soda. "That wasn't luck. That was plain sense. You must have dealt with city governments before."

Ethan said, "You bet we have. But they're tough, and in a town like this where we don't know anyone—"

"—You aren't going to get very far with straight opposition. True. You came to the right place. Care to step inside? This is the sort of conversation I'd rather have indoors." She stood up and let the swing wobble back and forth, pulled the screen door open and held it for them to go ahead.

Inside, the front room was so covered by piles of newspapers there wasn't anywhere to sit. Right by the door, two blue hard-side suitcases stood at attention, waiting to go somewhere.

"You leaving?" Ethan said.

"Right away," Ms. Burns said. "I was thinking I'd already be gone, but there's always something else to do. You're lucky—if you'd come a few minutes later, I wouldn't have been here."

Emily looked over at Ethan and raised her eyebrows.

Ms. Burns walked over to a table outside the kitchen. It, too, was piled with newspaper, but at one end a desktop computer glowed softly, and at the other end lay a file folder, which Ms. Burns picked up and thumbed through.

"First, you need to know that the referendum is going to pass."

"What referendum?" Emily said.

"You didn't read back far enough, obviously, although I buried the article about it under all sorts of congratulatory stuff about bringing new business to Gnarled Oak. There's a referendum on the ballot for next Tuesday. It's a measure to change the zoning along the river. Most people don't much care, I suspect, but the ones that do are the employees of the city on one side and the people that live along the river on the other. Unfortunately for your grandma, there aren't a lot of people left along the river. So the measure will pass, and the city council will meet the next day to accept the 'will of the people' and confirm the changes, zone the two or three blocks there commercial, and pave the way for Jaxton Chemical to buy the properties from the city for their new factory."

Ethan said, thumbing a couple of papers at the top of one of the stacks, "It's as bad as that?"

"Worse," Ms. Burns said. She wrapped her straw-colored hair back into a hairband and slung it over one shoulder. "Even with the zoning change, the city won't be able to force your grandma to sell. But they will be able to condemn the property as blighted and take it over under eminent domain. My guess is you don't understand a word of what I just said."

"Ah, so you're not omniscient," Emily said, smiling, "Although you are pretty good with the Sherlock bit. We actually do know about eminent domain. We had to deal with that in a town called LaPlaya, back where we live."

Ms. Burns scratched at her chin. "Really? You know the city can just take your property if it decides it's dragging down the property values, or whatever other excuse they use?"

Emily nodded. "We know. But that's not true with Grandma's house. It's not dragging anything down. It's one of the nicest houses in town."

"Doesn't matter," Ms. Burns said. "The rest of the properties there are pretty terrible—the city bought them and made sure they would be—so the whole zone can be condemned. Then they take the property— they'll pay your grandma something, surely—and sell it to the chemical company."

"But," Ethan said, "that's where I run into a problem. The chemical company isn't hurting for land where they are. They obviously cut down trees and got whatever zoning they needed to build their original factory, right? So why do they need this property? Why not just expand where they are?" Ethan drew out one of his maps, and pointed. "See, here's the land they need. It's right there, and they don't have to kick anyone out. So why go to all this trouble to get hold of land people are already living on?"

"You've asked a very good question," Ms. Burns said. "And I'd love to answer it, but I'm already late getting on the road. Here," she said, handing Emily the thick manila folder, "take this and go through it. It has pretty much everything you need to know, although the answer to that particular question isn't laid out for you. You'll have to read between the lines—even I don't know everything, although I have a pretty good idea what the answer is."

She dusted off her hands on her jeans and opened the front door. "I'm glad you came by. I was going to just leave it all and come back when it was over, since there wasn't anything more I could do, and here you are, all bright-eyed and eager. You don't have much chance against the people trying to put this thing together, but I sure as shooting wasn't going to get it done. Maybe you'll pass a miracle. Who knows?"

Ethan asked if he could carry her bags to the car, and she said that would be okay. "You're a gentleman. Patty would be proud."

"How well do you know Grandma?" Ethan said, racking the suitcases into the trunk of the beaten-up Celica.

"Not so well anymore. I spent some time out on her dock way back when. I guess you could say your Uncle Brock and I were an item, once. That was a long time ago." She smiled, and her eyes were far away. "But it was a good time, and your grandmother is a good woman. She always treated me well, and every other stray that washed up on her doorstep."

"Wait," Emily said, leaning against the driver's door so that Ms. Burns couldn't open the door right away, "you know Uncle Brock?"

"I did. I don't see him any more, not since he got back from jail. I hear, though, that he's doing pretty well, keeping his nose clean. He must be, too. Stuff like that has a way of getting around in a town like this. Either way, you two ought to be careful with him. He can be terribly charming when he wants to be, and he almost always wants to be for purposes of his own." She touched her shoulder and smiled again. "But tell him Penelope says hello."

Emily moved. "When will you be back?"

Penelope jerked open her car door, which seemed not to want to move. "End of next week. After the Fourth, after the referendum, and after the corpse of this town is laid out pretty in the morgue." She glanced sheepishly at the twins. "Sorry, I don't mean to be sentimental about it. I just hate seeing what's happening, and not being able to stop it."

Emily waved the file folder. "We'll see what we can do. We've had some success before."

"Well, good luck, anyway," Penelope said, climbing in behind the wheel, and slamming the door. She roared off toward the highway. The twins watched her go and thought it was a heavy load she'd left on their shoulders.

Turn to page 170.

If there was some reason Grandma's house wouldn't be there forever, you couldn't see it from the road. The house looked just the same—bright, shuttered windows and a robin egg blue front door, a shallowly sloping roof with its dark gray shingles, freshly cut patch of emerald grass between the porch and the white picket fence at the roadside. And, of course, the neon pink of the house everyone in town knew just by its color.

Dad turned right into the gravel drive that led to the side of the house, and before the car even came to a stop there was Grandma on the porch in her apron, waving a dishtowel.

Five feet, two inches of unconditional love folded the twins into a tight hug. "You two are at least twice as big as you were last year!" Grandma said.

"You say that every year, Grandma," Ethan said, his words muffled from being squashed into Grandma's shoulder.

"That's because it's true," she said. "Emily, how are you? You're growing like a weed."

"I'm fine," Emily said, stepping back half a pace and kissing Grandma's cheek.

"Hello, Mother," Dad said, leaning over the twins for a quick hug. "You look great."

"I'd look better if you were staying a couple days," she said, "But I suppose you have to get along to your big thing upstate."

"We do, yes," Mother said, pecking Grandma on the cheek. "Otherwise we'd like nothing better."

Grandma padded at the corner of her eyes with the dish towel. "You're staying for dinner, though, right?"

"Are you having peach pie?" Dad said.

"Do the big ones always get away?" Grandma said. "Of course there's peach pie. How do you think I get my grandchildren to come back every year?"

"We'd come back anyway," Emily said, prancing up the front porch and into the house, her duffel swung over her shoulder.

"I would never risk it," Grandma said, bringing up the rear as everyone paraded into the house.

Emily headed straight past the front room and padded down the short hallway to the door on the right, where she and Ethan had slept every year for as long as she could remember. Two beds, smaller and shorter every year, one on each wall. Emily thumped her bag down on the right-hand one and passed Ethan coming through the door.

"And you didn't want to come," Emily said.

"Well, it wasn't because of the peach pie, that's for sure."

The narrow hallway passed a kitchen on the right, a bathroom on the left, and next to the bathroom, the office where Grandpa once sat and watched the basketball games on TV. The door was closed, but Emily turned the brass handle and shushed it open over the thick carpet.

A high-backed, brass-tacked leather chair sat empty in front of a too-tidy desk, swiveled so that if you sat down in it, you'd be facing the ancient TV set against the wall. The desk was topped in glass, underneath which newspaper clippings had been mounted, each with a headline about Grandpa or one of the kids. Emily ran her finger over the glass above the article about her grandfather being made mayor of the town. She traced the strong jaw above his stylish coat and tie, his arm held up to the square, taking the oath of office.

"I miss him every time we come here," Ethan said from behind her, very softly. The carpet had muffled his footsteps completely.

"Yeah," Emily said. "I don't know how Grandma can stand it."

"Think about what would happen if she had to leave this place," Ethan said. "You think it's hard for her now, how would she get along if she had to start over, where there were no reminders of all the good times she had with Grandpa?"

"We can't let that happen," Emily said, turning abruptly. "We can't. Whatever we have to do, we'll do it, so that we don't have to watch Grandma try to choose which memories she wants to leave behind."

Ethan stuck out his hand. "Swear," he said.

She took it and shook just once. "I swear," she said.

He nodded and the two of them left the room, closing the door gently behind them.

Back to the front room, where Dad and Mom and Grandma had been joined by another man, shorter than Dad, with black hair and eyes and a couple days of growth on his face. Uncle Brock. The black sheep of the Tuttle clan.

"Here they are right now," Dad said. "You remember this day?" He pointed to a photo on the wall, one of dozens of every shape and size, black and white, color, faded and sharp, all framed behind glass, and all featuring the Tuttles, young and old. There was a whole section of photos of just Dad, then Dad and Mom, and then Dad and Mom and the twins, starting from the hospital when they were born and right on from there for fifteen years.

Dad had his finger pointed to one of Ethan and Emily standing on a riverbank, holding up a trout. Ethan had hooked it and Emily had netted it. They both counted it as theirs, one of the biggest fish either of them had ever caught.

"Sure we do," Ethan said, checking Emily's face, but of course she knew the day as well. They had been seven, on a campout with the family not too far away in the West Virginia hills.

"We need to do one of those again," Dad said, with a glance at Uncle Brock. "Sometime soon."

"Everyone's so busy," Grandma said. "I'll settle for having you come visit more often."

"As long as you're here, we'll keep coming back," Mom said, but as she did, it was like a shadow passed in front of the sun. They all knew the days of Grandma's little pink house on the river might be numbered.

At dinner that night, Ethan thought it was a good time to bring up the subject he'd heard about at lunch. "Grandma, have you heard about a new golf course in town?"

Grandma paused, a forkful of food halfway to her mouth. "I don't think so," she said, scanning his face to see if he was joking. "Where did you hear about it?"

"I didn't, really. There were just a couple of guys at Thusnelda's. Dad said they were talking about building a golf course, but they kind of clammed up when they noticed we were listening."

Grandma put the fork back down on her plate. "A golf course seems like a very weird thing to build in this town. I wouldn't think this would be a community that would be heavily into golf."

"Golf always struck me as strange sport anyway," Emily said. "I mean, all you really do is walk around and hit something with a stick."

Uncle Brock, halfway down the table, snorted into his fried chicken. "That sounds like a lot of games: hockey, except it's skating instead of walking; baseball, except walking is actually a good thing in baseball..."

"Yeah, we get it," Ethan said. "Even if *we* don't like golf, a lot of people do. There are a lot of golf courses scattered around the country on some fairly rich land."

"Well, that lets us out. There's no rich land around here at all." Grandma lifted the mashed potatoes and offered them down the table.

Uncle Brock took a healthy dollop, slung it on his plate, and passed the bowl. "I know they're trying to build something here along the river. That's why all the houses are derelict. They want everybody to move out, and they're buying up all the property they can. I don't think it's for a golf course."

"What is it then?" Emily said, ignoring a warning look from Mom.

Grandma gave her head a little shake, rose from the table, and went into the kitchen.

Brock leaned across the table. "She doesn't like to talk about it, even with family. Mom's getting a lot of pressure from Jaxton Chemical. They want to build a factory on this place."

"A factory?" Emily said. "Don't they already have a plant just up the river?"

Brock nodded. "This is a different kind of thing, I think. I'm not really sure what it is they want to do. All I know is they're putting an awful lot of pressure on the town, and the town is putting pressure on the people that live along the riverfront. It's getting so that most people would rather just sell and leave than try to fight it."

This was a new wrinkle that Ethan hadn't considered. First the golf course and now this chemical thing. "If they were going to build a golf course, they would need a lot of land, wouldn't they? This neighborhood is way too small."

Brock shrugged. "I don't much go in for golf. You couldn't build it to the south of town, way too many trees there. The forest is too thick. It would take forever and cost millions."

"What's north of town?" Emily said. "Wait, we came in from that direction, didn't we?"

"I don't think so," Ethan said. "Your head was in a bag, puking. I think we came in from the east."

"That's where the main road comes in from," Brock said. "North of town is a bunch of rolling hills. A long time ago, there were a lot of trees there, but there was some fairly intensive logging a while back. Now it's just scrub and grassland. There is a fairly decent-sized plot of trees down by the river, but everything else is pretty wide open. A lot of people like to go hiking there. It's pretty. Flowers and such."

"Do you hike through there?" Emily said.

Brock shook his head and forked in another mound of mashed potatoes. "Not much into hiking, either."

Ethan began to wonder what Brock *was* into.

Grandma re-entered, carrying a peach pie. "Come to think of it, I *have* heard about something going on toward the north of town. Some of the ladies were talking about it. I can't remember what it was they were deciding, but the city seems to be all excited to go on this big building project. It's weird. We've had very little change to our town for the last thirty or forty years. It was a huge scandal when I painted this place pink. That was the most exciting thing that had happened in town in a decade. Now, there's all this upheaval. Jaxton Chemical company, and now maybe a golf course?"

"Don't read too much into it," Ethan said. "I don't even know exactly what it was I heard."

The peach pie was sliced and heaping helpings were served out to everyone. Brock fetched a bucket of ice cream—he was into *that*, all right—and generous scoops plopped on top of the still-steaming pie.

Ethan loved how the creamy texture of the ice cream melted down into the crannies of the peach and sugar. It was just about the best dessert a guy could possibly ask for, and Grandma was so happy to be serving it.

Dad always said no son ever had a better mother, unless it was Ethan. Then Mom would always laugh and say, "Don't even try to put me in the same class with your mother. Maybe in fifty years, I'll be something like half as good as she is." Everyone would laugh, but there was truth in it. Ethan couldn't help watching his grandmother, paying attention to the small things she did. She seemed to fetch a napkin for you before you knew you needed it. She made sure the ice cream was good and hard, and melted in beautiful curlicues down into a pie you knew she had specially prepared for you. Her face lit up when the twins would tell a joke, or Brock told a story.

Everything spoke to how important to Grandma her family was: the pictures on the wall in the front room, the way she lovingly maintained her house, and how glad she was every year that the twins were going to come and spend Fourth of July. She lived for this family. She lived for being able to have family come and stay with her.

What would they do, what would any of them do, if this place weren't here? It was the home base of the Tuttles. It was like the mother tree that little seedlings had grown up out of. But still, there was the central trunk, and that trunk was Grandma. Holding up that trunk was this little pink house.

Ethan couldn't imagine what his grandmother's life would be like without it, and he was pretty sure Grandma couldn't imagine anything like that either.

He let the peachy goodness of the pie sit on his tongue for a moment before swallowing. This was paradise, and no one was going to pave it and put in a parking lot.

Next morning, Grandma put them to work. Weeding, scraping paint, edging the lawn, even planting bulbs in the gardens out front. Uncle Brock helped with that part, and it was from him that they found out more about what was happening, and why Grandma was so worried.

"Next spring, these daffodils are going to be super pretty," Emily said.

"If they're allowed to come up. If the house is even here. If they're not digging a big hole in the ground for a chemical plant," Brock said, stabbing a trowel into the soft black earth.

Ethan looked up and down the street. "This is a residential neighborhood. Can they build a factory here?"

Brock wiped his brow and gathered some more bulbs. "They can if the referendum passes. It's a vote to see if the town wants to change the zoning to allow heavy manufacturing here."

Ethan took off his cap and mopped his forehead. "Why is the whole town voting on this piece of ground? Why not just the people that live here? It's not like the people over on the north side are going to lose their homes. Why do they get to say what happens to Grandma?"

Brock shrugged. "That's how it works. It's America. We vote on things. It's kind of a tradition. Anyway, if the referendum passes it will clear the way for Jaxton Chemical to buy up land and build whatever they like." He stood up and rubbed the small of his back. "Whoo, it's hot. I'm going to make us some lemonade. Anyone want some?"

The twins said they did. Today might be heavy on the chores, but tomorrow it was time to do some investigating. There were too many questions about this town that needed answering. Ethan decided that in the morning he would take a little bike ride. The question was, should he go north or south? Jaxton Chemical, or the golf course?

If you think he should investigate the golf course, turn to page 43.

If you think he should investigate Jaxton Chemical, turn to page 167.

The park, just opposite city hall, had so many children in it Emily would have sworn they were springing from the ground.

From blocks away, she heard the shouting of children engaged in all sorts of watersports. Around the outside of the park, vendors displayed their wares, most of them edible. There was so much food, Emily was certain they could have fed a town three times this size. More, this was a place where everybody seemed to know everyone else. Hardly a person came to a booth who was not greeted by name. She met Xavier on the southeast corner, next to an oak tree that had to be at least a thousand years old. He was organizing the flyers they had made the night before.

It was hard to imagine a more festive scene. That made it kind of difficult for her and Xavier to get into the spirit of talking to people about a serious problem, but a serious problem is exactly what they were there to try and solve.

There was, of course, a booth for city councilmen and for the government to display its wares.

That was sort of how Emily had come to think of them, the city displaying its wares, because its services were, in fact, the things that it had to sell to the citizenry. The easiest things to sell were firemen—these gentlemen and ladies were prominent, all over the park—followed by police and school personnel. How does one argue that the city is wasting its money on firemen?

The citizens, in return, bought the services with their taxes. If the community activities were dominated by government, people would feel that they were getting value for their money, whether or not that was actually true. The parade route was lined by policemen, the city council members rode in the parade—on fire trucks, of course—and had a booth where they answered citizens' questions and fed them free hot dogs. Free, of course, meaning "paid for out of the city budget," which was also, of course, paid for by taxes. People seemed not to notice this and simply consumed the food as if they had been given something without their having to pay for it.

"It kind of bugs me," Emily said, around a mouthful of hot dog.

"What does?" Xavier said, at least that's what Emily thought he said, around a full mouth of his own.

"I feel like I'm being bribed," she said. "Here I have this lovely hot dog. It is delicious. I know that this hot dog exists because my grandmother paid taxes to the city, and the city used them, instead of providing necessary goods and services, to buy hot dogs. I ought to be outraged. But I must say, this is a very good hot dog."

"More than that," Xavier said. "This hot dog is so good, and there are so many of them, that no one will come to the restaurant today. So not only has this hotdog been paid for by your tax money, it has been used to make it less likely that the people of the city will support the local businesses their quality of life depends on. It makes my own employment less likely. And yet, as you correctly said, this is an excellent hot dog." He took another huge bite and looked longingly in the direction of the grills where more were being prepared.

Emily tried very hard to make the hot dog not taste good, but she failed. Slathered in relish and covered in mustard and ketchup, it was just about the perfect summer treat.

"And in a minute," she said, "I'm going to go over there and get some cotton candy."

"Good news for your conscience," Xavier said. "The cotton candy is being provided by Mrs. Taylor. She has some kind of special sugar recipe that she uses. I'm sure it's disgusting, but everyone in town loves it, and if she didn't come out here to the fair and hand some out, people would be outraged."

Xavier polished off his dog and licked his fingers. "So how is that better?" he said. "I mean, when the government gives me something, I know it comes from my tax money. When I get it from Mrs. Taylor, I know that it doesn't come from tax money. But why should I care? I don't pay taxes anyway."

"You should care because there is a difference between government charity and individual charity. There's a difference between enforced community and voluntary community. The government cannot give me anything that it hasn't already taken away either from me, or from someone else. But Mrs. Taylor doesn't have that problem. She can give us things of her own free will and choice."

Xavier reached the end of the cotton candy queue and picked up the thread of Emily's argument. "So, the money that she earned working at The Princess Dress on Main Street did not come unwillingly from anyone. All that money was willingly given to her in exchange for her seamstress services, which people valued, because it made their clothes magical."

"She's a seamstress, not a fairy godmother."

Xavier waved that away. "Don't interrupt. On the other hand, by your argument, it doesn't matter if I think the roads are crappy, or that the police are too slow to respond to an emergency, or that my house burned down, I still have to pay taxes to the city, and I don't get to decide how much I pay, or whether what I pay is actually worth the value I'm receiving."

"That's right," Emily said. "When you put it that way, it sounds like a raw deal."

"Of course, the counter-argument is that without those taxes, there are services I couldn't get at all. There is no road-grading fairy godmother, for instance. If Cinderella hadn't been part of a kingdom that had built convenient roads between her simple country house and the castle, the pumpkin carriage couldn't have gotten there."

"Silly boy. You think the king built those roads?" She pointed to the ribbon of road far off in the distance that headed out toward the interstate. "That road there was cut by the Monongahela—the natives, I mean, not the river. All we did was pave it."

"You make a good point," Xavier said. "But I doubt there's anyone else in this park that will see it that way."

The line for the cotton candy stretched back thirty yards. It seemed like the entire town had queued up in front of them.

"This had better be some awfully good cotton candy," Emily said.

"Count on it," Xavier said. "It should alter your life. Not that your life isn't terrific already, but you know what I mean."

"Like the El Diablo?"

Xavier said, "The precise opposite of the El Diablo, in fact."

Emily agreed that the cotton candy was good, maybe the best cotton candy she'd ever had, but she did not believe that her life had been altered thereby.

Their early lunch came to an end, and then it was time to fan out across the park and try to get some work done. Easily half the town lounged in the park, eating food, gabbing, and watching performances on the portable stage.

"This was a good idea," Xavier said. "Pretty much, if we can get half the people in this park right now to vote no on the referendum, it will surely fail."

"That's just the problem," Emily said. "Getting these people to vote is going to be a major chore."

"Why is that?" Xavier said. "I can't even vote yet, but if I could, nothing in the world could stop me."

Emily shrugged. "I don't really know why. People just don't vote in America. I mean, some of them do, but there are an awful lot of people who register to vote, but then never bother to actually do it."

Shoulder to shoulder, they marched into the park again, this time fortified with backpacks filled with flyers and clipboards containing voting information. Ahead of them, a line of people stood waiting for their turn to fill up a cup full of soda.

At the back of the line, a couple wrangled their children, trying to keep them in line.

"That's as good a place to start as any," Xavier said. "Those are the Petersons. I've known them a long time."

The two teens approached the Petersons, smiles pasted on their faces, although their insides were filled with butterflies.

"Hey, Mrs. Peterson, Mr. Peterson," Xavier said. "This is my friend Emily. We are in the park today encouraging people to come out and vote no on the referendum on Tuesday."

The Petersons underwent a fascinating transformation during this little speech. Where they had been open and friendly, welcoming, with smiles on their faces, at the mention of the referendum, their faces fell, and Mr. Peterson shuffled uncomfortably.

"Thank you," Mrs. Peterson said, taking one of the flyers. "We haven't decided how we are going to vote on the referendum."

"What kinds of questions do you have?" Xavier said. "We're just kids, but Emily and I have been studying this issue for quite a long time. Emily's grandmother lives in the little pink house." Again, as every time it was brought up, the mention of the little pink house earned a smile.

"We love that house," Mrs. Peterson said. "But my husband has been struggling to find work that's closer than an hour away. He drives all the way into New Haven to go to work at a factory there, and we would love it if he could work a little closer. He has exactly the kinds of qualifications that they'll be looking for at the new chemical plant. We're hoping he can get a job there."

"But you know, if they build that chemical factory where they're planning to, they'll have to bulldoze the little pink house."

"That's why it's so difficult for us to make a decision," Mr. Peterson said. He placed his hand on his child's head and gently guided his child back into line again. "I know it's selfish of me, but I love this town, and I don't want to have to move. The factory could make it a lot easier for me to stay here."

What could they say to this? It sounded like a decent argument. After all, he was going to need to feed his family some way, wasn't he?

"Are you sure you're registered to vote?" she said, finally.

Their faces brightened up again. "Oh, yes," Mrs. Peterson said. "We always make sure we registered. We vote in all the elections."

"Well, thank you, have a lovely day," Xavier said. They moved off toward another line.

"That was interesting," Emily said.

"Yeah," Xavier said. "I was sure the Petersons would be an automatic no. They've lived in this town almost as long as I have. I know they love it here. And I'm pretty sure their kids go boating up and down the river, as well. If they're struggling with how to vote on this referendum, we might be in bigger trouble than I thought."

In the middle of the park, a roped-off area provided space for families to have picnics. Dozens of blankets were spread out on the grass, and families munched on fried chicken and potato salad. The children mostly ran off to the playground and the foam pit over on the north side of the park, leaving the parents to lounge under the shade of the wide oak trees.

"Maybe we'll have more luck here," Emily said. They approached a youngish man, in his twenties, lying on a blue and green checked blanket reading a book.

"Hey, *Fablehaven*," Emily said. "I love that book."

The man looked up. "Brandon Mull is pretty terrific, isn't he?"

Xavier said, "We don't want to take up any of your time, but we're making sure that people are aware that there is a referendum on Tuesday and asking people to go to the polls and vote no."

The man shook his head. "I never vote." He went back to looking at his book.

"You never vote?" Emily said. "Without wishing to interrupt what is really an excellent book, can I ask you why not?"

"You can *ask*," the man said. He laughed a little bit to himself. Then he closed his book on his finger, making sure he had marked his place, and looked up at her.

"It's like this," he said. "I used to vote. Back when I was 18 years old, I thought voting was the coolest thing that I could possibly do. I was excited when I got my driver's license to register to vote by mail. But then a couple of elections came along. I voted for president, but obviously that didn't make any difference at all. In this state, the presidential winner was already determined a long time before I even walked into a voting booth. I thought on the state level, I could have more impact, and I do, but still not enough to make any very significant difference. I get to vote for state representatives and state senators, and I've found that although my vote may count, my voice doesn't."

"What does that mean?" Emily said. "I thought your voice and your vote were the same thing."

"Well, not quite. The difference is that although my vote does affect who it is that gets elected, it doesn't seem to make any difference in terms of what that person does when he gets elected. A lot of guys come along and talk about the fun things they're going to do when they get into office, how they're going to behave, but the truth of it is, I don't see much difference between one party or the other when it comes to that. There really aren't a whole lot of guys who make much difference when they get in office. So even though my vote counted, my voice didn't.

"Plus, you have to admit, voting for a particular candidate, who then is going to vote on all the pieces of legislation, is a pretty crude instrument when it comes to expressing your personal preferences in public policy."

Emily began to wonder what sort of a person they had wandered into here. He spoke like a political scientist, not like some guy having a picnic on the Fourth of July.

"So then we get to local elections. Now here, my vote actually matters. In fact, it matters quite a bit, probably far more than it should. I mean, in this city, there are only five city councilmen. None of them gets more than a couple of hundred votes. My vote makes a relatively significant difference, when you look at it that way. But again, most of the city councilmen that are running believe the same things, and do the same things when they get into office. So it really doesn't matter if I vote for Joe or for Jill; when they get into office, they're going to run the city pretty much the same way."

"But we're talking here about a referendum. Isn't that different?" Xavier said. "You said that your vote didn't make much difference, because the individual pieces of legislation were going to be voted on by people who couldn't tell you, or probably didn't even want to tell you, while they were campaigning, how they were going to vote. But this is actually a piece of legislation all by itself. It's like you get to be one of the representatives."

The man sat up on his blanket, a curious smile on his face. It was obvious he had done a great deal of thinking about this. "It does seem like that, doesn't it? But the truth of that is, a lot of the time the referendum doesn't make any difference, either. Let's say that 2000 people go to the polls next Tuesday."

"That sounds about right," Emily said.

"OK. Those people are going to split a thousand people each. If I go, and my mother goes, and I get my brother to go as well, and we all vote, that's three votes out of a thousand. It's not a lot, but it's something. So let's say that we are even successful, and the referendum is defeated. Or passes, depending on which side you want."

"Defeated," Xavier said. "Definitely defeated."

The man's mouth turned up at the corners. "OK then, you win. The referendum is defeated. Congratulations."

"Thank you," Xavier said, drawing himself up to his full height and placing his hand on his chest. "I think it was all due to my personal efforts."

"That's very humble of you," the man said. "But here comes the problem. Why was that particular piece of legislation on the ballot in the first place?"

"Well, because..." Xavier said, and then stopped. He opened his mouth a couple of times as if he were going to say something more, but then he didn't.

"Cat got your tongue?" the man said.

Xavier finally found his voice. "Actually, I don't know why it's on the ballot. I suppose it's because there are people who want to do something, and other people who don't want them to do it."

"And your supposition would be correct," the man said. "There are people who want to do something, and there are other people who want to do something else. But behind those people, behind both sets of people, are other forces. Normally, if a government decides to do something, and it makes a lot of people angry, they don't do it, do they?"

"No, they don't," Emily said. "I have some experience with this. Politicians tend to try to do things that are going to help them get reelected. If a lot of people are angry about a policy they propose, they usually back off. If they don't, people don't vote for them."

"Bingo," the man said, "And this town is fairly angry about bulldozing a bunch of houses to build a chemical plant, isn't it?"

"Well, I thought it was," Emily said, "But then we talked to a couple of people today who are probably in favor of the referendum. So maybe it's not as clear cut as I thought."

"It never is, but that's not actually the point. Yes, it does make some difference how many people are angry about it. And most people would be pretty clear on the injustice of forcing a bunch of little old ladies out of their houses in order to build a chemical plant. So why would the politicians do that, if it's going to get on the evening news and make them look bad?"

Emily thought fast. There had to be something in it. There always was. But what could it... Oh, wait. "Money," Emily said.

The man's eyes crinkled. "You have quite the intelligent girlfriend here," he said to Xavier, whose face turned beet red. Emily noticed, however, that he didn't deny it. Maybe he was just really interested in this discussion of politics.

"You're absolutely right, but why did you say that?"

"Because it always comes back to money, somehow. Maybe not exactly *always*, but it seems to me that economics is behind pretty much everything. Somehow, it always comes back to incentives, what people can get, and what they want to give. Or, I guess, what they're afraid of."

"So your guess was right on," he said, talking to Emily now. "There's money involved."

He shifted a little bit on the blanket, and leaned back on his hands. "I don't want to give you the wrong idea. It's almost never something like a direct bribe. Politicians normally don't get into politics with the idea that they're going to make themselves rich by getting paid off by corporations. It just sort of creeps up on them, and not all of them either. Most of them do a pretty good job, the problem is they lose sight of what their job actually is. And in this case, I don't know how the money works. I'm not sure why the city is so excited about condemning these properties to hand the land over to the chemical company. But I guarantee you, if you dig, you will find there's money involved. Suppose, just for instance, your wish really is granted and the referendum fails. Does that money go away?"

Emily and Xavier looked at each other and back to the man.

"I don't know," Emily said. "I don't know about the money in the first place, not for sure."

The man stabbed the air with his finger. "And neither do I. But if the money does not go away, then no matter how the referendum comes out next week, the government is going to find a way to make the project happen. Usually, there are millions of dollars on the line. Those millions won't go to them directly, but they will come to the community. And if they don't manage to get the project built, those funds go away. No politician wants to be the guy who let millions of dollars get away. So even if the referendum says no, it's a rare politician who is going to be able to let the people of the town tell him what he ought to do. Most politicians feel like they got a job to do, and that job is to run things. And running things means bringing as much money into that organisation as possible."

The man finished, a little out of breath, and leaned back again on his elbows, swinging the book up in front of him. "I wish you good luck with this, really I do," he said. "But I got to be honest; I think I can affect the world far more by reading this book than I can by casting a vote next week."

"Well, happy Independence Day to you anyway," Xavier said.

"And back to you, my friend," the man said sunnily. "I hear our taxpayer-funded fireworks are going to be spectacular tonight."

The four of them met back up in front of city hall, away from the park where the festivities were taking place. A few floats were parked here, some of them with wheels removed, as their trailers had to be taken for other activities that day. They looked sad and forlorn,

their means of mobility taken away from them, fringes
spread along the ground like a starfish. Shannon sat
on one of these, a large representation of the Liberty
Bell, plucking gold crepe paper and letting it fall to the
ground in a golden rain. Ethan sat on the same float at a
different corner. He stared off into the distance, toward
the river, his hands clasped in front of him, back rigid,
shoulders back as if he were sitting at attention. They
said nothing to each other.

Emily and Xavier came around the city hall building, folder full of flyers still bulging and clipboards held
under their arms. Shannon looked up when they approached, but Ethan didn't turn his head from whatever
he was staring at.

"So how did it go?" Shannon said, in a voice that
said she already knew the answer to the question.

"Not quite as well as I hoped," Xavier said. His voice
was still chipper. It seemed impossible to make him
depressed or sad.

"What does that mean?" Shannon said.

Before Xavier could speak, Emily spoke up. "It
means that as friendly and as good as people try to be,
the truth is, no one wants to talk to us, no one wants to
register to vote, and more or less no one is going to go
vote in the referendum."

"And the ones that are," Xavier said, slumping down
onto the float next to Shannon, "are split as evenly as
you can be between voting no on the referendum and

voting yes. I think the biggest reason is people are hoping that the promises the chemical company has made will actually come true. It *would* be nice if there were some more jobs in this town.

"The facility they have right now is only fifteen minutes up the road," Shannon said, bitterness evident in her voice. "And that doesn't seem to make any difference at all, does it?"

"Not very much," Xavier admitted. "But this is a different kind of factory. It's much more a place where they make things, not where they're doing research. Maybe that will have a wider appeal to the people of the town. Maybe that will match up with their skills better."

"It's not going to matter," Ethan said from the far side of the float. He still didn't turn around to look at the group. "No matter what we do, that factory is going to get built. And no matter what they promise the people, they're going to hire from Pittsburgh, or from coal country in West Virginia, not here. This town has a lot of things going for it, but that factory is not one of them.

"So, I guess we're just going to let fate take its course?" Emily said. She couldn't believe that her brother was giving up.

"Fate, chemical company, the city council, all of it. Face it, we can't fight them."

"What about publicity?" Xavier said. "You have that famous uncle, right?"

"Uncle Ben, yeah. He doesn't have a wide audience, and I wouldn't be surprised if there was no one in this town that listened to him."

"And I suppose it's better than nothing."

"It's not *much* better than nothing," Ethan said.

"It's a wonder anybody wants you to come here at all," Shannon said. "Heaven knows I don't."

Emily was sure this would get a rise from her brother, who never took an insult lying down, but this time, Ethan said nothing, just let his shoulders sag a little bit and seemed to get smaller there at the opposite end of the float. The four of them sat in silence, listening to the sounds of music from the party over the city hall building. Every now and then, Shannon would pull another piece of crepe paper off the float, tear it into little pieces, and scatter it into the growing pile at her feet. A stray cat came wandering through the square, sniffing the wind, probably looking for a meal. It slunk around the side of the city hall building and disappeared.

Finally, Xavier said, "You know what? This is a holiday. It's Independence Day. And the people who made Independence Day happen were people who would never have sat here on this float tearing up pieces of crepe paper and feeling sorry for themselves. Maybe I haven't got tea that I can dump into the river. Maybe I don't have any foreign friends who are going to come and bail us out if we start a revolution. But I do have an appetite and a nose for hot dogs. I'm going to go have a great evening, watch some fireworks, and do everything I can do between now and the referendum to stop this vote from destroying my town. If that means talking to one person, twenty people, or 200,000 people, then that's what I'm going to do. So unless we want to sit here and be sad sacks as if the sky were falling, I say we march back over there to that park, grab some grub, and make our own kind of party." He stood up, dusted off his hands, and held out his hand for Emily.

Emily sat still for a moment, then turned her face up toward him and saw his hand. A broad smile creased her face. "I'm in. I don't see any way we can have an impact on the election, but I would sure rather have a good time waiting for the axe to fall than sitting here and wishing it was over. So, I'm for a hotdog and some ice cream, and maybe even a little cotton candy." And she dropped her hand into Xavier's and stood up. Neither Shannon nor Ethan moved.

Xavier said, "I guess you're not coming. But just so you guys know, we'll be over at the park, talking to as many people as we can."

"Yes, generally making a nuisance of ourselves," Emily said. "After all, that's what teenagers are best at."

With that, the two of them turned and walked back toward the park. Out of the corner of his eye, Ethan noticed that Xavier did not let go of his sister's hand.

"Well," Ethan said, turning to Shannon. "I don't really want to third-wheel it with them. So should I just go home and watch the fireworks on my cock? Or do you have a better idea?"

"You can go with them if you want," Shannon said. "I don't want to stop you. I know it's like the two of them are kind of together, and I don't want you to feel like you have to be with me. I can take care of myself."

If you think he should stay with Shannon, turn to page 471.

If you think he should go home, turn to page 6.

Eventually, they reached the windy road that led down into the river valley where Grandma lived. The trees grew close to the road there, high summer foliage mixed with colorful brush.

By this point, Emily had started feeling a little better, probably because there was nothing left to throw up. Ethan loved to watch the trunks of the trees fly by and count the flowering dogwoods away back from the road in the forest. The car topped the rise and started down the twisty road that led into Grandma's town. Emily groaned.

"Almost there," Mom said. "Crack the window again."

North of the town, quite a ways north, lay the sprawling metropolis of Pittsburgh where the Monongahela met the Ohio and the Allegheny. South, a two-lane road followed the river up into the West Virginia highlands. A few other villages dotted the landscape up that way. Through the trees, a tall smokestack, currently inert, rose above the landscape. Some chemical company had a plant there, and a long four-lane road ran from its front door to the freeway a few miles off to the east.

Grandma's house itself sat right on the banks of the Monongahela. In the dim past it had been a fisherman's shop, and still kept the dock, sticking like a thumb out into the river. Grandma had lived there all her life.

Having the twins come and visit, she said, was "like having her own children back home. I never want to leave this house. I want to die here, sitting on my back porch, looking out over the rolling river."

While some family members had anticipated she wouldn't last that long, Ethan was pretty sure she was going to get her wish. Assuming the universe would ever allow her to die in the first place.

She was getting well up in years now, and although she still had a twinkle in her eye and a memory like a steel trap—not to mention ears that could hear a teenager in stocking feet stepping across the kitchen to the cookie jar—she was having more and more trouble getting around.

The house had long since started to show wear, and Ethan wondered why Uncle Brock didn't do more maintenance there. Not that anyone seemed to know what it was Uncle Brock did or didn't do. There had been some trouble about him a while back, but Ethan didn't really know what that was all about. Mom and Dad only seemed to talk about it when they thought the twins couldn't hear. He was living there, with Grandma, but you sure couldn't tell from the state of the place. One day the little pink house would fall down around Grandma's ears, and then she would get her wish about dying in the house for sure.

The Tuttles rolled down the blacktop ribbon into the Y-intersection where their road met Main, and there was one of the highlights of the trip—Thusnelda's Malt Shoppe, the best, and for a long time the *only*, burger joint in town. It was a central destination for people in the area, and the twins had heard stories about it growing up.

Thusnelda—whoever that was—specialized in a particular kind of burger that Ethan found fascinating but had never had the guts to actually try.

It went by the warning label of "El Diablo."

A whole pound of meat, stuffed with jalapeno peppers, topped with lettuce, tomato, and a hot sauce with a reputation for being able to kill downstream fish a mile away.

A few minutes later, Ethan found himself staring at the shop's menu board, attempting —not for the first time—to work up the guts to try El Diablo. If he succeeded in downing the entire thing, he would get a T-shirt that would be the envy of everyone in town. In all the years they had been coming to visit Grandma, Ethan had only seen two of these T-shirts, and they both belonged to the coolest kids in town. It was either that or the Wolfie burger with mushrooms. Emily walked up behind him and whispered in his ear.

"Don't do it," she said. "You'll regret it tonight when you can't leave the bathroom."

"I will not," Ethan said. "I'll eat it if I want to, and *only* because I decided I want to."

Emily laughed as if she knew something.

If you think they should order El Diablo, turn to page 183.

If you think they should order the Wolfie burger with mushrooms instead, turn to page 286.

"Anything you want, except that."

Shannon rolled her eyes. "I knew it. I knew you were all talk."

"It's just not a good idea, that's all."

"So you have a better one?" Shannon spat.

"Yeah, I have a better one. It's do nothing at all, because doing nothing at all is better than this stupid idea." He didn't remember when he'd been this angry.

"You're just a coward," Shannon said.

"It's not cowardice to refuse to do something that's totally stupid," Ethan said. He picked up a rock and whizzed it across the street, where it bounced three times before getting buried in the weeds.

"You just think it's stupid because you didn't think of it."

"You only think it's a good idea because you *did*. Seriously, breaking into city hall? How is that a good idea in any universe?"

"It's better than letting the chemical company take over and bulldoze the town. But I guess you wouldn't understand because you don't live here." Shannon sounded less and less angry, and more and more defeated.

"I may not live here, but my grandmother does, and even if she didn't, I know what's right and what's wrong. I know when it isn't a good idea to do something illegal, just because I think something worse might happen if I don't. You can't get something good by doing something bad. That's just not the way the universe works."

"You sound like my Sunday school teacher."

"If you're trying to insult me, you'd better come up with something better than that. I think most Sunday school teachers are pretty wise. And all I know is, we still have a chance to win the referendum right now, but if we get arrested for breaking into city hall, that chance goes away immediately. There is no way we could win then."

The two of them sat, staring at each other, each of them wishing the other one would dry up and blow away.

"To heck with it. We probably would get caught. There's no way we're ever going to stop this thing. I guess we're licked." Shannon slumped flat onto the float, casting up a flutter of bunting.

"Although I don't think I've ever said this before," Ethan said, smiling a little rueful smile, "I think my sister Emily has the right of it. Or maybe it was Xavier. But we've got a couple of hours left before the fireworks, and then fireworks over the river. That's a sight to see, even if it may be the last time it ever happens."

Ethan extended a hand to Shannon. "I know we haven't exactly seen eye to eye on things, But will you come and have some ice cream with me and watch the fireworks? Whether this thing goes good or bad, I think it would be a good idea for us to celebrate as much of it as we can."

Shannon looked for a moment like she was going to take his hand, as his sister had taken Xavier's, but then, at the last moment, she shook her head. "I'm sorry, I know I'm being a serious jerk, but the truth is I just can't get into it. The fireworks would only make me extra sad for what I know is going to come after."

Ethan tried to play it off like he understood. "That's OK. And hey, we might win."

"And what if we do? " Shannon said, wandering off away from city hall, toward the quiet part of town. "Aren't they going to go ahead and build the factory anyway?"

"I don't see how they can. The referendum is for the zoning change. If they don't change the zoning, they can't build the factory."

"Then maybe I'll go into West Virginia and play the lottery or something like that. Maybe then I can write a bribe large enough to keep them from tearing my town in half." And with that, she disappeared around the side of the library. Ethan took a long slow walk back toward Grandma's house, looking at the fireworks as he went.

Emily was disgusted. "Breaking and entering, that's a lovely way to make sure that not only does Grandma's house get bulldozed, but we get a chance to go to jail for not being able to stop it."

"I told her that. I'm not totally stupid. But now we have nothing."

"Just because we don't want to go committing a felony doesn't mean we're not going to do anything. I mean, we've done a bunch of things already."

"Right. And those have been so successful." Sarcasm dripped from every word.

"We don't know if they've been successful yet. They don't look very successful, I've got to grant you that, but you never know. We haven't actually played the game yet. We don't know if what we've done has maybe made a difference. And in the meantime," she said, "there have to be other things we can do that are less risky than breaking into a government building, especially at the height of a contentious political battle.

"OK, Watergate was a stupid idea. I get it." He slumped back down in the chair, put his feet up on the coffee table and sank back as if he wanted to disappear. Emily, not feeling too chipper herself, wandered across the room to the big overstuffed chair by the window and flopped into it.

For a few minutes, they just sat there, listening to Grandma's clock tick and watching shadows crawl across the floor. They only had a couple of days left. What could they possibly do in that little time?

"Maybe we're thinking about this all wrong," Emily said.

"That would be a relief," Ethan said. He didn't move at all, as if no possible idea could ever get him out of the chair again.

"I mean we've been thinking about how to directly oppose the government."

"We do that a lot. Because it's filled with fun and merriment," Ethan said. If possible, he sank deeper into the chair.

"Of course it's not." Emily began getting a little testy herself. "We don't oppose the government because we don't have anything better to do. We do it because there is an injustice, or something needs to happen and the people in power don't seem to want to do anything about it. We only do it when we think we really need to."

"And now we really need to, maybe worse than we've ever needed to before, and everything we do is getting us nowhere."

"Maybe with something like this, something that's a little more substantial than letting somebody operate a taco truck, or putting a road somewhere, maybe in this kind of a circumstance, we aren't going to be able to fight the government directly."

"That's what Shannon was thinking of, fighting indirectly, stealing their secrets."

"No, not like that. But what if there were a way for us to use the government against itself?" Emily let that statement hang there for just a moment,

After thirty seconds or so, Ethan's head came up a little bit. "I'm listening,"

"It's alive. I wasn't sure. For a minute there, I thought I was talking to a chair."

"Very funny," Ethan said. "What do you mean, use the government against itself?"

"Well, there are a lot of different parts of the government, right?"

"Way too many, yeah."

"Ok, but each of them wants something, right? That's why they exist. Either they want something, or the population wants something, and they want that particular part of the government to give it to them. So what if the two things are in conflict? What if one part of the government wants one thing, and another part of the government wants something else?"

"That doesn't happen," Ethan said. But the slump was a little less, and it looked like he might reanimate himself after all.

"Of course it does. If you want something, and there's somebody who wants something different, that's just normal. Surely, different branches of government, and different levels of government, they're looking out for things that sometimes they can't both have."

Ethan rubbed his chin. "I seem to remember something. I can't bring it to mind right now. But something like that. Are there times you can think of when a government agency stopped something from being built?"

"Stopped something from being built? Well, there must be… Government builds things, so government must also have the power to stop things from being built."

"That's what I was thinking. So what if one part of the government wants to stop something from being built, and the other part of government wants something to be built."

"Clash of the Titans," Ethan said. He heaved himself up out of the chair and started pacing in a circle around the coffee table. "I guess whichever branch of the government is more powerful, that's the one that's going to win."

"And how do we know which one is more powerful?"

"We don't. That's why they play the games." He smiled a little. It was the first sign of life she had seen from him and a couple of days. "Regardless, it's one of those questions that has to be settled on a field, so to speak. That takes time. Once the lawyers get involved, it could go on forever."

"That's what I was talking to Grandma about earlier. I mentioned the lawyer thing; those fellows are awfully useful when you want to bog things down in red tape and not let anything happen."

"True. The problem is, they're very expensive."

Emily nodded. "That's exactly what Grandma said. I told her she could have my paper route money, but obviously that's not going to do any good. We don't have deep pockets for lawyers. But government does. They have lawyers on one side, they have lawyers on the other side, and they put them in the arena and they fight to the death. But no matter what happens, no matter who wins, it takes a long time. It gives us time to make other things happen, to rally public opinion, whatever we decide we're going to do."

Ethan blew out a long breath. "I don't know," he said. "That's a lot to think about. I don't know how we would even go about doing that, even supposing that there was a branch of the government that could stop this thing from being built."

"And we don't have a lot of time, either. I think we need to do some more research."

"What kind of research?" Ethan said, but he was moving toward the door as he said it.

"Research on times when something was going to be built, but it got stopped, because some government agency decided to block it."

Ethan went to the door and put his hand on the knob.

"Where are you going?" Emily said.

"We only have the one laptop," he said. "If we're going to both do research at the same time, and we probably better if we are going to maximize our time here, we're going to both need to be on computers at the same time. So I'm going to use the one at the library."

Emily arched an eyebrow. "The library? Just for the computer, of course."

Ethan's face was as blank as a newborn's. "Of course. What else would I be going there for?" And he slid through the half open door and was gone.

Turn to page 421.

Emily and Ethan stood at the back of the line at the height of Thusneldsa's rush hour, moving slowly forward. They could have gone over to a different line, but that would have defeated the purpose.

When they reached the front, Emily gave the cashier a bright smile. "It's Xavier, right? Remember me?"

It was very clear that he did. He swallowed, and tried unsuccessfully to keep his own smile tamped down. "Yes," he said. "I thought you were just passing through."

"Nope. We have people here. You seem like the kind of person that knows stuff about the town. A guy we could count on to have ideas."

"Now is not a good time," he said, grimacing at the line stretching out behind them.

"Probably not," Emily said, "But you can get me a Wolfie Burger and fries—"

"I'll have a Pete's Dragon—" Ethan interjected.

"Plus two raspberry shakes. And we'll be in the back corner. I eat really slowly." She fished a twenty-dollar bill out of her pants and handed it over, getting the plastic chit in return. Just as she hoped, Xavier's eyes stayed on her the whole way back to her table.

"You certainly got his attention," Ethan said, a little crotchety about the whole thing.

"Yep. But that's the point, right? We need his help. Who better to help us than a guy who sees half the town come through his restaurant every week?"

It took a while for the rush to dissipate, but eventually, a sweating Xavier tossed himself onto the bench next to Emily like a sack of frozen peas.

"Is it always like this?" Ethan said, munching a fry.

He shook his head. "Lately, it almost never is. You're just lucky."

"We need your help," Emily said.

"So you mentioned."

She told him about the new developments in the trouble with the little pink house.

Xavier said, "It all stinks. That rope swing of hers should be named a national monument."

"It's all going away unless we do something," Emily said.

Xavier slumped back, tilting his head to look at the ceiling. "Still don't know what we can do. The city council gets whatever it wants. I don't even think there's been a dissenting vote on anything since Town Hog Day was passed a couple years back."

"Town Hog Day?" Ethan said.

"You don't want to know."

"We could work out something, I know we could. There's the referendum, and plans are being drawn up right now out at Jaxton Chemical to take over the land as soon as the votes are counted," Emily said. She spooned some shake into her mouth.

Xavier's stare, never leaving Emily for long, intensified. "You know this… how?"

She waved the spoon. "That is not important. What *is* important is that we have to stop it. Can we get together and talk about what we can do? There has to be a way."

Xavier blew out a breath. "Okay. It can't hurt anything. But we're going to be short of time—even shorter than you think, because I'm working a lot—and I think we need more heads working the problem."

"You have someone in mind?" Emily said.

"Always. But in this case, I think we need Shannon."

Xavier saw something in Emily's face and said, "We're not a couple. Both of us are what you might call free agents, romantically speaking. Not that we should be speaking romantically. I mean, she's very smart. Works in the library. Has all sorts of constructive ideas. We could invite her to the meeting. If she'd come. She might. I could ask her." He swallowed again. "Am I talking too much?"

"Yes," Ethan said, testily. "But that seems to be something we'll just have to put up with. If you need to invite Shannon, do it. When can we meet?"

"Monday morning would be best, I think," Xavier said. "I don't think she's working until the afternoon that day. I'm off in the morning, too." He paused a moment. "There's just one thing."

Ethan crumpled up his burger wrapper and set it on the tray. "Which is?"

"Shannon doesn't really like... people."

"Like *any* people?"

"Out-of-towners. Like, well, like *you* people. I'm not sure how excited she'll be to have people come in from outside with their own ideas and agendas. That's not really her thing. She's worked harder than anyone to stop the rezoning and the loss of the riverfront houses. She's incredibly passionate about it and also getting kinda frustrated, as you can imagine."

Ethan scowled. "We have to invite her, though?"

"We don't *have* to. But we should. If she decides she likes you, she's a great resource. And I'm sure she'll like you. I mean, *I* like you. A lot." His face got slightly pink. "That is, I like the, um, idea that you're trying to help the town, and, uh, that you like the, uh, Wolfie burger. You did like it, didn't you? I didn't overdo the mushrooms?"

Emily laughed. "You're talking too much again," she said, but she put her hand on his arm when she said it.

Turn to page 6.

"It's got to be city hall. The editor will still be here. Where's she going to go on a holiday? It's the biggest thing in this town. No editor could miss it," Emily said.

"Suits me. That's good thinking," Ethan said. As they left the library, the humidity hit them in the face like a damp rag. They waded through the afternoon heat toward city hall.

"Wow. I can't believe people live here," Emily said. "I need SCUBA gear just to get from one place to another."

"Smells great, though," Ethan said, inhaling. Fresh cut grass. His favorite. They tracked across the lawn to the front of city hall.

It wasn't much to look at. Clearly built in the seventies, when apparently all architectural schools taught their students that one-floor, brick buildings with flat roofs were a design for all time. Emily got to the glass front door first and held it open for Ethan.

"Thanks," he said. "Our papers are wilting." He tapped his back pocket.

"It's a wonder they don't collapse in a soggy heap," she said.

Inside it was blessedly cool, but also dark. To the right, wooden doors led to the city council chambers, or so the sign said. Ahead, a vinyl-tiled hallway led to a cashier's cage. A sign above it said Utility Bills and Impact Fees. Not the way to go. But to the left was another glass-fronted cage that said City Recorder.

"That one," Ethan said.

Emily took the lead. She stood in front of a clerk, a youngish man who couldn't have looked more bored if he'd been assigned the part in a movie. He didn't look up, just kept glacially making marks on a form. She wondered if she should clear her throat or something to get his attention. But after fifteen or twenty seconds he looked up with one eye and said, "Sorry, we're closed."

Ethan pointed to a sign on the wall that said 9-5, Monday-Friday. "It's only 4:45. You should be open for the next fifteen minutes."

"Not on a holiday weekend."

Ethan's face got a little red. "The holiday isn't for another couple days."

"I'm sorry," Emily said, shooting Ethan a nasty glance. "This will only take a second. We'd like to see a map that tells what kinds of things can be built where in the city. If you could just get us one of those, we'd get out of your way."

"You want a zoning map?" the clerk said, clearly not believing.

"We do, yes. Please."

"We have no zoning maps," he said. "They're all being redrafted pursuant to the referendum next week."

"We'd be happy to take an old one. You can't have any use for those any more," Emily said, grabbing Ethan by the arm.

"They've all been destroyed. We don't have any. Besides which, we're closed." And the man got up, grabbed his form from off the desk, and disappeared down a hallway. The office behind him was totally empty of people.

Ethan peered closely through the glass. "Never mind," he said. "Look at that." On the back wall hung a huge map of the city, with patches in various colors. "Tell me what that looks like to you."

"It looks like… a map."

"A zoning map. Each of those colors is a zone. I'm sure of it."

"What do they all mean?" Emily said, pulling out her phone.

Ethan shrugged. "I don't know. There's a code in the bottom corner, though. I think I can read it, if I squint."

"Your eyes are better than mine, then. I can't read those tiny letters."

"Do you think you can get some good pictures from here? Maybe if you zoom all the way in."

Emily did; it was blurry, but she didn't need to be able to read the street names. The areas would do just fine. Ethan busied himself writing down what he could read of the code, trying to match it up to what he saw on the map.

"I think Grandma's house is zoned R-1, whatever that means."

"The legend doesn't help?"

"The legend tells me that the zone is R-1. It doesn't come with a helpful definition of what R-1 means. Not hard to guess, though, because Grandma's house is in a place with just houses, so R probably means something like... riverside? No, that can't be right. There's a lot of that red in places nowhere near the river. Residential, maybe? That could be it."

"What about the north end of town?"

"Same color."

Emily checked the photos on her phone. "I need to brace it against something, or it's too blurry." She propped it on the counter, shooting through the small hole in the glass. "So if it's zoned for houses, can the city build there?"

"Beats me. I would have thought no."

"Unless they rezone." She looked up, eyes distant. "That's the referendum. Rezoning. The clerk said so."

"And if they rezone, nothing can stop them from building there. They can condemn whatever they like that's in their way. We've seen that before."

"We gotta get back home to Grandma," Emily said. "I'm done here."

"First the editor. We need to talk to her more than ever, now."

They punched the crash bar to get out and heard the door click behind them. Ethan tried it. "Locked," he said.

"We're done in there anyway."

They mounted their bikes and pedaled fast over to Klickitat Street, only consulting the map once. It wasn't a big town, after all. They reached the editor's house. It had a wide front porch and a vaguely decrepit look. No car in the driveway. No garage.

"It doesn't look like she's home," Ethan said.

"We have to try. Maybe her car's in the shop, or her husband has it."

They mounted the stairs. The porch creaked under them as they went to the front door. Ethan's shoe scuffed some peeling paint off the porch boards. It smelled strongly of old paper.

Emily rapped on the door. No response. "There's no bell," she said.

Ethan pounded with his fist, hoping that if he made enough of a nuisance of himself, even if she didn't want to answer, she'd have to. But either she was more stubborn than he was, or she wasn't home.

Emily wandered over to the edge of the porch and shaded her eyes from the declining sun. "I don't like dead ends. This town is starting to get on my nerves."

Ethan grabbed a newspaper off a stray stack to the left of the door. He rummaged in his pockets and came up with nothing. "Lend me your pencil."

Drawing it out, she handed it to him point-first. He scribbled a note on a corner of the newspaper, tore it off the paper, and stuck it into the screen.

"Where are we going now?" Ethan said.

"I think maybe home, first. Back to Grandma's. I want to check something with her."

When they got there, Emily showed her the pictures on her phone, and Ethan read off the legend he had copied down. Grandma nodded and said that was residential zoning, all right, and yes, the referendum was to change it. "To industrial, I think. At least for my section. I don't know about the north."

"We need to go in there and see what we can do, maybe warn people," Emily said.

"Don't go tonight," Grandma said. "One more day won't matter. I need some help with dinner, and then we need to weed the garden."

The twins stayed and Ethan had to admit it was pretty great to work with Grandma. She didn't seem like an old person; she just was who she was. She showed them how to make really crispy fried chicken, some of the best he'd ever tasted. Then she pulled weeds with them and told them stories about their father—all the embarrassing ones they'd never gotten to hear before. When the mosquitoes got too aggressive, they headed back inside and played Uno until it was time for bed.

"Good night, Grandma," Emily said, kissing her on the forehead.

"Good night, you two. It's like old times, some of the best of my life, having you here."

The next morning, the twins wolfed their breakfast and headed out at warp speed on their bikes. But when they reached the road into the north section of town, it was blocked. A barrier stood across the road, and behind it was a policeman, sitting in his car, lights flashing.

The twins pulled up on the other side of the barrier, craning their necks to see down the road.

The cop opened his door and got out, hitching up his belt. "Can I help you?" he said. But it didn't sound like he really wanted to help.

"We need to get back in there to visit some friends," Emily said. It was worth a try.

The officer shook his head. "Nobody goes back there. Road's closed. We had a report."

His radio crackled. "Dispatch, report of a man with a gun. Officers en route," it spat out.

The twins' eyes widened.

The officer twisted a dial on his radio, turning it down. "You kids get along now. Don't try going in there, or I'll have to arrest you."

The twins rode off, as slowly as they could keep their balance. "What do we do now?" Emily said.

"The city closed the road because of us," Ethan said. "Because we were snooping around city hall asking for zoning maps."

"That's a stretch. Not everything is about you, you know. You heard the thing on the radio about the gun."

"I did, yeah," Ethan said, his eyes closed in disgust. "But the road was closed before that, wasn't it? No prizes guessing why."

"Maybe we can get in there along the river?" Ethan said, and turned right, heading west, the sun on the back of his neck.

But that didn't work, either. Construction equipment, both active and inactive, blocked the way right down to the water. "Well, dang. How do we find out what's going on back there?"

Ethan put his bike down and walked down to the bulrushes at the river side. He picked up a rock and skipped it. He got three bounces before it sank.

"Everywhere a dead end," he said.

"We've done what we can. We didn't really get sent here by Mom and Dad to save the town, anyway. I'm sure the referendum will fail. Who would vote for it?"

"So, what's your plan?"

Emily ticked it off on her fingers. "One, ride over to Klickitat and find out if the editor got our message. Two, ride down to the rope swing and get some *summer* happening. We've been here three days and all we've done is go to the library and city hall, pull weeds, and ride our bikes around in some of the hottest, dustiest parts of town. I want some water and some swimming and some *vacation*, dang it."

That sounded good to Ethan.

They didn't even have to get up on the porch to see that the note was still there. She hadn't been home. "Rope swing it is," Ethan said.

It was, he had to admit, a pretty good summer vacation.

The weekend filled up with grilling, fireworks, and doing chores around Grandma's. They worked hard, moving things around the yard, pulling weeds, painting, repairing, and cleaning. When they were done, Grandma's place looked 100% better.

Tuesday, the referendum made that irrelevant.

Packed into the city council chambers, the crowd howled for blood when the results were announced, but the vote wasn't even all that close. Grandma sat on the front row, looking defeated. It was a look Emily had never seen on her grandmother before.

"What will happen now?" Ethan said.

"Let's go home, children. Nothing is going to happen tonight."

The next day, she got a letter from the city, informing her that the property had been condemned, and offering her a lot less than their previous offer as a settlement. She had sixty days to vacate.

"I won't do it," she said, tears welling up in her eyes. "I'll make them knock the house down around me."

Mom and Dad got back two days later. "We tried, up at the state," they said. "But there's nothing we can do. The city has all the cards."

"And they played them perfectly," Grandma said. "My own city. My friends—or, I thought they were." She tried to pretend she wasn't upset, but the twins had heard her crying through the thin walls.

Late that summer, the Tuttles came back one last time to clean the house and pack up Grandma's things. They had one more burger at Thusnelda's and one more day with the rope swing. By now, all the other houses on the block had already been knocked down. Grandma's little pink house stood alone.

She made sure it was clean inside and out and locked the door behind her, walking out to the car.

"Why are we bothering to clean it, if they're just going to... you know," Emily said, standing in the front yard for the last time.

"It was good enough for the Okies. It was good enough for my grandmother, when she left Germany. It's what we do. We take care of our things, even if those things aren't ours anymore." Her voice cracked. But she held herself together.

Until they rolled out of the driveway and down the street.

On both sides of the street, people came out and stood, waving as she passed by. There was no cheering—there couldn't be—but the whole town turned out and sent Patricia Tuttle off in style.

She sobbed as if her heart would break, all the way to the interstate.

THE END

"One thing we know," Ethan said, "is protests. We know how to make these kinds of things work."

"Yeah," Emily said, "But we also know that a protest that turns violent is one of the best ways to make sure nobody cares about what you're protesting for anymore. Once you establish yourself as thugs, nobody pays any attention to your message. Their brains turn off."

The twins stood there and watched their worst fears about this protest materialize. Xavier chugged across the grass to the knot of people shouting and screaming at city hall. At first, they were mostly simply waving their placards and chanting, but increasingly, the placards came down like hammers toward the policemen. The cops' faces went from conciliatory to defiant to downright angry.

Behind them, another policeman arrived, this one with a bullhorn and a chest label that said "Chief." He thumbed the switch to blast a siren over the crowd, and in the resulting quieter space made an announcement.

"This is an unauthorized protest. You have no permit and no authorization to be here. You cannot be in this space. This is public property. If you do not disperse, you will be arrested."

The effect of this was something like throwing cooking oil on a growing blaze on a stovetop. Immediately, the protesters screamed louder and one of them hit one of the policemen with her placard. The policeman reached out, grabbed the placard and tugged it out of the hand of the protester, pulling her onto the ground next to him. He whipped the handcuffs off of his belt and clasped them on her wrists as she lay there, the crowd screaming for blood, and the other policemen physically restraining them from doing anything to the officer making the arrest.

The policeman with the bullhorn thumbed another switch, and the screech from the bullhorn made everyone momentarily cover their ears. He said, "I will tell you only one more time. Violence will not be tolerated. There is no one here authorized to be protesting. You will disperse or you will be arrested."

While he was making this speech, a large man shoved his way to the front and began screaming at the policemen, his face only an inch away from theirs. One of the policemen put out a hand to his chest to push him back a step. The man grabbed the policeman's wrist.

As big as he was, he was no match for the policeman, who simply tugged him forward, overbalancing him, stuck out a leg, and dropped him to the ground. As soon as he hit the turf, the policeman dropped onto his back, his knee in the middle of his spine, and cuffed his hands.

"Anyone else?" the police chief said. The crowd continued to howl and scream that this was unfair, that they were being forced off of public property for no reason, but the fight had gone out of them. The cops dragged the two violent protesters to their feet and hustled them around to the back of city hall, presumably to the police station there. The crowd began to break up. The police chief made a couple more announcements, each one increasingly threatening, and one more person was arrested when the policemen tried to push him out of the square. It was dusk and the light was bad, with the sun out of sight behind the hills, but Emily was pretty sure that other person was Xavier.

They rode sedately home in the gathering dark. All around them, the familiar smells of an early summer night drifted by. From far off, they could hear the gurgling of the river. Here and there, scattered among the trees and the houses, they caught the flash of fireflies. Summer flowers, roses and chrysanthemums, added their scent to the beauty of the evening. But Ethan could see very little of it. He thought of the high spirits in which they had begun the evening, whizzing down the streets toward a grand adventure in the center of town.

And now, this. Their one friend in town was probably arrested. People who were trying to help keep the riverside properties from being taken over were shamed, arrested, and increasingly powerless. When they reached Grandma's street, Ethan took stock of what the actual situation was. House after house sat empty, windows lifeless, yards gone to weeds. On the three blocks along the river, he counted only four houses that had not been left abandoned. He resolved the next morning that he would make the acquaintance of those four people and get their stories. Maybe it was enough to start something.

But tonight, it wasn't about starting things; it was about ending them. Emily seemed to feel the same. She was quiet, as quiet as he had ever seen her. They coasted slowly up Grandma's drive to the front door of the shed, dialed the combination of the lock, and put their bikes away. Then they went and sat on the back porch and looked out over the river.

The moon had not yet risen, and stars winked overhead. The old river gurgled in the dark. From some distance across the water, a nightingale trilled.

"I don't know what we're going to do," Emily finally said.

Ethan didn't either, so he said nothing.

But they couldn't very well just let Grandma be forced out of her house. Zoning or no zoning. Referendum or no referendum. There had to be a way for them to help their Grandmother. There had to be a way for her to be able to keep her house.

"We've been in tight spots before," Ethan said. "We've had situations where it looked hopeless. We've always been able to rally some help before. Maybe we can do it this time, too."

Emily sighed and held out her hand for a firefly. It danced around, as if deciding whether it wanted to land on her, and then drifted away toward the river in the darkness. All of a sudden there was a flitting of large, black wings, and the light winked out.

Ethan let out a laugh. "Well, if that isn't an excellent metaphor for this whole evening. We have a beautiful firefly, and all it does is attract a bat to come by and snatch it out of the air. "

Emily punched him in the shoulder. "That's not very funny," she said. "But I have to admit, it's pretty accurate." And they went upstairs to go to bed.

The phone rang, early enough in the morning that nobody was terribly glad to hear it. Emily rolled over in bed and tried to go back to sleep. It was someone for Grandma, after all.

Except it wasn't. "Emily, it's for you," Grandma said, sticking her head into the room.

"For me?" Emily said.

"That's what the woman said," Ethan croaked, a pillow over his head. "Can't you take it and leave me in peace?"

"It's after nine. You can get up now, too, slugabed. The shower's open. Use it," Grandma said. After a moment, they heard her voice from the kitchen. "She's coming. Please hold on a moment."

"Who calls you?" Ethan said, making no visible motion toward obeying Grandma's instructions.

"I don't know. Mom and Dad, maybe."

"They don't call *you*, princess. They call *us*."

"Goodness. Well, there's a simple way for me to find out, isn't there?" Emily tossed on a robe and went out into the kitchen. Grandma handed her the phone with a twinkle in her eye. Emily couldn't miss it. She cocked her head, covering the mouthpiece.

"Not telling," Grandma said. "Answer it."

"This is Emily Tuttle."

"And this is Xavier Bugatti."

Emily coughed. "Sorry... Your last name is *Bugatti*?"

"One cannot choose one's last name, alas," he said.

"Not quite true," Emily said. "I cannot choose my *maiden* name, but I will have the liberty of choosing my married name."

A short pause ensued. Xavier cleared his throat. "Might we change the subject?"

"Yes, I'd like that. Why aren't you in jail? Or are you in jail, and you've chosen to use your one phone call on this fascinating conversation?"

"I am not in jail."

"You made bail? How clever of you."

He blushed so hard Emily could feel it through the phone. "I was released the moment the crowd dispersed. It was a case of mistaken identity. They meant to arrest Xavier Cugat."

"Who?"

"Please, may I ask for another change of subject? I do really have something I want to ask you."

"By all means. Fire away."

"I want you and your brother to invite me to lunch."

Emily turned to look at Grandma. She was frying sausage and paying no apparent attention. Emily tapped on the counter. Grandma's face tightened in an effort not to smile.

"Hello?"

"Um, yes, Xavier. Sorry. We were just discussing that."

"I should tell you, not just me. I want you to invite Shannon as well."

Emily pursed her lips. "Will you tell me the nature of this lunch? Shall I prepare something special? Will there be others?"

"Just the two of us. After my narrow escape from life as a hardened criminal, I'd like to discuss how to get in even more trouble. And possibly save your grandmother's house."

Emily covered the receiver. "Grandma!"

"Yes?" she said, not looking over.

"Xavier wants to come here for lunch. What should I say?"

Grandma's face broke into a beatific smile. "You should say, 'Would you like fresh chocolate chip cookies for dessert?'"

Turn to page 474.

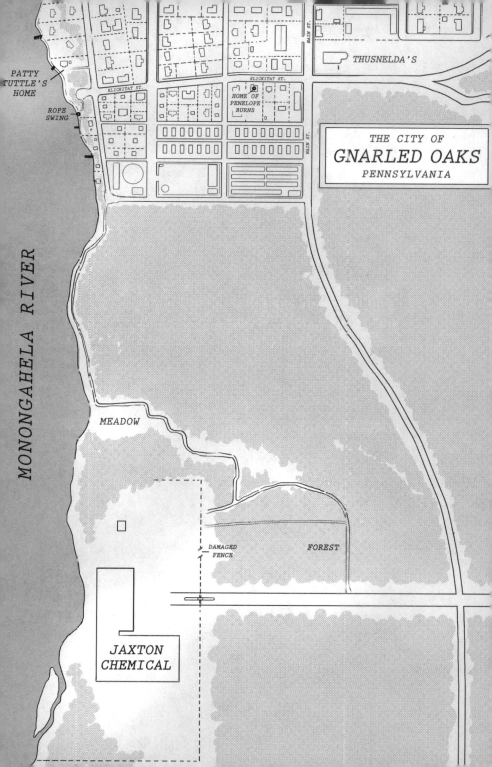

The next day, they rolled their bikes up the driveway
to the street and stood for a moment, adjusting their
position on the pedals and looking up and down the road.

"Where to?" Emily said.

"I was thinking we would ride south," Ethan said.

Emily gave him a look. "Just—ride south?" she said.
"OK, I'm game. But I can't help thinking you have a
destination in mind."

Ethan shrugged, which was as good as an answer,
and headed down the frontage road along the river.
Within four blocks, the houses ran out, and they found
themselves riding along a path, winding along with the
river, with trees on one side and the water on the other.
No guardrail, either, just the water ten or fifteen feet off
the western edge of the road. They rode along for half
an hour or so until the road came to a ninety-degree
turn to the left. Ethan pulled up and waited for Emily.

A wide meadow ran away to the south. Birch trees
sprouted here and there, and the meadow was carpeted
in summer flowers.

"That's very pretty," Emily said. "I don't remember
seeing that before."

"I don't think we've ever come this way," Ethan said.

"Is this what you wanted to see?"

"No," Ethan said, a beginning of a smile on his face.
"I was thinking we would make this left and head a little
further south as soon as we can."

He took the lead again. Emily was content to let him, as she had no idea where they were going. Every time there was a way to go further south, they took it, until after half an hour, they were well outside of town.

The road came to a T intersection, and Ethan turned to the right, toward the river, but they hadn't gone more than a few feet before they hit a fence blocking off the end of the road. It had a sign on it that said "No Trespassing." What made it actually prevent people from trespassing was the topping of razor wire on the crown of the chain link.

"Well," Emily said, "that certainly is a unique landscaping feature for this town."

"I don't think we're in town anymore," Ethan said. "Still, the owners of this property seriously don't want us doing anything here. I wonder where this fence line goes?" He flashed his sister a sly look.

"Are you going to tell me where you think we are?" Emily said. "I know you have an idea."

Ethan nodded. "I'm pretty sure I know who owns this land. I wasn't 100 percent sure, not having seen a very good map, I mean, one that was detailed enough to really give me a good idea, but from what everybody said, and from a quick dig on the Internet last night, I was pretty sure if we rode along the river far enough we would come to the headquarters of Jaxton Chemical."

The chain link fence lay crumpled and rusted in places. It had obviously been trying vainly to stand, untended, for a long time. The other side of the fence, generally, was kept pretty well maintained, and there was no place where the razor wire was absent. They were able to see across fields, sometimes to parking lots that never had a single car. Every so often, they would come to a gate leading out of the compound and into the forest, usually with a rutted dirt track.

"One of these times, we'll have to follow a road out. See where it goes, " Ethan said. But this wasn't the time for that, since both of them wanted to make sure they stayed close to the fence line to keep from getting lost.

They came to a section of fence that had fallen down completely, the razor wire spilling into the forest like a deadly silver vine. "We can get in here," Emily said, but not as if she really wanted to try it.

"I'm not sure," Ethan said. "I know we *can* get through here, but there's nothing here but that small building all the way across the field. It doesn't look very important, and I don't know what we would learn by going in there." Still, neither of them was prepared to immediately dismiss it. Here was a way to sneak around the chemical factory and find some dirt on the company before the referendum coming up next week.

If you think they should go through the fence line, turn to page 246.

If you think they should keep going to the front gate, turn to page 317.

"Grandma, can we take over the dining-room table for a bit?" Ethan asked. Or thought he did. His mouth was full of chocolate chip cookie, so there was no telling what other people could understand.

Grandma seemed to have the same superpower that Mom did. "Yes, you may. You guys have a project or something you're working on?"

"Something like that," Emily said, working her way around the overstuffed chairs in the living room. "We got some stuff from the town paper's editor. We want to see what all she gave us."

Grandma closed a drawer in the kitchen and poked her head out. "Penelope's a lovely girl. We used to be good friends." She cleared her throat. "I'm going over to Marjorie's house tonight to play bridge. I'll be late—I don't want you two still up when I get back."

The twins couldn't help looking at each other out of the corner of their eyes. "Grandma," Ethan started to say, but she cut him off.

"No, now listen. I know it's your big vacation, but you need to get some sleep. Travel always takes it out of you. You're not going to want to stay up late every night and then not be able to stay awake for fireworks and such later on, are you?"

"Uh, no," Ethan said, unable to imagine any such thing regardless of how much or how little sleep he'd gotten.

"There, then." Grandma hung her apron on the peg by the door and fluffed up her hair. "How do I look?"

"Marjorie will be jealous," Emily said, and planted a kiss on her cheek. Grandma smiled.

"Cookies in the jar."

"We know," Ethan said, brushing crumbs from his shirt.

A moment later the door closed.

Ethan dropped the thick folder onto the table with a whack. "Now. Let's see what we've got here."

Emily flipped open the folder and grabbed an inch or so of paper. Some of it was typewritten, obviously on one of those old typewriters no one used any more. Some of it was other things, newspaper clippings, photographs, handwritten scribble.

"I got something here on a napkin," Ethan said, holding it up. "It's a series of numbers. I don't have any idea what that's supposed to mean."

"Is it attached to anything?" Emily said.

"Nope." He waved it around, loose.

"Wait," Emily said. "Let me see that."

Ethan tossed it over frisbee-style. "Look here," Emily said, her finger on a corner. "This looks like rust. The shape would be right for a paperclip. Are you sure it wasn't attached to anything?"

"Absolutely sure. But there's three more inches of document here. Maybe we'll find it later."

"But seriously, why would we be able to find it, if Ms. Burns couldn't?"

"Well, who says she can't?"

"It's pretty obvious, isn't it?" Emily slapped her papers on the table and shoved back in her chair. "This stuff is just going to be clippings and scrapbook material. I'm telling you, if she had something, she would have gone to the cops with it."

Ethan shook his head. "No, don't you see? That's exactly what she couldn't do. Even if there is something in here that is totally incriminating, absolutely proof that something shady was going on, how could that go to the cops? These are the same guys that share offices with the people that are breaking the law."

Emily scoffed, but Ethan's eyes were shining.

"Put yourself in her position," he said. "She lives here. She knows all these people. Let's say she found evidence that, I don't know, there's some kind of secret deal to sell the property to the chemical company because they've discovered a platinum deposit there."

"A platinum deposit? Why not dilithium crystals?"

"Stay with me. Let's just say that's what it is. Who has to be involved?"

"The city, sure. All the city council, or at least a majority of it. The guys that run the chemical company. The mayor."

"Okay, right. That's a lot of people. Those are the people that run this town. They make decisions about everything. Now maybe the cops aren't involved, but could you count on that?"

Emily thought for a second. "Probably not."

"Definitely not," Ethan said, rising and pacing back and forth. "Every one of the policemen in this town, and there are going to be, what, six? At most? This place is Mayberry. Every one of those policemen is a personal friend of the rest of the city administration, or they couldn't have gotten hired. Even if they don't know what's going on, even if they're totally in the dark about the arrangement, are they going to believe the reporter? The woman watching over them, making sure they do the right thing, pointing out to people when they screw up?"

"But they'd have to believe her, if she had proof." Emily was still playing devil's advocate, but she was leaning forward again. Ethan's argument was getting to her.

"No, that's just it," Ethan said. "They might believe her. They might even know she was telling the truth. But would they just march into the city office and start arresting people? They couldn't. They know these people. They'd have to discuss it. Talk it over. And then they cover their tracks."

"That's pretty cynical."

"The cynical part is taking away an old woman's house to make money off it by selling it to a huge corporation."

"We don't know that's what's happening."

"Yes, we do. That is what they're doing. The question is only whether they're doing it legally, though unethically, or whether they're doing it illegally *and* unethically. But there isn't any question what they're doing."

Emily reached out and took up a paper. "Okay. That's true. I don't know if there's anything here, but you've convinced me that there could be."

"And here's my clincher, Em. Where is the woman?"

Emily looked up. "What do you mean where is she? She left town."

Ethan just smiled.

"She left town. She went on vacation."

"Over the Fourth of July. In a small town where that's the biggest thing that ever happens. Over the date of a referendum on the very question we're talking about here. And the city council meeting that follows. She's on vacation."

"But... we saw the suitcases. She was leaving."

"She was, sure. We did get lucky, getting there when we did. She couldn't have planned that. But she did plan to be gone. And now she's gone, and whatever happens it can't be her fault, because she's not here."

Emily thought about it while Ethan bounced into the kitchen and came back with a couple of cookies. He handed her one.

When he got around to the other side, Emily said, "There's one more thing you didn't mention."

"What's that?" Ethan said, sitting and leafing through the top part of the stack.

"We have another complication beyond finding an incriminating needle in this haystack. If we do come up with something—not saying we will, but if we do—we can't use it."

"Why not? She gave us this stuff so we could use it."

"Yeah, okay, we can use it, but we have to figure out how to do it so it doesn't get back to Ms. Burns. She left town so she wouldn't have to see this. She found it and wouldn't use it. She's terrified that it will get back to her. So we have to protect her."

Ethan munched his cookie. "You're right. And here I thought this was going to be fun."

An hour later, papers were strewn all over the table and part of the floor. It was an impressive collection Penelope Burns had put together, with articles from all over the region, various papers, occasionally with something circled in them. Often, though, the articles gave no clue as to why they had been curated. There were articles about Native American artifacts, about hydrodynamics, even a couple about a river monster called the Monongy that was alleged to inhabit this section of the Monongahela.

The photos were interesting, but quite obscure. Often the photos were unlabeled, and frequently they had been taken at some distance. Blurred figures shook hands in a car park. No notations indicated who the men were. Five people sat behind some kind of platform—probably the city council, although there wasn't any titling on the photograph, so Emily couldn't be sure. Why that photograph, unless there was something about the two figures to the extreme right, a man and a woman, whispering together? And it looked like there was someone behind them, holding a piece of paper. Emily couldn't tell from the photo, which seemed to have been taken from the audience between the shoulders of a couple of watchers.

Two hours. Emily knew more than she ever wanted to about the inner workings of the city government. She knew the names of all the city employees (there were sixteen of them, including two who made up the parks department, which was the same as the number of parks in the town). She knew the members of the city council. She even had begun to figure out the succession in the council—one of the members had been there twenty-two years, one of them fourteen, and two of them eight. One, though, was different. He had been elected a couple of years before and was up for re-election this year, though it did not appear that he had any opposition.

But if there were a smoking gun in here somewhere, some indication of shenanigans, she hadn't found any of it. Her eyes were beginning to cross.

"I have to take a break," she said, rubbing her face.

Ethan waved at her. "We should probably go to bed anyway. If we're still up when Grandma comes home, she'll empty the cookie jar as punishment. Then what will I eat?"

Turn to page 206.

The dirt road didn't actually go anywhere but back to the jet-black ribbon of asphalt that ran straight away from the Jaxton Chemical front door.

"Actually, I'm just as glad," Emily said. "I'm tired of walking. I'll be glad to get some wind in my hair."

"We're out of sight of the guards, anyhow. We should be fine," Ethan said, pedaling out for the right side of the road.

For a while, they were. Two or three times, cars came along the road, but the road was straight, and they heard them coming well before they arrived. The road was flat and wide and a pleasure to ride on. Emily got to where she could ride along without touching the handlebars, resting her arms.

"That's better," she said. "That's like summer at last. I feel like we've been up to our necks in all this political stuff, and we haven't had any time for any summer vacation."

She swerved to miss a rock in the road, and a car slammed into the back of her bike.

The first thing she remembered after that was some people talking. She didn't know who they were. Her eyes weren't opening.

"We never heard it, Dad. I swear."

"I know. It was one of those electric jobs, going slow. Almost silent. You'd have been fine, except that Emily

179

swerved. They had no time to dodge her. Nobody's fault, son. It's an accident."

Then the first voice started crying. That seemed pointless. She was fine, wasn't she? Except that her eyes wouldn't open. She should just drift back off to sleep.

The next time, a stabbing pain woke her up. She cried out. This time her eyes tried to open, but something kept them closed. Was she blind? She tried to reach up and rub her eyes, but her wrist was imprisoned by some kind of strap. A machine spat out a series of hysterical beeps.

A voice said, "Don't, Emily. Just lie still. You'll be fine. I'm here, darling." That was a voice she knew. That was Mom.

"Where…" she tried to say, but her voice wouldn't work. She tried again. "Where am I?"

Mom's voice had a break in it. "You're in the hospital. Do you remember what happened?"

"No. We were in the forest. Did a tree fall on me? Is Ethan okay?"

"Shhh. Just rest, dear. You're going to be fine."

Resting. That sounded good. Except she was supposed to go swimming, wasn't she?

It took two weeks, but Emily eventually got the bandages off. She asked for a mirror, but nobody would bring her one.

"They had to drill a hole in your head, Em," Dad said. "You can see it later."

The doctor pronounced himself astonished, but pleased. "She's incredibly tough. I think a lesser person might have been killed. Or if her brother hadn't acted so quickly. You saved her life, young man."

"You owe me, Em," he said, but his voice broke and he couldn't meet her eyes.

"Owe you nothing," she said.

Two days later, she got out of bed, and three days after that, she walked out of the hospital. They had dinner at the little pink house. The front yard was covered in flowers and stuffed animals.

"Wow. All this for me?" Emily said. "I don't know anyone in this town."

"Ah, but I do," Dad said, "and what's more, your grandmother does. She knows everyone. Right now, you're the most popular kid in the whole place."

It wasn't until the second helping of mashed potatoes that Emily remembered. "Oh my gosh! The house!" She looked about wildly, as if bulldozers were going to punch through the walls any second.

"The house is fine," Grandma said, patting her hand. "Thanks to you, sort of. People rallied around here for days, taking care of me, asking what they could do. I just told them, 'help me keep my house.' The mayor came out and made a speech about it and everything. They'll probably try again one day, but for now, I'm not packing."

"That's... wonderful," Emily said. "It was totally worth it."

"NO!"

The whole family yelled it at once, and Mom half rose out of her chair.

Grandma took Emily's hand. "You know those pictures on the wall in the front room?"

Emily nodded. All the family, every one of them.

"Those are just pictures, and that's just a wall. I love them because of what they remind me of, not because there's anything magic about the walls, or the frames. I'd trade a dozen houses for one day with you, and don't you forget it. Don't you ever forget it."

Emily smiled. "I won't. But I do have one question."

"What's that?"

"Do I have to wait for my hair to grow back before I go off the rope swing? I don't feel like I got a proper summer."

"Absolutely not," Grandma said. "Summer begins as soon as you finish your dinner."

THE END

Emily had meant to poke him a little bit, to tease him, but not to make him actually go through with it. Everyone knew that you couldn't actually *eat* El Diablo, because it would kill you, your children, and probably your parents and close relatives. But there Ethan was, seriously considering doing it.

I should tell him I was just kidding, Emily thought. She opened her mouth to say something, but before she could, she heard the fatal words come out of his mouth.

"I'll have the El Diablo," he said.

Behind the counter, the cashier's eyes grew wide. "You're serious," the young man said.

"I'm serious."

The cashier shook his head. "No one orders El Diablo. No one is crazy enough to do that."

"My name is Ethan Tuttle, and I'm crazy enough to try almost anything."

The teenager punched a couple of buttons on the register, a worried look on his face. "Thanks for telling me your name," he said, "so I'll know what to have carved on your tombstone. My name's Xavier, by the way. Ex-A-vier, like Professor Charles... the X-men comic books? Nevermind."

"Why are you talking me out of the burger? I thought you were here to sell food," Ethan said.

"I *am* here to sell food," Xavier said, calling the order back into the kitchen, whereupon a gale of incredulous laughter exploded from behind the grill. "El Diablo is not food. It's a deathwish." He punched up the order and handed over a plastic tab. "You're number 12."

Ethan took the tab from the cashier and turned to go back to the table. Emily thought he looked a little bit pale. No doubt El Diablo would take care of that in a moment.

"And for you, Miss?" Xavier said, eyes on Emily.

"I'll have the Hogzilla," she said.

"That's a fine choice," Xavier said. "Every pretty girl in town gets that burger."

"Ooh, flattery," Emily said, trying not to blush. "Does that come with fries?"

"No extra charge. But, um, yeah, *did* you want fries with that?"

Emily said she didn't and went back to the booth. Ethan had apparently already told their parents what he had done.

"That sounds like no fun at all," Mom said.

"It sounds like something I would have done when I was your age," Dad said.

"Did you?" Ethan said.

Dad got a small smile on his face. His eyes seemed to take him someplace far away. "Yes. I've never regretted it," Dad said.

"Seriously?" Ethan said.

Dad nodded. "Seriously. Of course, there was a girl involved."

"There often was," Mom said, patting his hand. "I think it's time for you to go and see about those shakes."

Turn to page 293.

The day dawned overcast, with a threat of rain in the afternoon. Referendum Day. Ethan rolled over in bed, cracked an eye, and tried to go back to sleep. But he couldn't.

Immediately, his mind seized on a hundred million things that could happen today, and ninety-nine million of them were bad. That there was almost nothing he could do to make any of them go away or matter less did not seem to make any difference to his brain, which had gone from dead zero to red line and in a matter of seconds.

He checked to see if his sister was still in bed and found that she had already gone. Her bed was rumpled, but she wasn't in it.

Ethan vaulted himself out of bed and down the hallway. Grandma hadn't yet arisen, and there was none of the usual smell of frying bacon and eggs.

Ethan expected to find Emily in the front room, possibly in the kitchen, but she was neither of those places. She wasn't curled up in the chair by the window, reading her book. She wasn't in the kitchen getting an early start on breakfast. No heaping bowl of fruity cereal graced the kitchen table.

Ethan thought he had an idea where she might be. He grabbed a piece of bread, popped it in the toaster, and went out onto the back porch.

There was his sister, sitting on the porch gazing intently out over the river. She did not look up as he sat down next to her. "I'm making toast," he said.

She gave the barest nod and continued gazing at the river.

Minutes went by, and Ethan went back in for the toast. He brought a slice out to her and sat down next to her again.

After a moment she said, "Do you ever think, this could be the last time we ever get to sit here like this?"

"It's not that bad," he said. "It isn't as if they're going to evict Grandma tomorrow, even if the referendum doesn't get a single no vote."

She sighed. "No," she said, "But it won't be long after that. Grandma is tired. She doesn't want to fight these people anymore. She just wants to be left alone. And if the referendum doesn't go our way, she's not going to get very much for this property. The city will buy it, but they won't give her a very good price. Probably even less than they're offering her now. And then what will she do? She needs the money from the sale to find some other place to live."

And all at once, Emily was crying.

Ethan, like most boys, didn't have any good idea what to do with that. Angry girls were a problem, but he could deal with that. Crying girls? No idea. So he just sat there, munching his toast, and every now and then he would reach over, put his arm around her, and pat her shoulder.

He had no idea if it helped; maybe it did, maybe it didn't, but it was all he could think of to do.

After a while, Emily stopped crying, wiped her nose with her arm, and ate some toast. "Sorry about that," she said. "I didn't realize how serious I was taking this whole thing."

"You didn't?" Ethan said. "You should have asked me. I could have told you."

She laughed a very little, took a ragged breath, and finished off her toast. She wiped her hands on her jeans just as the first rays of the silver morning struck the hills across the river.

"It's awfully beautiful here," she said. "Remember when we didn't want to come?"

Ethan said. "What are you talking about? It was you that didn't want to come. I always like to come to Grandma's. I was *begging* to come here."

She punched him in the shoulder. That was better.

"So what are we going to do today?" he said

"I don't know what impact we can have downtown, but I don't want to just hide out."

"Maybe if we went downtown, staying away from the polling place, we could be useful for a last-minute flyer distribution, or something like that."

"It doesn't really matter to me what we do," Emily said, strength coming back into her voice. "All I know is, I'm not going to sit here and wait for the axe to fall. We're going to go downtown. We're going to talk to people. And we're probably going to get in serious trouble. But we're going to go to where the action is, and we're going to be there all the way to the end tonight."

Ethan nodded and breathed in the cool morning air. The river gurgled away down toward the end of the dock. Uncle Brock's boat bobbed gently on the swells. "It's a really nice morning. Let's hope that's a good sign for today."

It wasn't long before they heard the banging in the kitchen that meant Grandma was up.

But still, for a long while they couldn't bring themselves to go back into the house. The scenery was just too beautiful, and both of them felt as if they were perhaps seeing it for the last time. Although they knew that the house would remain, at least for a while, possibly for a long while, still there was something about this day.

Once the referendum was over, and the verdict of the town was in, the clock would begin to tick. And yet, they kept hope in their hearts that they would not lose. Somehow, the town would come to its senses and vote the referendum down.

"You know, even if we win, the job won't be done," Emily said.

"I know that. It's kind of frustrating. I mean we've done all this work and tried so hard to get people to come out and vote, and if they don't..."

"And if they don't, and we lose, then it seems like it was all for nothing," Emily said. "I know. But even if we win, everyone seems certain that it won't mean that the battle is over. They'll just try something different. It feels like there's no way we can possibly stop them, no matter what we do. And yet, here we are getting ready to go downtown and watch the polls all day, in the hope that when we're done, we will have won at least a small victory."

"We do what we can. Embrace the struggle. Victory or defeat is in the hands of those who act."

In the kitchen, Grandma began banging on her pans and calling out to them. "Breakfast is up," she said.

When Grandma calls for breakfast, all you can do is go in. They had Grandma's usual spread: hash browns, bacon, eggs, all good things. It was a merry meal, and Ethan couldn't help feeling like this is what it would be like on the morning of an execution. Possibly a little dramatic, but still, he felt the weight of the day's events settle on his shoulders and knew that the others did too.

Once breakfast was over and the meal cleared up, Grandma put on her Sunday dress and prepared to head out the door. She stopped, as usual, in the front room. She turned a slow circle, looking at each one of the photos of her family.

Emily stood with her and watched this little ritual. "Why do you do this?" Emily said.

Grandma kept turning in her slow circle. "I'm saying hello, and goodbye, to each of them. I do it every time I go out of the house. It helps me remember that I'm very lucky, and that the most important things in my life are not the things I have, but the people that love me."

Emily thought that sounded like an excellent idea, so she stepped across the room to stand in front of the picture of her own family. There they were, the four of them, with the mountain in the background. The day of the photo had been a fall day, cool, and Emily could still remember the feel of the breeze on her face and the amazing comfort of knowing that her family was around her. In her heart she wished them luck, and then it was time to go.

Grandma stood at the screen door, looking out to her front porch. She squared her shoulders like a gladiator going into the arena and marched out the door.

The three of them headed toward the center of town, where the voting place was. Ethan wondered if there might be more traffic because the referendum might draw more people, but it looked like any other Tuesday. A few children, out for summer vacation, rode their bikes around the park. A couple of kids played hopscotch, which Ethan hadn't thought anybody did anymore.

Emily stopped for a second and asked if she could play. The little girls, only too happy to have a grown up, or a *more* grown up, play their game with them, let her play for a few minutes. Ethan stopped across the street and watched.

Grandma kept going, slowly walking the three more blocks to the center of town. As she did, she would stop and wave at people out sweeping their porches or cutting their grass.

She knew everyone in town, of course. She also seemed to be one of the most popular people there. *Not a surprise*, Ethan thought. *My grandma is awesome.*

But he also saw Grandma's connection to the place. How knowing everyone in town, and being admired and liked by them, added joy and purpose to her life. Losing that would be like losing a child. Ethan couldn't imagine what that would feel like, but he knew that for Grandma, it would be one of the worst things that could possibly happen to her. It was a terrible, sinking feeling. As if a sword were poised over their heads, ready to fall.

Emily finished and sauntered back across the street, her cheeks a little flushed from the exertion. "That's a harder game than I remember," she said.

Ethan smiled. "Probably you're just getting old," he said. She punched him in the arm.

He nodded up the street toward Grandma, her dress flapping in the early morning breeze. "This is going to be really hard on her, no matter what happens."

"It already has been, or weren't you paying attention?" Emily said. "Whatever happens, we need to make sure that she knows we're with her, and that it's not her house, but Grandma herself, that's really important to us."

They hustled up the block and fell into step on either side of her.

Grandma reached out to take Emily's hand, and Emily grabbed it with shining eyes.

But none of them said anything.

They rounded the final corner, and there was city hall. Ethan was happy to see that there were a few people in line outside the building, which meant there must have been quite a group trying to get in to vote.

It was still early, not even ten o'clock, and Ethan thought that was a good sign. Heavy turnout would almost certainly be in their favor.

A "Hey guys" floated over the grassy expanse toward them. Xavier sat on the steps of the library, watching the line snake its way into city hall across the way. He beckoned them to come and sit with him.

"Go ahead," Grandma said. "I can take it from here."

"We'll be here when you get finished," Emily said.

Grandma nodded, a little absently, her mind already on the voting ahead. She went to join the back of the line.

The twins strolled across the greensward to the library and sat down on either side of Xavier.

"So," Ethan said, "how long have you been here?"

"Long enough to know that there are an awful lot of people coming to vote in this referendum today."

"Heavy turnout works in our favor, I think," Emily said.

Xavier shrugged. "I think that's right, but I guess it could go either way."

They sat there for a few more minutes, in that kind of silence that exists when people have done all they can and simply wait to see what happens. A steady stream of people kept coming.

"Is it usually like this?" Ethan said.

Xavier turned his head toward him. "My friend," he said, "If you think there's ever been a time when I wasted a perfectly good summer day sitting on the steps of the library watching people go into city hall to vote, you really have an incorrect opinion of what sort of fellow I am."

"So that means you don't know?"

"I do not know, and until just this moment I couldn't imagine any possible need for such knowledge."

A few moments more, and Emily said, "Grandma's about to go in. I want to go and take a look at how this works."

She got up and held her hand out for Xavier. It was a hand-holding sort of day, and she knew Xavier wouldn't waste it. He was only too happy to take Emily's hand, and together they walked across to join up with Grandma just as she reached the front door.

Ethan trotted along in their wake.

He didn't recognize any of the people in line, but he knew that none of them were from the village in the north. He hoped they would come. He would have thought they would come early, to get it over with, but maybe they had their own plan.

Grandma gave the twins a tight smile and nodded to Xavier. The line reached the front, and Grandma opened the doors and went into city hall.

Ahead of them sat a table. Behind it sat three people with pencils and ledgers and expectant smiles on their faces.

Grandma said, "It's nice to see you, Mrs. Welsh, Mrs. O'Connor."

"And, of course, you, too, Patricia."

"Can I see some identification?" the woman in the middle said.

The man on her left snorted. "As if everyone in town didn't already know who you were, Patricia."

"That's all right, Fred. I'm happy to show my ID to anyone that asks, especially for a purpose like this." She pulled out a driver's license and handed it over. The woman in the middle made a mark on her ledger and recorded a number.

She handed the card back to Grandma, along with a sheet of paper and a pencil. "You're still voting by paper," Emily said.

Grandma laughed a high, nervous laugh. "We've been doing it this way for a couple of hundred years in this town," she said. "Some of us are too old to adapt to the modern ways."

The woman in the middle waved her pencil at the three teenagers. "You guys are too young to vote," she said.

"We're just here to watch," Ethan said. "If that's OK, I mean."

"These are my grandchildren and their friend. It's OK with me if they watch," Grandma said.

The woman in the middle shrugged and the three poll watchers transferred their gaze to the man in line behind the group.

Grandma went a little way off to the small table with partitions set up around it to make places where people could sit for a moment and fill out their ballots without being observed. The ballot was pretty simple. At the top was the name of the town, and underneath it the text of the referendum, asking about rezoning the area indicated, both by a map, and by a legal description.

Right in the center of the area stood the little pink house. Grandma voted no so hard Emily thought she might tear a hole in the paper. Then she smiled, folded the paper up, and carried it back to the table.

A tall wooden box sat at the end of the table with a slot in the top.

"I just drop this in here?" Grandma said.

Fred nodded his head. "No trouble guessing which side you're on, is there?" he said.

Grandma shook her head violently. "It's a terrible idea, and I hope the town agrees with me." She slipped the paper into the box and slapped the top of it with a crack that rang through the hall. Then they went back outside, and Grandma stretched as if a weight had been lifted off her shoulders. "I'm headed back home," she said. "I assume you guys will stick around here and try to get into trouble?" Her eyes twinkled, but there was something a little sad behind them.

"I suppose we will," Ethan said. Emily nodded.

Xavier said, "I'll be here to make sure nothing bad happens."

Grandma laughed and patted him on the shoulder. "I know I can count on you, Xavier." She marched off in the direction of the street to head back to the little pink house.

The twins watched her go. Xavier was the one who broke the silence. "If we don't win, it's going to be one of the greatest tragedies in American history."

The day sweltered on. Actually, Ethan had to admit it wasn't too bad. He had experienced a lot of Fourth of Julys where the weather was significantly worse. They didn't have all that much to do, even, but somehow they felt like they needed to be where the action was, and the action was at the polling place. Even Shannon drifted in and took up a position on the steps with the others.

There was actually a fair amount of action there. All through the day, a steady stream of people arrived, walked into city hall, and came back out again. None of them, however, looked like the people that the four friends were waiting to see.

"Maybe they won't show," Shannon said.

"Maybe they will and they just aren't here yet," Ethan said.

"Maybe, if we all had thick ice cream shakes, we wouldn't care so much," Xavier said.

"No," Emily said, "this is one time I think even a thick raspberry shake will not help me to feel less anxious. I'm kind of feeling like I want to ride my bike out there."

"Is that such a good idea?" Shannon said. "Didn't that guy almost blow your head off one time when you tried that?"

"Yeah, but that was before we were friends," Ethan said. "I'm sure he wouldn't do that now."

"I didn't bring my bike," Xavier said.

"I didn't bring mine, either," Shannon said.

"We could ride out doubles," Ethan said, but he sounded like he hoped no one would be interested in that. Fortunately for him, no one was.

It wasn't until about 6:00pm that the group arrived to give them hope. It was far from the whole group, but Ethan thought he recognized a couple of the women. As they walked across the village green, they saw Ethan and Emily with their friends and came over to say hello.

Ethan stood up and went to greet them. "We were afraid you wouldn't come," Ethan said.

"Of course we will come." The woman acted as if it were an obvious thing. "This means far more to us than it does to you."

When she said it like that, it was obvious. "Sorry," Ethan said, "I was just thinking of my grandma."

The woman smiled, a broad, toothy grin that showed off her brilliant white teeth. "Your grandmother is a wonderful woman," she said. "Helping her, as well as ourselves, makes this a double pleasure."

They all introduced themselves, saying that the men had not been able to make it the last time the group had been out to the village. "They were working, out toward Pittsburgh. But we got hold of them, and they were only too happy to come."

The group went into city hall.

Shannon said, "I hope that's not all we're going to get. It's not even close to enough."

Ethan smiled at her. "It's not all we're going to get," he said. "I have a good feeling about this."

Ethan's hunch turned out to be correct. About half an hour later, two large minivans pulled up, and following them, a line of huge fifteen-passenger vans. They parked along Main Street as if they were the advance guard of a parade, and people began to get out.

"Holy mackerel," Xavier said. "It's the whole darned village."

It was. Not just the adults, but the teenagers, the children, everyone came. There were so many of them that they filled up the entire courtyard between the library and city hall, as the adults queued up to get in to register and vote.

"Somebody should get in there and make sure they let them cast their ballots," Shannon said, and hustled off, volunteering herself.

"I'll go with her," Ethan said, charging into city hall.

It was a good thing, too, because the voter registration people were not excited about these people voting. It was, admittedly, a little weird. They had identification, but it came in all sorts and varieties. Some of them had military IDs. Some had driver's licenses. Others had passports. And some of them had even brought old work IDs, with a picture and a cell phone bill.

"But these don't have street addresses on them," the woman was saying. "They are all delivered to PO boxes."

"We don't have anything else," an elderly woman was saying. "These are all the identification we have. But we've lived here longer than the town has been around, some of us."

Some people were talking on cell phones, try to get clarification, others were standing patiently, waiting for the people ahead of them to have decisions made about whether they could vote.

Eventually, one of the ladies said, "I've just spoken to the county. They say that the thing to do is to allow these people to vote, but only with provisional ballots."

A general groan resounded through the hall. Shannon leaned over to Ethan. He liked it when she did that. "What's a provisional ballot?" she said.

Ethan said, "A provisional ballot is where they let you vote, but they attach information to the ballot that allows election personnel to figure out whether the votes should be counted."

"What if they decide that it shouldn't?"

"Then the vote doesn't count," Ethan said, "And sometimes it can take a while for them to make that decision."

"So even if they let these people vote today, some of their votes won't be counted?"

"At least not for a while," Ethan said. "But it's better than not voting at all."

Even as it was, with the decision made, it took forever for all the people to get through the line.

At one point, Xavier came in and said, "I counted ninety-five people. We know how they're all voting, so if they count all those votes, we have an excellent chance of getting over the top with this thing."

The polls were supposed to close at 8:00pm, and Grandma arrived about then. There was still a line going out the door. She stared in bewilderment. "Who are all these people?"

Emily smiled and put her arm around a middle-aged gentleman. "These are our friends. They live in the north end of town where the city is trying to build a golf course."

"This is a lot of people," Grandma said. "Have they been here long?"

"Since about six. We're down to just the last few, now. Oh, you should have been here a couple of hours ago."

Eventually, around nine, the last of them managed to get through. The four friends met in the middle of the courtyard, surrounded by a huge group of people from the village who had brought picnic baskets and were camping out on the village green to wait for the voting results.

"You guys were inside," Emily said, "how many of their votes do you think they will count?"

"Tonight?" Shannon said, "About half."

"I think most of them will end up being counted eventually," Ethan said, "But I don't think they'll be counted tonight. There was some seriously weird identification presented. But they all had something, just like we told them."

Xavier got a smug look on his face. "Unless we lose by a lot, it doesn't actually matter if they count them tonight. We know we have those votes in the bag. If it's close, or if we win, we have nothing to worry about. The only question is, if we are behind, will they allow those votes to be counted, or will they try to invalidate them?"

"I'm sure they'll try to invalidate them," Shannon said, bitterly. "That's kind of how the game is played."

"It's a sad game," Ethan said. "But there are difficulties both ways. We don't want people voting who aren't eligible to vote, do we? But we want to make sure everyone's vote counts. It's a tough line to walk. I felt like the ladies in there were doing the very best they could to walk it."

"Usually, that's how it is. Most of the time you can trust the people who are closest to the situation. The people who are actually part of the decision. It's the ones above them, the ones that have the agenda, that you have to watch out for," Emily said.

"But we've done our best," Xavier said, "And I believe that that entitles us to refreshment."

"We don't have time to go all the way out to the burger place," Emily said.

"No," Shannon said, with a flashing grin that Ethan was sure he had never seen before. "But there is time to go to the soda shop on Main Street."

It was almost 11:00pm when the haggard-looking election people came back into a packed city council chamber and said they had completed their count.

"It was most irregular," the woman said, "because of the number of provisional ballots. We had more than fifty of them that are not included in our totals this evening, and that may end up not being counted at all."

"Never mind that," a woman said from the front row, "what's the total of the votes you could count?"

It was obvious that the election staff had meant, earlier in the evening, to draw out the process and make it dramatic. But they had no energy for that now.

"The referendum fails," the clerk said. "By a total of 571 votes to 515 votes."

For a result that was so close, the amount of wild cheering that ensued was a surprise, but Ethan and his friends had no time for the goings-on in the chamber. As soon as they had the totals, they sprinted out to the steps of city hall and shouted the news to the assembled village. That was when things got really crazy.

The party lasted three days. The twins and Shannon and Xavier got so many hugs and kisses that their faces began to chap. Ethan ate all he could and didn't make a dent in the mounds of food that decked every table. Shannon, as good as her word, appeared to comprehensively re-evaluate her opinion of Ethan and kept herself threaded through his arm whenever he was around. As for Emily and Xavier, the less said the better. Neither of them complained.

The twins got to the point where they wanted to sleep in the village rather than riding back and forth to Grandma's house every night, but Grandma said that Mom and Dad would insist, so every night, before they fell over from exhaustion, they headed home to tuck themselves in at Grandma's.

"I'm very proud of you," Grandma said. "I didn't think we could pull this off."

"It's as much because of you as it is because of us," Emily said, snuggling down in bed. "If you hadn't been our grandmother, we might be lying in a couple of shallow graves in the forest. They were pretty hostile until we evoked the name of Saint Patricia."

"Everyone loves you, Grandma," Ethan said. "The goodwill you've built up in this town is one of the most powerful electoral forces we could have had working for us."

"Even so," Grandma said, "it was barely enough, and I'm sure the city isn't finished with us yet."

"Maybe not," Ethan said, through a gigantic yawn that threatened to split his face in half. "But I have a feeling our new friends will be a lot more vigilant from now on."

"I hope you're right," Grandma said, turning off the light. "Now get some sleep."

THE END

They tidied up the best they could, but there were still piles of paper and photographs all over the place when they went to bed. They were more tired than they imagined, because neither of them could really remember having lain down, and then the light was streaming through the windows and roses were waving in the gentle breeze, casting shadows on their walls.

"Wow. Morning already," Ethan said, rubbing his eyes.

"I'm showering first," Emily said, not even rolling over.

"Suits me," Ethan said. "Today is absolutely a rope swing day. I'll let the pure waters of the Monongahela carry off the dirt from my skin."

Emily tried not to laugh, but it was impossible to think of the Monongahela as pure, though it must have been, once. At this point on the river's course toward the big city downstream (*yet north of here*, she had to keep reminding herself), it was still not too bad. People ate the fish they caught. And there was the rope swing, one of the best parts of the Fourth of July holiday. After all, there was still time. The referendum wasn't until after the weekend.

Grandma intercepted them as they were about to dash out the back door and down to the water's edge. "You can't leave my dining room looking like a news-paper office," she said, whacking her stirring spoon on the edge of a skillet. "And you can't go swimming until you've had something to eat."

Ethan reached for the cookie jar.

Grandma whacked the lid with the spoon. "Something *good*," she said.

"Your cookies *are* good," Ethan said. "A man could live on them for days. Months, even. He'd never need any other sustenance."

"Excellent. You know how to say 'sustenance.' I must congratulate your English teacher. Do you know how to say, 'Don't argue with Grandma?'"

It turned out he did. A few minutes later he and Emily were seated at the table with a heaping plate of eggs and sausage in front of them, and some orange juice to wash it down.

"Now that you'll be sitting still for a minute, what did you find in all those papers last night?"

Emily swallowed fastest. "Not a lot. I mean, we know all sorts of things about the town government, but I don't think I saw the words 'referendum' or 'golf course' in anything I looked at."

Ethan shook his head. "Or me, either. There was a lot of background about Jaxton Chemical, though. Those guys are not the friends of this town. No matter what their PR machine makes it sound like."

"How do you come to that conclusion?" Grandma said. She had stopped cooking and cleaning, and stood by the stove with her arms folded.

"Couple things," Ethan said, waving a fork. "One, the big draw to get them to put their plant where it is now is that, one, it wouldn't block anyone's view of the river or access to it. It did that, okay, but now they want to put a new plant right where they promised they wouldn't put their plant the first time. There was a big interview about it, the guy made all kinds of promises, which they're now breaking. Ten years later, but still."

Grandma frowned. "I remember... I was in those meetings. They did talk a lot about how they wouldn't be building inside the city limits, how they were trying to minimize impact on the area, stuff like that."

"Right. Anyway, that's only the first thing. The second thing was something I didn't think about when I was reading last night, but this morning when I woke up, there it was. Jaxton Chemical promised park space for the city if the town gave up on its opposition to having a bunch of big trucks roll through town."

"The trucks don't come through here," Grandma said. "They kept their word on that."

"Yeah, they did then. But what about now? Did you get parkland? I don't see any. And yes, the trucks are not rolling through town, but that's only because they cut a new road that bypasses the town altogether. Where that bypass hits the major state road, you have two or three businesses that compete with the city's established places—"

"Like Thusnelda's," Emily finished. "I get it. There was an article about that."

"Inevitable," Grandma said. "You get one or the other. Either you have big trucks coming through, or you have to give them another place to go. That will take their business traffic outside of town."

"And their business with it. But that's just it," Ethan said, wiping his mouth with a napkin, because Grandma was watching. "There was all kinds of discussion about letting them build their factory because it would increase business in the town. But it didn't. There was no increase in business in the town at all. I saw the budget figures. I thought that was weird, that they all go back to the same year, the one right before the chemical factory got built. Every year there's an economic report in the *Au Courant*, and every year that report goes back to the same year. It's ten years now, the graph. It's flat. City revenue hasn't increased."

Emily abruptly jogged out of the room. She was back in a second with three old papers. She slapped the first one on the table. "Main Street Businesses Prepare for Boom," she said, reading the headline. "Ten years ago." A second paper landed on the first. "Main Street Business Struggles to Invite," she said. "Seven years ago. This article is about how they need to get the city to update the road and sidewalks to attract more business, because they aren't getting the traffic they thought they would. And then this," she said, whacking a third paper down to complete the stack. "County Opens New Industrial Park. This one isn't from the *Au Courant*, because it's not about Gnarled Oak, but look at the map. The industrial park is right outside the city limits." She stabbed a finger down on it. "Big box stores. MegaMart, Royal and Shedd's bookstore, Home Station hardware. It's right on the junction between the bypass road and the state highway."

"We pass it coming into town. Four years ago there was nothing there. Now there's all kinds of stuff."

"Stuff we want," Grandma said. "We were thrilled when the MegaMart opened."

"Everyone?" Emily said. "What about Broadbent's?"

"Anna Broadbent was excited, too. She said it would make it easier for her to get things in bulk. Then she'd resell them at her store."

"It's not happening," Ethan said, his eyes on the map. "There was an article about how she and her whole family were trying to find ways to attract people back to her store."

"We've seen this before," Emily said. "Business gets government to grant tax privileges—"

"Lots of those," Ethan said, "I had a quarter-inch of documents about that."

"—based on how much economic benefit their buildings are going to be to the surrounding community. The community buys the promises and gives the tax breaks, but the larger benefits never materialize. In fact, the things the town was most afraid of—like bleeding off traffic from its businesses—those things happen anyway. Now the big business is back, asking for more, when they never delivered on their original promises. They only made them to get the city council to go along with the original proposal."

"Holy smokes," Ethan said. "I didn't put it together..." He dashed out of the room. A moment later he yelled out, "Can you guys come in here a second?"

Grandma and Emily came into the dining room to find five neat stacks on the table.

Ethan looked at Grandma. "How well do you know the people on the city council?" "Pretty well," she said. "Some of them better than others."

"Susan Cook?"

"Old friend. She's one of the ladies I play bridge with."

"Been on the city council for fourteen years. How about Charley Butler?"

"He was one of your grandfather's fishing buddies."

"He's been there forever. Twenty-two years."

"And one of the nicest guys you'll ever meet. What's this about?"

"Just a minute. What about Art Willoughby?"

"Art moved to town about ten years ago. He pitches horseshoes."

"Friend of yours?"

"About like anyone," Grandma said, her good humor starting to fray.

"Eight years on the council, He got elected right after the Jaxton plant got built."

"And?"

Ethan's eyes twinkled. "Just two more. Carter Osterhout?"

"Don't know Carter that well. He's on the other side of town."

"Also eight years on the council. Do you remember who he replaced?"

Grandma thought a moment. "Hank? I'm assuming you know, Mr. Smarty Pants. Was it Hank Harlow?"

Ethan nodded. "Your memory is terrific, of course, Grandma. Hank Harlow. Didn't he live here someplace?"

"Down the street. The house is still there. Nobody lives in it."

"And the new guy."

Grandma made a face. "Grayson."

"Dick Grayson. Used to work for Jaxton Chemical," Ethan said.

Grandma looked like she'd bitten into a lemon. "Everyone knows he's a plant. Got on the board so he could do Jaxton's dirty work."

Ethan smiled so big it was a wonder his face didn't split. "That's funny. I think there are three Jaxton plants on the Council."

"Three?" Grandma said.

"Of course," Emily said, walking around the table to take a look at the stacks. "You don't suddenly put three people on the Council. Everyone will know what you're up to if you do that."

"Right. You have to get your pieces in place long before you plan to act. Osterhout and Willoughby. There are clippings here about them, but there's other stuff, too. I didn't have time to read it. But you can bet I will now. What if they've been there all along, doing Jaxton's work and waiting for this moment?"

"Doesn't make sense," Grandma said. "Why this moment? What's so special about now?"

Ethan shrugged. "I don't know. But something has happened. And I bet that whatever it is, we'll find a clipping about it in these stacks someplace."

Emily said, "But not in the next few minutes. I'm going out to swing on the rope, and get wet, and play like I won't ever get to play here again. Just in case that turns out to be true."

They were three swings in when the cashier from Thusnelda's rode up. He parked his bike against a tree and sat down under the branches to watch them. At first, Ethan didn't care, but after a few minutes he went over to see what he wanted.

"Nothing," the cashier said. "I just come here for fresh air and sunshine."

"I remember you from the malt shop," Ethan said. "My name's Ethan." He stuck out his hand.

"Xavier," the cashier said. "Not havier, but ex-avier, even though I think it's spelled the same."

"That's right. I remember now."

Emily came up, wrapping herself in a towel. "I'm Emily." She shook hands with Xavier and tried a smile on him.

It seemed to work. He brightened considerably. Ethan said, "You remember Xavier from the malt shop?"

Emily raised an eyebrow. "Yes. As a matter of fact, I do."

Ethan walked back in the direction of the knotted, ancient rope tied thirty feet up in a gnarled oak that overhung the river. "You come down here to swim?"

"That I did not," Xavier said. "I don't swim in the Monongahela."

Ethan took hold of the rope and tugged it to make sure it was still strong. Satisfied, he jumped and wrapped his legs around the rope. "Well, I do!" he said, and swung off the bank and far out over the river. Just before the rope pendulum would have begun to swing back, he let go and, with a yell, plummeted into the greenish water.

"Why don't you swim in the Monongahela?" Emily said. "I mean, it's not the cleanest, but it's better than it was. It hardly smells at all any more."

"It's not the smell or the cleanliness," Xavier said. "I have brothers and we used to bathe together. Gross water is practically what I was born in. No, the reason I don't swim in the river any more is that I don't want to swim someplace that is the lair of a beast."

"A beast?" Emily squeezed some of the water out of her hair.

Xavier seemed to like watching her do that. "Yes," he said. "A beast."

"Like Bigfoot?"

"More like Nessie, but the principle is the same."

"You have the Loch Ness Monster swimming in the Monongahela? What, is she traveling? This is her summer home?"

"You've really never heard of the Monongy?"

Emily thought for a moment. "Yes. It was in a copy of the paper I read last night. But I don't believe everything I read in the paper."

Xavier said, "There are even some people right here in town that don't know about it. But it's a real thing. The University of Pittsburgh even had a team out looking for it a few years back."

"And they found it?" Emily's skepticism was surely sharp enough that even this guy couldn't miss it.

"Of course they didn't find it. Where would be the fun in that? But just because they didn't find it doesn't mean it isn't there."

Emily sat down at a tree a few feet away. Ethan splashed about in the river, showing no sign of coming in closer to shore. "Should I tell my brother? He might be eaten at any moment."

"Very funny," Xavier said, almost as if he thought it were. "There are no reported cases of the Monongy eating anyone. Although it did eat a plane once."

"A plane?" She had a momentary vision of a huge creature leaping from the river and snatching a plane from the air.

"Training flight in World War II," Xavier said, scooting closer to her. "Crashed in the river. A massive shape rose out of the water and swallowed it. It was never seen again."

"That would probably be hard to digest," Emily said. This boy had nice freckles across his nose and curious orange flecks in his green eyes. "Even for a monster."

"Yeah, well," Xavier said, "still. I'm not going out there. Just in case this time the Monongy decides to try something softer and pinker."

Ethan didn't bother with the towel, just ran up the bank and grabbed the rope again, dragging it up to the highest spot on the bank for the longest swing possible. He glanced over. "What?" he said.

"Nothing," Emily said. "Just wish I had my camera, that's all."

Ethan jumped and physics did what it does. Halfway through his arc, Xavier said quietly, "If the Monongy leaps out and eats him, you'll really wish you had that camera."

That was when Emily decided this guy needed to be a part of whatever they were doing.

So she told him about the house, which he knew all about—it wasn't a big town, after all—and about the fight to save it, which he was interested in, and about the dining room full of newspaper clippings and photographs, which seemed to deepen his interest to the point that he couldn't take his eyes off her.

He confirmed their impressions of Ms. Burns, too, and offered to help sort through things. "There's no way she'd leave town over the Fourth. She goes to everything that happens in this town, whether she's welcome or not."

"I don't want that house gone any more than you do. It's an icon. It brings in massive tourist dollars."

Emily frowned. "It does not."

Xavier nodded. "It does not. But it should. And I feel like I've spent far too little time there myself. From this point on, I suspect I'll give in to the irresistible pull that house has for all that know it."

"Not just for the cookies?"

"Wait, there are also cookies?"

Emily punched him in the arm. He seemed to like that. "We could use your help. There's so much to sort through. We don't feel like we can get through all of it in time."

"I agree that rope swinging into the river is the best way to fix that problem." He sounded totally sincere.

"Okay, obviously not, but I couldn't stay there and sort. My eyes were crossing."

"Your eyes look fine to me," Xavier said. Then nothing happened, nothing in the world, for a long moment.

And then Ethan trotted up, dripping, and said, "Hey guys. You coming in or not?"

Emily woke from her dream and dropped her towel. "One more time," she said, and did. Then the three of them went back to the house because it was getting on for lunch, and they were beginning to feel a little bit guilty.

Halfway through, with sandwiches and partially-drunk milk glasses to one side, they dove back into the piles of material.

"This time," Ethan said, "whenever we come across anything about members of the city council, we need to put those to the side. Maybe if we both read them—sorry, all three of us—we'll see something we wouldn't by ourselves."

Xavier picked up the top sheet from Emily's stack. "What about things like this?" he said, and turned the paper around. The article headline was "Morgantown Secures $17 Million in Grants."

Ethan shrugged. "I don't know. I don't even know where Morgantown is. Maybe it got in here by mistake."

Emily took the paper from Xavier. She cocked her head while reading, the way she did when something didn't make sense. "I don't think she'd have put this in here by mistake."

"You saw her house," Ethan said. "There were papers all over the place. This could have fallen in sometime, and she would never have known it."

"I don't think so," Emily said. "It looks like Morgantown is a city a hundred or so miles from here. Maybe it's a town like this one."

"Okay, maybe it is," Xavier said, reading over her shoulder, and standing very close to be able to do so, "But what difference does that make? So the town got $17 million. Good for them. What does that mean for us?"

Emily shook her head. "I don't know. But I have to think there's something here we're missing."

"Then we're missing it," Ethan said. "We can't do everything. This is all we have to work with, and maybe it's enough, and maybe it isn't, and maybe we have to just do the best we can with what we have. We have one lead that we like, so let's go after that one, and if we have time for the others, great. If we can even figure out what those are."

Hours fled, and the three friends did finally get to the bottom of the stack. They had built a neat pile at the end of the table, where there were a couple of dozen articles about members of the city council. But almost all of the articles were about one of them—Carter Osterhout.

The profile was, at first, nothing to get excited about. He had a short stint as a high school principal, then got hired at Jaxton Chemical in the public relations department, where he worked for three years. At that point he was promoted to director of PR, and he stayed there for ten years. Eight years ago, he moved to Gnarled Oak, and two years after that ran for city council. Two years later, he quit Jaxton and started work at a paper mill outside of town.

"That's a weird resume," Xavier said. "I would have thought he would quit Jaxton before he'd run for city council."

"Why?" Emily said. She was stretched out under the table. "A guy has to work somewhere."

"But if you're going to put a plant on the city council, wouldn't you want to maintain some separation? He's working there for two years after he wins a seat. He's a Jaxton representative on the council. That's not hiding anything," Xavier said.

"Then that's not what they're hiding," Ethan said. He had four articles spread in front of them and was swiveling his head back and forth between them, as if it were a find-the-differences picture. "The key is something else, or somewhere else."

Emily whistled, long and low. "It's some*where*," she said. "Look at this." Her hand stuck out from under the table and held up a photograph. Xavier sat down next to her and plucked it from her hand.

A newspaper photograph, black and white, with a number of people in it. Below the photo was a key with the names of the people in the picture. Fourth from the right, in the second row, was Carter Osterhout. "Great. He hasn't aged well. What am I missing?" Xavier said.

"Let me see," Ethan said, sticking his head under the table. Xavier showed the photo to him.

Ethan picked out Osterhout right away. Then he saw something else.

"In the background," he said. "Is that what I think it is?"

Xavier flipped the picture around, and his eyebrows went up. "I completely missed that." Behind the people was a marble sign, the kind you put on the side of the road as people drive into town. It said, "The Rotary Club of Central West Virginia Welcomes You to Morgantown."

"Osterhout lived in Morgantown," Emily said. "Where's that article?"

"I buried it," Xavier said, climbing to his feet and rummaging through some of the papers. "But I'll find it."

"Do we have anything else about Morgantown?" Ethan said. "I don't think I had anything in my stack."

"Not just Morgantown," Emily said. "Any town like Gnarled Oak will do. Do we have other articles that don't make any sense?"

"Two of those," Ethan said. "One about Springlake—I think that's in Maryland—and one about Walford's Ferry in Missouri. They both talk about how the city got grant money in some way. I didn't read closely, because I thought this was just more random chaff, stuff that got stuck in the folder. But once there were three of them, I started to wonder. Everybody take one."

Xavier said, "Could we use another hand?"

The twins looked at one another. "Boy or girl?" Ethan finally said.

"Her name's Shannon. She won't like you."

Ethan shrugged. "Can she think?"

Xavier said, "Where's your phone?"

Half an hour later, a tall blonde with deep blue eyes pulled up on her bike and knocked on the door. Ethan went to answer it.

"I heard you needed help with something," she said.

"I'm Ethan." He opened the screen door and held it for her to come inside.

"Shannon," she said. "Just back here?"

"Yeah. We're working on some stuff we got from the editor of the paper."

She shook her head. "Don't care. Where's Xavier?"

Xavier poked his head out of the dining room. "I'll fill you in. And be nice. These guys are on our side."

It took a few minutes, Xavier talking Shannon through what they'd been working on. She didn't seem interested, but her eyes narrowed when she heard the latest development, and the beginning of a smile showed through—the first human quality she'd displayed. Ethan felt a bit distracted with her there. She might be prickly, but there wasn't anything wrong with her mind. He tried to concentrate on his task.

Emily knocked on the bottom of the table.

"No, get up here. I'm not handing them to you," Ethan said.

Emily stuck her head out. "But it's so comfortable down here. Cooler, too."

The day was getting hot. The kids exchanged a glance, and Ethan finally shrugged. Maybe Emily had a point.

They flopped onto the floor and rolled over to lie side by side. Everyone took an article.

"It's a federal grant for development," Ethan said. "The Department of Housing and Urban Development gives cities money to improve their lands. The city has to use the money for building projects, and when they do, the government turns loose cash."

"Not just a little cash, either," Xavier said. "Springlake got $20 million." He put the article down for a second. "Man, that's a lot of fries."

"You always think of things in terms of deep-fried potatoes?" Emily said.

"It's kind of an occupational hazard," Xavier said. "Speaking of which, what time is it? I'm on at three."

It was two fifteen. "I have another couple minutes. It's a ten minute walk from here," Xavier said.

"Bingo," Emily said a minute later. "I got him."

"Who?" Xavier said, scooching over to look at her article. And lay his arm along her side.

"Osterhout. He wasn't just *in* Morgantown. He was part of the bid process. He helped put the whole thing together."

"That makes sense," Ethan said. "He knew how to use the grant process because he'd done it before. So he comes here, gets on the city council—"

"And uses the same process in Gnarled Oak," Xavier finished. "That's the key. They have the grant money ready to go. But if they don't build, if they don't redevelop—"

"—meaning 'bulldoze this house'—" Emily said.

"—then they don't get the cash. That's a lot of incentive, no matter how small the grant is."

"It's bound to be tens of millions. The later the articles are, the more money the cities get. Grandma's house is the key to $25 million or so," Emily said.

Ethan rolled out from under the table and stood up, tossing his article on the table in disgust. "Well, if they're going to get millions, they ought to offer them to Grandma instead of keeping them for themselves."

Xavier's head appeared. "You know, that money could be really good for this town. That much money could mean new playground equipment, new expansions for the elementary school, roads, maybe a park…"

"Which is all great, but two things:" Emily said. "One, that money came from somewhere. It's not like the government has it in a vault someplace. They get it from taxes. They get it from the rest of us, and they give it to Gnarled Oak. Is that fair?"

Xavier opened his mouth to reply, but Emily held up a finger. "And two, far more importantly, to get the money, they have to kick my Grandmother out of her house. Are you telling me you want this money more than you want my grandmother to stay in her lovely house? Because I know you're not saying that."

Xavier was not a dumb kid. "No. I am not saying that. I would never say that. *Thinking* that gives me the collywobbles."

"Extra points for the *101 Dalmatians* reference," Ethan said. "I like this guy."

Emily and Shannon said nothing.

Ethan went on, as Xavier looked like a man just hauled back from the lip of a fatal fall off a cliff. "If the people of the town want the stuff you were talking about, then they should pay for it themselves. Take the rope swing for instance. Who put that up there?"

Shannon shrugged. "I don't know. It's always been here."

"My grandfather put that up. Years ago. He used that great rope, and it's still there, which is great, but the thing is, even though everyone in town uses the rope, Grandfather paid for it. He didn't have to. Nobody made him. He did it because he wanted to. That's how those things ought to be provided. The people that want them should pay for them."

"That won't work, though, will it?" Shannon said. "There aren't enough people who want to pay for the park to, you know, pay for it. If we didn't do it by taxes, we wouldn't have a park."

"Then maybe you shouldn't have a park," Emily said, arms crossed and a dangerous look still on her face.

"Risking your righteous wrath, my lady, I think that's kind of selfish," Xavier said. "Cookie?" He held one out to her.

She took it and humphed, but seemed mollified. "It does sound selfish, I admit, and that's why a lot of people won't say it out loud. But think about what's really happening when you pass a tax to buy a park. Is it right that everyone should pay for it?"

"Seems so."

Emily nodded. "It does. But see what's behind it. What if I don't want to pay for it?"

"Well, you, uh, that is, you can always, um…"

"I can pay for it, or I can be fined and even go to jail. That's the way it works. If I don't pay my taxes, the government can escalate things until I surrender and pay up."

Ethan excused himself and went down the hall. This was a conversation he could already see the end of, and he didn't need to be there to dance on the poor boy's ashes.

"I don't want you to go to jail."

"I believe you," Emily said, taking the opportunity to pat Xavier's arm. "But that's how it works. Taxing power is a blunt instrument. It's a chainsaw, not a scalpel. You might only want to cut off the little wart, but there's a good chance you're going to cut a whole lot of other stuff at the same time."

"So if people don't want to pay for the park, they still have to," Xavier said, munching a cookie himself, and concentrating.

"Right. The city can fine you for not paying. If you don't pay that, they might send the police to arrest you and bring you before a judge."

"Sounds like a fun TV show..."

"The question is, how badly do you want this park? Do you want it badly enough to have the police pull guns on people that don't want to pay for it? Because that's the end of that road."

"Gee, it sounds pretty horrid when you say it like that. I used to really like that park, too."

"Not saying you shouldn't. Parks are great. I love them. But I would be willing to pay for them. I would *not* be willing to have the government harass some poor old lady if she didn't."

Xavier touched his arm where Emily had patted him. "Your compassion does you credit. All the old ladies in town are grateful." He thought for a second. "I wonder why more people don't just decide not to pay their taxes when government is spending it on things they don't like."

"You want to get arrested?"

"I don't. No."

"Neither do they. Even less, probably, not being handsome and fit. It feels selfish, too. It's just a few bucks. They bite the bullet and pay. We all do. But that doesn't mean we shouldn't understand what it is that's really going on."

Xavier's eyes were wide. "You said... Am I handsome and fit?"

"I don't believe I said that. Which does not mean it would not have been true if I had."

Ethan chose that moment to re-enter the room. "What did I miss?"

"It's what I missed, I think," Xavier said, shaking his head as if to clear it. "Anyway, I've now been thoroughly educated about the evils of community taxation. But I don't think we're any closer to figuring out what to do about Osterhout, or even if he's doing anything illegal. It doesn't sound like he is."

"He might not be. But he's doing something I don't like. We don't like. So the question is how to stop him. If he's doing something illegal, so much the better, that just makes it easy to stop him. If not, then we need to see if there's something here we can use to get leverage to derail his plan."

"His plan being to get this house, I understand," Xavier said, with a glance at Emily. "But I think telling people that the city council is using the expertise of one of their members in order to secure millions of dollars in federal grants is probably going to earn them admiration, not scorn."

"Definitely. We have to humanize the situation. We have to get people to understand what's going to happen to Patricia Tuttle. That's how we can win," Ethan said.

"It's also possible that there's more here that we haven't uncovered yet," Emily said, waving her arms over the piles of paper on the table.

"Undoubtedly there is. But what's the best use of our time?" Shannon said. "It's Thursday. The Fourth is on Friday. The referendum is the Tuesday after that. Can we assume that if we can't come up with something cool between now and Monday, we're likely to lose, and all of this is pointless?"

The other three seemed to think that was right.

Shannon nodded. "Great. Well, we know what we have to get done. The problem is how to do it. And Xavier and I have to get to work. This has been fun."

Emily stretched and yawned. "I've been at this too long. I should get out and do something. Take a walk, or a bike ride, or something."

Ethan glared at her. "I'll just sort through mountains of potential evidence, then, while the three of you go off and do whatever you're going to do."

"Thank you!" Emily said brightly. "That's really great of you. I'll bring you a cookie and a glass of milk."

Ethan's scowl deepened, but he accepted the cookie.

"I'll admit," Shannon said, "when I got here I didn't think there was going to be anything to this. But you two are... pretty okay... I guess."

To Ethan that sounded like high praise, and he watched her ride away with a weird feeling in his gut.

"Be back in a minute, big brother," Emily said, holding the door for Xavier.

"Should I wait up?" Ethan said.

Emily took her bike, but since Xavier didn't have one, she walked it, crunching over the gravel side-by-side with the tall, awkward boy. But there was something about him. Not everyone would have spent most of his morning and part of his afternoon looking through dusty files trying to save someone else's house. She had to admit, that was pretty cool.

He walked with his hands in his pockets, kicking at loose stones. The smell of roses drifted on the lazy breeze. He had said he was on duty at Thusnelda's at three, and it was nearly three now, but he seemed not to be in much of a hurry.

"Do you like your job?" Emily said, in lieu of walking along in uncomfortable silence—though the silence had its positives, too.

"I don't. No one likes that kind of job. Well, let me take that back. I like parts of my job. It lets me meet interesting people. Cool people, sometimes," he said, tossing the barest glance in her direction, then hurrying on, "but not nearly as many cool people as I was hoping it would. Back when Thusnelda's was the only shop in town for grease and sugar, the place was packed all the time. I remember going there when I was a kid, and it was like Disneyland for me."

"Disneyland? Seriously? Have you actually been to Disneyland?"

"No. So I'm having to imagine a place that's a lot like Heaven, only the music is better."

"I'm pretty sure Heaven's music rocks. Still. You were saying."

"Uh, yeah. Okay. Anyway, so I used to go there with my folks sometimes and it was great. Lots of people from town, of course, but there were always a few people from out of town, stopping there because of the freeway exit not too far away and there not being anywhere else to stop for a bunch of miles in any direction."

Emily stepped awkwardly around a pothole and bumped into him. He didn't move away, just gently pushed back so she wouldn't fall. "And that doesn't happen now?" she said.

"It doesn't. The only people that come to Thusnelda's are people that live here—and they are, undeniably, great people, but I know them all already. And there are people that are coming into town to visit someone. Like you. I mean, there aren't a lot of people like you. Or any, actually. But I think you know what I mean without my sounding any less intelligent."

She smiled, and that got a bright smile back from him. "I do know what you mean. What's changed?"

"The Jaxton bypass, is what. They ran that special, Jaxton-only road out to the freeway, so now there are two exits in a couple of miles, and the Jaxton one has

MacBurger and a Gas-N-Blow and everyone stops there instead."

Emily checked her watch. "You're late," she said, not speeding up to get him there any faster. The blocks stretched ahead of them. She thought she could see a red-and-white rotating sign at the end of them, a mile or so off.

"I am. No one will care. There won't be anyone in the place at three in the afternoon. They don't really need me, but the owner is a friend of my father's, so they took me on because what's a teenager going to do in the summer?"

Emily swallowed and looked over at a bank of black-berry bushes lining the road. "I can think of a couple of things."

Xavier didn't say anything, but if she hadn't known she was imagining it, she would have sworn his temperature had gone up a couple degrees. His face did look just a little redder. It was cute.

"Yes," he said. "There are other things. Um, like rope swinging. Or, say, saving the world. Just to mention a couple at random."

"We saw something like what's going on at Thusnelda's back at a beach close to our house where we used to go for vacations. It wasn't pretty. A lot of people lost their jobs."

"That could happen," Xavier said, with a small shrug. "The shop can't be doing very well."

It was the shop in the distance, Emily could see it now. When they arrived, there was no car in the parking lot, just as Xavier had said there wouldn't be.

"You could come in. You know, for a shake or something. My treat."

"I really shouldn't. I need to get back to help my brother. We don't have a lot of time on this thing."

"I get off at ten today, and I gotta go straight home. But tomorrow I don't work at all. I was thinking of a swim."

"Going to risk the Monongy?" Emily said, with a smile and a wink.

He definitely blushed this time. "It depends. You know, on the inducements."

Emily pursed her lips. "Okay. You can have two cookies this time."

He laughed, easily, brightly. Hopefully. "That's a date." He stopped, his face draining of color. "I mean, it's not a *date* date. It's just a, you know, a, um..."

She touched his hand and swung herself up onto the seat of her bike. "See you then," she said, and rode off in a shower of dust.

When she checked back over her shoulder, he was still standing there. And she could see his smile for blocks.

Turn to page 312.

The first shot was followed by silence, as the echo rolled across the water. But then the whole riverbank opened up. A fusillade of shots banged out above them, and the shots were returned, obviously from over the river. Bullets pinged off the deck above and glass shattered. One shot came down through the open door and buried itself in the decking. Ethan crouched lower and prayed.

An engine growled out on the water, and then a larger gun barked, answered by screams and then cries of "Stop! Don't shoot!"

A voice—familiar, Ethan thought—rang out, amplified by bullhorn. "Drop your weapons and lie down on the bank!"

There was shouting and someone still cried out in obvious pain, but the shooting stopped. The sound of the boat engine increased, then cut to a low rumble, very nearby. "Mr. Tuttle," the voice said, this time closer and without amplification. "What a surprise."

This time Ethan knew for sure who it was. It was Eve Hamilton, the officer from over the river.

"It's not what you think," Brock said, from the stern. He sounded shaken but not hurt.

"I'll just bet. Hank, this time I think you'll find the hold contains more than just bilge water."

The boat rocked as the mountain that was Hank boarded. Ethan heard the jingle of the smuggling ring, and the low chuckle as Hank discovered the cartons of cigarettes.

"Bingo," he said, bass voice vibrating the planking. "We got a full load here."

A creak, and Emily's lid raised up. Her eyes shone white and wide in the dim. Ethan set his jaw. They couldn't let this happen.

Emily shook her head no. But Ethan was determined. He knew what had happened, and Hamilton did not.

He unrolled himself from under the desk and charged up the stairs.

Into madness.

They were, indeed, moored next to the chemical company, but not at the main building. In fact, they were just across a grass-and-concrete landing from a smallish, single story building. But the landing wasn't empty. Five men lay there—three of them on their faces, as instructed, but two writhing on blood-slick grass, holding legs and arms and moaning. Each one was flanked by a uniformed policeman, guns pointed at their backs.

Brock sat, slumped on the port side of the stern. He didn't even seem surprised to see Ethan standing at the top of the stairs.

On the water, a larger boat chugged, holding against the current, blocking Brock's boat from any chance of escape. It bristled with men, all of them armed, weapons leveled at the men on the bank—but also at Brock. And at Ethan.

Hank held a carton of cigarettes beneath his open mouth. And Hamilton stood like a fantasy warrior-hero, one knee up on the bow and a look on her face Ethan couldn't read.

"Brock isn't a smuggler. I mean, he's a smuggler, obviously, but it's not his idea. He's being threatened."

Hamilton's face moved to disbelief. "Really."

"Really. I heard the whole thing. One of these guys," he said, pointing at the five on the riverbank, "told him he'd burn my grandma's house down if he stopped running cigarettes. I don't really understand why cigarettes, but that's, I mean, there they are."

"They're bootleg," Hamilton said. "Tax-free. The cigarettes are evading taxes and being smuggled... Where, Brock? Pittsburgh?"

Brock nodded.

"That's what he said. It's not Brock. It's those guys. Brock wanted out. He was being blackmailed."

"Extorted, actually," Brock said.

"Uh, right. Extorted."

Ethan felt a hand touch his leg and almost threw himself into the river. Emily came up the stairs and stood behind him.

"I heard it, too," she said. "Our uncle is innocent."

"I know," Hamilton said.

"You have to let him go," Emily said. "He didn't do anything wrong."

"I said, I know," Hamilton said.

This time the twins heard her. "You... Wait, you do?"

Brock turned his head and a jagged smile peeked through his curtain of jet-black hair. "She said she does. She's not given to a lot of untruth, this woman."

"But... how?" Ethan said.

Brock, in answer, pointed toward the boat console. Ethan saw nothing. "I don't get it," he said.

Emily, though, came around Ethan and ran her hand over the water side of the panel, where there was nothing. "The box," she said. "It's not here."

Hamilton also pointed, with a similar smile on her face, up toward the top of her boat's bridge. The twins thought they could make out a familiar conical shape there, pointed toward the shore.

Ethan stared at Brock. "You set this up?"

He shoved himself off the stern and ran a hand through his hair, slicking it back. "Mutually. Not by myself. But after last night, when we got... acquainted... I thought I saw a way to get these guys what they deserved, and maybe get out of it myself."

"I thought you liked smuggling."

"Exaggeration. I tolerate smuggling. But I don't like bullies. It turns out Eve, er, Officer Hamilton, and I have that in common."

Ethan's face broke into an incredulous grin. "You're a hero."

Brock shook his head and looked embarrassed. "I'm not. I didn't really… It was mostly her. And, you know, them."

Ethan shook his head. "No, Uncle Brock. It's you, too. You're a hero. I'm going to make sure everyone knows about it."

Emily climbed up on the gunwale and shined her flashlight at the bank. "Where did the cigarettes come from?"

Hamilton came over to stand by her. "That's the interesting thing, here. That building there is where they were bringing the cigarettes out of."

"It has to belong to Jaxton, doesn't it?"

"Seems like it. All this land does. The smugglers might just have been using it without the company's knowledge. But there's something missing from this picture." She gave Emily a second to look it over.

"Guards. Where are the Jaxton guards?" Ethan said.

"Smart boy. Yes. I don't see them, do you? And I would have thought as much gunfire as we had here this evening would have brought them double-quick. I think Jaxton Chemical is going to have some explaining to do."

Emily came over to stand by Brock. "They're going to let you go, aren't they?"

"I'll have to do a lot of debriefing. We'll have to move fast to get the rest of the gang. But yeah, I think so."

Hamilton said, "I'll need Brock to spend some time at headquarters to make sure we have his testimony accurately transcribed and so he can identify the ringleaders. But we won't be charging him with anything. He's done what he needed to to convince us he's on the level."

The scene broke up slowly. Emily, Ethan, and Brock stayed on the boat while the customs officers cuffed the smugglers. About halfway through the proceedings, two fat guards came trundling up in a golf cart. One of them tried to get officious and order the customs people around, but Hamilton backed him off. In moments he was spluttering about how Jaxton had no knowledge of any smuggling and how it must have been one of the employees gone rogue.

That theory got some support when one of the downed smugglers proved to have Jaxton corporate ID on him.

"That's worth a phone call to the news, don't you think?" Ethan said, already dialing.

"You two really shouldn't have been here for this," Brock said.

"We thought we were going to catch you," Emily said. "We should have known you'd turn out to be one of the good guys."

"I'm just glad you weren't hurt. If I'd brought you back with a bullet wound, your Dad would have drowned me in this river."

"Hello, Channel Four? My name is Ethan Tuttle. There's been a raid on a smuggling operation at Jaxton Chemical."

The story broke widely the next day, with reports from all over. Officer Hamilton was hailed as a hero for unmasking the smugglers, but Uncle Brock got some play as well for being the "undercover local man" who busted the ring. Jaxton Chemical denied wrongdoing, but two of the smugglers were employees, and not just in the last couple months. The company simply refused comment.

The people of Gnarled Oak had a comment, however. The referendum failed by ten to one.

Two days later, on the last day of vacation, the twins went out to the rope swing and found that it was already being used. Uncle Brock, looking tanned and peaceful, stood holding the rope. Someone splashed about in the water, down below.

"Hey, you two. You're just in time. I need someone to retrieve the rope."

"Who's your friend?" Ethan said.

A woman with long, golden hair splashed ashore.

"I think you know Eve Hamilton," he said.

Emily said, "What's she doing here?"

Brock's smile blazed out. "Debriefing," he said, and swung out over the river.

THE END

Mom and Dad stayed around for a little while, but pretty soon said they needed to be on the road. They hugged the twins goodbye, and everyone went out to the front porch to wave and watch them drive away.

"Have a nice time!" Mom called out the window. Both of the twins yelled back that they definitely would. After the car was out of sight, they remained on the front porch for a few minutes, just taking in the atmosphere. Across the street stood an old house, even older than Grandma's, that was obviously no longer lived in.

"What happened to Mrs. Casper's house?" Emily said.

"Nothing happened to the house," Grandma said, "or to Mrs. Casper either. It's what's happened to this entire area."

"Yeah, Emily and I were just talking about that." Up and down the street, there were many of the same kinds of houses, houses that had been built a hundred years or longer ago and lived in ever since. It was a beautiful part of the world. A lot of people were excited to live so close to the river. Even though there were no major cities close by, lots of people wanted to live in a small town along a pretty river.

"I heard something about Jaxton Chemical," Emily said.

"Something about them wanting to build a factory close by," Grandma said. "Not close by—right here. The chemical company wants to locate their new factory on this exact spot of ground."

"How bad do they want it?" Ethan said.

"Very badly," Grandma said. "They've been sending me letters for months now, trying to get me to sell."

"Are they offering a lot of money?" Emily said.

"They could be offering me millions of dollars—" Grandma said, "—although I will tell you that they aren't—but I don't want to sell this house. My husband and I raised our family here. This is the only place I've ever wanted to live, and all my memories of my whole life are in this place. It's worth more to me than any money could possibly be."

Ethan thought about his own home and how much he enjoyed living there. He could not imagine having someone come and force him out of that home, and he had only been living there for the last few years of his life.

What if he had grown up in that house, had a family there? There were some things that were worth more than money. Grandma looked worried. She turned to go back into the house.

"Wait, Grandma," Emily said. "There must be some way we can stop them. I mean, you own the house. If you don't sell it to them, then they can't build their factory. Right?"

"It's not that simple," Grandma said, holding the door open for the kids to go in ahead of her. She let the screen door slam behind her and went into the big family room with all the pictures. "They have powerful friends on the city council. The city council is able to make rules for when property can be taken away from people."

"Taken away from people?" Ethan said. "The city council can't just take people's property away from them. Can they?"

"You would think that they couldn't," Grandma said, "But the truth is that they have lots of weapons they can use. One of them is a thing called condemnation. They can decide that a particular part of the city is blighted. That means it isn't fit for people to live in anymore. Then they can condemn all the houses in that area. They can also use a thing called eminent domain."

"We know a little bit about that," Emily said. "We saw some of it when the government decided to build a new road to a beach we like to go to. They used eminent domain to take over the land, built a new road, and killed off all the businesses that didn't get traffic any more."

"It can be very hard for people who are in the path of what the government wants to do," Ethan said. "Is that what's happening here?"

Grandma nodded. "And not just to me. There are rumors that the city is also working on taking over a section of ground to the north for some project. My friends at book club think it's an amusement park, or maybe a golf course. I don't think there are any houses up that way, but there is a lot of pretty forestland. I'd hate to lose it. I'd hate to lose any of it."

She sank down into her favorite chair, facing the wall with all the pictures of her children in their younger days. For a long moment she didn't say anything, just sat there facing the wall, thinking whatever it was that she was thinking.

Turn to page 418.

Emily thought the building looked promising. It sat all by itself off in the middle of a green field, squat, lone, and mysterious.

"I want to go see that building," Emily said.

Ethan's eyebrows raised. "Really? I wouldn't have thought you'd be interested in that."

She kept her eyes toward the river. "I want to save the house. I'll take some chances to do that."

Ethan scanned right and left. Lazy, sunny, humid summer day, not a person in sight. Bees droned back and forth, doing their work with the clover. An occasional bird chirped in the branches above, but just the one cheep and no more, as if it was too much effort to sing an entire tune.

"Okay. The coast is clear, I guess."

"Leave the bikes," Emily said. "Just in case we have to make a getaway."

Let that not be ironic foreshadowing, Ethan thought.

They dumped the bikes upright against the fence and trod gingerly over the rusty, downed chain link, not wanting to risk getting cut. Beyond it, the grass stretched neat and green from the fence to the building and right down to the river. The company cared a lot more about its lawn than its fencing. A wide concrete path led away from the squat gray structure and off south toward the rest of the complex.

Emily found herself trying to walk softly and laughed a little at herself. As if her footsteps would make any noise over the sounds of the river and the light breeze in the trees. But Ethan was doing it, too, walking exaggeratedly like he was sneaking across the field. In the sunshine. With no cover.

The thing to do was run. So Emily did, all at once, the nervous tension releasing itself in a mad dash across the field. It took ten strides. Five seconds. And she was under the eaves of the north side of the building.

It had no windows, at least not on this side.

Ethan joined Emily a moment later, having sprinted himself across the field. "That was unexpected," he said.

She crept along the side of the building, trying not to touch the sides, making as little noise as possible. Right up against the building, a concrete apron ringed the place. Their tennis shoes made soft sounds against the stone. They came around to the front of the building, or what they judged to be the front, facing the river. There were two windows on this side, one on either side of a door. The whole building was not more than fifteen feet by twenty. The door was solid, no window.

From the door to the river, the grass was matted down, as if a troop had walked over it carrying something heavy. Emily pointed. Ethan shrugged.

She scooted down and crawled to the door, making sure that her head stayed underneath the level of the window. She crouched there for a while, listening intently, just in case there was someone inside, but she heard nothing. The river rushed by about twenty feet away. The concrete path that led toward the rest of the compound showed wear from tires, but there was nothing on it now. From a crouched position, underneath the door handle, she reached up and gave it a twist. It turned easily and the door popped open. Immediately, she popped up onto her haunches, like a rabbit startled in a field, ready to make a break for it, but there was no shout from inside, no cry of alarm.

The door sat open three or four inches, and finally Emily grew brave enough to stand up and pull it open. After all, she could just pretend to have gotten lost, right?

There was no one inside. The back of the building was lined with white crates. In front, the floor was open, but two drafting tables stood on either side of the open floor in the middle, and on them were architect's drawings of buildings. On the one to the left, the building looked like a manufactory of some sort, exactly as she would have expected the new chemical plant to look.

On the other drafting board was a very different structure, a neat-looking chateau, surrounded by wide fields of grass. Ethan went right, Emily went left, and they had a moment to study the drawings. Sure enough, when Emily looked closely, in the right-hand corner of the drawing page it said 'chemical facility, August.'

Ethan said, "Well, that answers the question about what's going on in the north part of town."

"What is it? Emily said.

"It's a golf course. And it's supposed to be located just north of town, exactly where we thought it might be."

"Yeah," Emily said, "this building sits on land that bears a really close resemblance to a stretch of river we're both quite familiar with. Look," she said, flipping a page over and exposing an aerial view. "See the river right here? This is where the rope swing is right now. This right here, fifty yards farther down, would be Grandma's house. Only now it looks like a chemical bottling facility."

"Smoking gun, wouldn't you say?" Ethan said.

"Smoking so hot the bullet hasn't exited the barrel yet."

Ethan pulled his cell phone out of his pocket. "I want to get a picture of this."

"Dang," Emily said. "I left my cell phone at home."

"That's okay," Ethan said, "I'll take pictures of that when I'm done with this one. Come and hold the pages." He snapped away at the twelve or thirteen pages of architectural drawings.

"It's too bad," Ethan said. "This looks like a really nice place to play golf."

"It probably would be," Emily said, "if they didn't have to kick a bunch of people off their land to build it." Emily flipped the pages back down and made sure it looked exactly as it had before they got there. "Come take pictures of mine, now," Emily said.

They turned toward the other drafting table just as the door whipped open and two men in khaki uniforms said, "I don't think you'll be taking pictures of anything."

The next day, they had a meeting at Jaxton Chemical. It wasn't a pleasant one.

"I appreciate you coming on such short notice, Mr. and Mrs. Tuttle," the man said. He sat behind a polished glass table in a room at the chemical headquarters. "This won't take much of your time. We don't believe that your children meant any harm, but they were trespassing, and I'm having a devil of a time persuading my executive team that they should not press charges."

"Surely," Mrs. Tuttle said, "you're used to having kids come through that downed part of the fence all the time."

"These are the first to do so with a camera," the man said. He kept his eyes on the paper before him. "At issue here," the man said, "is the desire of the Jaxton Chemical to protect intellectual property. It's not as simple as a matter of trespassing, although that is certainly one of the possible charges, but your children took pictures of documents and violated our property rights."

He looked over at Emily and Ethan. They sat morosely against the wall, trying desperately to pretend this was all going to go away without causing any more trouble for them.

"That means," he said, "you stole from us."

Ethan swiveled in his seat for a second. "We *didn't* steal from you. I know what property rights are," he said.

"You just don't respect them, is that it?" Just a little of the steel beneath the velvet flashed out.

Mr. Tuttle put out a hand. "Mr. Barfuss, perhaps you could just tell us what it is you want us to do and what our options are."

"Certainly," he said, as if by asking him to proceed Mr. Tuttle was doing him a great favor. "We are prepared to return the cell phone, with the pictures removed, of course, and to waive the charges of theft, if the children promise not to trespass on our land again. I think you'll agree that this is a generous offer."

"It certainly is," Mr. Tuttle said. "It's so generous that I can't help wondering what the catch is."

"No catch at all," Mr. Barfuss said. "We understand what it's like to be fifteen years old on summer vacation. We don't believe the children meant any harm, but we are most interested in protecting our rights in this matter. As you see, we have not even called the police."

"Also very generous," Mr. Tuttle said. "I think we can promise you that our children will never again trespass on your land."

"Excellent," Mr. Barfuss said. "Of course, I should mention that if they were to do so, or if they were to in any way publish or distribute the results of their illegal activity, we would be forced to press charges." He spread his hands as if he were powerless in the matter. "I'm sure you understand there's nothing I can do about that."

"Absolutely," Mrs. Tuttle said, dryly. "I understand quite well, I believe."

"Excellent," Mr. Barfuss said, "then we need say no more about it. You and your children are free to go, and I hope we can all put this unpleasant matter behind us."

The adults stood, and shook hands, and a few moments later the Tuttles found themselves outside the main building, looking up at the flagpoles, and heading for their car.

"We're really sorry," Ethan said. "We were just trying to help Grandma."

"Yes, well," Dad said. "You almost never help anybody by committing crimes."

"It's them that's committing crimes," Emily said, indignant. "They're probably bribing the city council and already making plans to bulldoze the property and throw the people that live there out of their houses."

"I see," Mr. Tuttle said. "So you believe they are violating Grandma's property rights."

"I don't *believe* they are. They *are*. The stuff in that shed as good as proved it."

"You did say you know what property rights are. All right, then, why is it important to preserve them?"

"It's an unalienable right. It's in the Declaration of Independence."

Emily muttered, "Not in the final draft."

Ethan glared at her. "But it should have been. Anyway, without property rights, people are slaves. The government can make them do anything. Just like this."

"So only governments can violate property rights?" Dad said.

Ethan sensed a trap. "Well..."

"Or is it anyone in power that can do that?"

That was easier. "Anyone in power."

"And you think that has to be defended against."

"With everything we have."

Dad sighed. "Then it's a good thing for you Mr. Barfuss doesn't agree with you, because if he did, you'd be headed to juvenile detention."

Ethan's face flushed.

"You were the one with the power in that shed. You were where you shouldn't have been, doing what you shouldn't have been doing, and you thought you could use your power to take something of value from someone at your mercy."

"They're big, and we're small," Ethan said, but it sounded lame, even to him.

"So property rights are only for little people? You know better than that. What's big? What's little? Who decides?" He shook his head. "It's no good, son. Either everyone has these rights, or no one does. What you did is exactly what you're accusing them of doing. You're no better than they are."

"But they're trying to throw Grandma out of her house!" Emily said.

Mrs. Tuttle put her hand on Emily's shoulder. "And they may yet succeed. We are no longer in any position to stop them, however much we might wish to be. In fact, after dinner tonight, I'm taking you two home." Mrs. Tuttle sounded very sad. "Your father is going to stay for a couple of days, at least through next week's referendum, before he comes home. I think the chances are good he'll be needed to box things up."

"But they can't be allowed to win!" Ethan said, "It's not fair."

"Fair or not," Mr. Tuttle said, "you two are leaving. I realize you thought you were doing something to help, but you've put Grandma, the opposition forces in the town, and all of us in a terribly awkward position. I have very little hope that we'll be able to save the house now."

Dinner that night was somber, without much conversation. Even Grandma's peach pie, baked specially for the occasion, did nothing to lighten the mood. As soon as dinner was over, the Tuttles packed the children into the car.

They said tearful goodbyes to Grandma and rolled slowly out of town. The last they saw of the little pink house, Grandma and Dad were there on its front porch, waving goodbye.

"I don't think we're ever going to see that house again," Emily said.

"I hate it," Ethan said, "And it's not fair, but I think you're right."

THE END

"Do you think you're really going to be able to hear anything?" Ethan said.

"I'm going to be able to hear a lot more than that vacuum cleaner," Brock said. "At least, I hope so."

"You will have to dodge the guard, though," Brock said, dousing the boat's lights and gunning the engine. He headed upstream until they were about two hundred yards up the bank.

"We're too far," Emily said. "If I have to land here, it's an awfully long walk back. Doesn't that increase my chances of being caught?"

"You don't have to walk back," Brock said, with a grim little smile. "In fact, this will do just fine, I think. The watch is vigilant, but I think it will be a lot easier to get by them if we don't make a lot of noise doing it." With that, he cut the engine. Immediately the boat began to drift backward down the river.

Brock steered the boat as best he could, slowly drifting closer and closer to the bank. The soft glow of the clock on the dashboard was the only illumination. It said 9:57. "If I remember right," Brock said, whispering now, "the watch generally passes by here about 10:15. Sometimes there are a few minutes on either side."

"I didn't see any of them when we were here before," Ethan said. "Wouldn't it be just our luck if we came upon them just as we were tying up on the bank."

They were still about twenty-five yards from the bank when they heard a man whistling. The boat had not yet drifted back to the chemical plant, and the way the property was constructed, thick forest lay to the south of the company's property, meaning that the chemical plant property ended in a hard green line— one minute grass, sloping gently down to the riverbank, the next minute a solid line of forest, brush and trees. As close as they were to the bank, the trees obscured them from whatever was happening on the chemical plant's lawn. But there was a jingle of keys, and the whistling stopped abruptly. A walkie talkie crackled, the noise carrying cleanly across the gurgling of the river.

"Yeah, all clear here. I'm heading back."

There was a click and the squawking radio cut off. The whistling resumed, growing fainter as the man walked up the lawn toward the chemical building.

In the ghostly light, Emily's grin was easy to be seen. "That was lucky." She turned to Brock. "You really have some skill with this, don't you?"

To this, Brock said nothing, just kept pressure on the wheel, drifting the boat closer and closer to the bank.

It slid up against reeds along the line of the land and slowed dramatically. "There's no place to tie up," he said. "But we should be able to get ourselves stuck in here pretty good. It will also help to hide the boat. You might get your feet a little bit wet jumping out, but you should have a nice easy run up to the building. Nobody will bother you for at least an hour, if my memory serves on the rotation of the guards."

Ethan and Brock grabbed fistfuls of sturdy cattails, slowing the boat even more, but its momentum was still strong, and the current kept pulling them down the bank. They dragged the boat as close to the shore as they could, miring it as much as possible in the vegetation, but it was never going to stop completely.

"We won't be able to get it to a standstill," Brock said. "You're going to have to jump for it." He handed her a flashlight. "We'll drift down the river away, then motor back up. When you hear us, give us a flick of the light, and we'll come inshore close enough to pick you up."

Emily's face was pale in the faint moonlight.

"Are you sure you want to do this?" Ethan said.

"I'm sure," Emily said.

Her voice sounded anything but, but she gave a nod and set her jaw, climbing up on the port gunwale. The riverbank was still three or four feet away. It was a hefty jump, and Ethan thought that Emily would have second thoughts about it. But all at once she gave a mighty spring, and leaped.

It was a good jump, and she landed with a foot or so to spare on the hard ground. She pumped her fist. "Come back and get me in ten minutes," she whispered, and then she was over the side of the boat.

Emily hadn't really thought she'd have to do this by herself. But now, with the boat gone and her support with it, she found herself wondering what it was she had gotten herself into. She crouched for a long moment next to the cattails, her dark clothing hiding her against the flowing river and the waving vegetation. There was hardly any breeze, and the moon shone only fitfully. She listened as if her ears might fall off, but heard no sound other than the natural ones of the surroundings, underscored with a mechanical hum from the machinery powering the air conditioning systems of the buildings in front of her. Her eyes alert for any movement at all, she crept forward slowly across the grass, keeping low in a crouch, heading for the brightly lit row of windows.

If she remembered right, the only offices that had people in them were the third one from the left and the one on the corner, where the conversation they'd listened to took place. As she watched the third one from the corner, the light went out. So that one was safe now—assuming that the person who had occupied the room would be headed out the opposite way toward the parking lot and not taking a stroll down by the river. She glanced in the direction the guard had gone, but there was no sign of him, or any other individual. She was alone.

That didn't make her less frightened. She was ready to bolt at the slightest sound, already picking out the closest patch of thick woods to dive into, but no shout came. There was no one to pay any attention to her at all.

She slinked quietly up to hug the building, the way she imagined the Grinch did on Christmas morning. It had looked from the river like rough stone. When she got there she found it was really some kind of final veneer over the outside of the building. Probably concrete underneath. If she stood up, her head would be even with the bottom of the window, possibly a little bit taller.

Would it allow her to see inside? Crouched as she was, she could see nothing, but of course no one could see her either. She hadn't seen any cleaning personnel, nobody on the interior of the building who might suddenly come into one of the offices and look out, but that didn't mean there wasn't anybody there. Slowly, she raised herself up until she was even with the window sill of the north corner office. If she stood on tiptoe, she could just get her eyes over. She took a quick glance inside. The light was from the inside of the building, so she could see in very well, but anybody looking from the inside would have a hard time seeing her.

There was no one at home. A single office chair, a high back with armrests, probably leather, sat behind a polished walnut desk. The desk was empty, just a phone sitting on the edge, but there was writing on the whiteboard, and books on the bookshelves. The contents of the white board were not terribly interesting, mostly dates and places, it looked like for some kind of a trip. None of the dates or the places meant anything to her at all.

Time to move on. The ground sloped upward slightly as she went along the edge of the building, so that her head was farther up over the windowsill at each step. By the time she got to the other corner she would be shoulders above the window and be able to see much better. Of course, that was the window that had someone behind it, so it might not be a good idea to be that exposed. She moved to the fourth window, only three from the end. This was the one with the plans on the drafting table. It confirmed her suspicion. These were plans for a new building.

And given the proximity of the blue ribbon along the bottom of the plans, she figured it was probably the new plant that was supposed to be built right on her grandmother's property. This office's whiteboard, however, was interesting. It had dates as well, but the very first one she knew right off; it was the referendum date.

Below that were written several additional dates, leading to the last item on the menu, which was groundbreaking. Emily's blood boiled. This was awfully presumptuous, with a referendum not even having happened yet, to assume they would be given the go-ahead and be able to build their building.

We'll see about that, she thought. They don't know who they're messing with. She wished for a camera, or a piece of paper, or anything to record what she was seeing. She really wasn't very good at the spy business at all. Still, at least she could try to remember some of these dates, and maybe those would be helpful later. Neither of the next two offices yielded anything of interest, and the only remaining one was the corner office, where the executive had been having the conversation they overheard. She was excessively cautious here. Coming to the edge of the window, standing straight up with her face at the siding, and then leaning over just slightly until one eye came past the sash of the window.

The man they had overheard was staring right at her.

Emily froze. Every muscle in her body wanted to jerk her head back out of sight but she knew that if she moved, she would surely be seen.

She couldn't imagine how she was not being seen right now, but a second passed and then two and then three, and the gentleman inside the room kept his gaze locked on her, but did nothing.

He seemed lost in contemplation, even though his eyes continued to bore directly into hers. Ten seconds went by, and fifteen. Emily's legs began to tremble with the strain of holding so perfectly still. Just as she decided that she would try to slowly slide her head back out of sight, the man blew out a long breath, and swiveled around in his chair to face the opposite direction. He hadn't seen her after all.

Then it was Emily's turn to let her breath out, although hers was much less violent.

She felt that she had been there forever, that staying any longer was tempting fate. She had learned all she could from this anyway. Drawing the flashlight from her belt, she flashed it out at the river. Nothing particular happened, and she thought she would have to get back to the riverside in order to be able to be seen. Maybe she could flash the light downriver where it would be easier for Brock and Ethan to see it.

That wide open expanse of green was no less intimidating returning to the river than it was coming up toward the building, so Emily did it at a run, sprinting down toward the water and ducking into the cattails at the riverbank. Again she crouched and listened, but no one shouted or called after her. She had not been seen, as far as she could tell. She pointed the flashlight down the river and blinked it several times. After a minute or so, she was rewarded with the sound of a motorboat chugging its way up toward her. Again as before, it went on by, up the river, and then abruptly the engine cut out.

Emily watched for the boat to drift down into view again and felt a great sense of relief as it did so.

She was just reaching over to grab hold of one of the stern cleats, when a voice behind her called out, "Hey! You! Stop!"

Emily, startled, slipped and fell face down in the mud. She was coated from head to foot. Mud from the riverbank oozed into her pants. The man shouted again. Brock, leaning over the gunwale of the boat, extended his hand. Emily tried to drag herself out of the cattails and mud, but it clung to her, sticking her to the riverbank. Brock reached down as far as he could, his fingers brushing the back of her hand.

"Now or never," he said. She managed to raise one arm out of the muck, and he grabbed hold of it. With his assistance, she was able to stagger to her feet and throw one leg over the side of the boat. Something tugged on her from behind, but she felt the grip slip free, and she was tumbling into the bottom of the boat.

Ethan, standing at the wheel, threw the throttle forward, and the boat leaped away out into the middle of the river. Angry shouts followed them, and eventually, a beam of light, glancing out over the river. Just a flashlight, not a spotlight, or something that might have had a chance of illuminating them as they sped away. Emily lay on her back, staring up at the stars. Brock bent over her, his face broadly smiling.

"Well, that was an adventure. I hope it was worth it." Emily shook her head fractionally.

"I don't think it was. I didn't get a chance to see much, and I couldn't hear anything at all. I should have taken the device with me."

"Wouldn't have helped you," Brock said, pulling her to her feet. "It's attached to the box, and without the box it doesn't do anything. You couldn't have carried both."

"And it wouldn't have done any good anyway," she said, slumping onto the box at the stern of the boat. "There was just the one guy."

"The one in the corner office?" Ethan said. Emily nodded, even though she knew he couldn't see her. Her face was caked in mud, the front of her shirt and pants as brown as the water itself.

"You're a fright," Ethan said, turning his head around. "So you didn't get anything at all?"

"Well, there's something on the whiteboard in the corner office that I didn't really understand. One of the other offices has an architectural drawing that's definitely of the place where Grandma lives, only now it has a honking great factory on it."

"So, that was a major risk for nothing then," Brock said.

"Not for nothing," Ethan said merrily. "We got to see Emily faceplant. That's not nothing."

Emily sighed and tried to brush the mud off her face. "I'm sorry, that was a stupid idea," she said.

"What are you talking about?" Brock said. "Eavesdropping, trespassing, a little breaking and entering—always a great idea."

"You sure have some interesting ideas," Ethan said. "Where do you want me to take this boat? Home, unfortunately, is thataway." He tossed his thumb over his shoulder.

"True," Brock said. "At some point, we'll have to kill the engine and drift back. But the river's wide enough there that I think if we wait fifteen minutes or so, there's no way they're going to see us, even if they're still out there waiting. And I don't see why they would be. After all, it's not like you got anything valuable," he said.

"Nope, only a little more angry. Okay, illegal activity is probably not the way to go. But they're certainly planning to take over that land. They've already decided they're going to. As if none of this stuff we're doing with the referendum, or research on them, or publicity, or any of it makes any difference." Emily blew out a frustrated breath.

"Then we better get some help. We're smart. We can find people in this town that have ideas. There has to be *something* we can do."

Turn to page 144.

"We know a thing or two about protesting, don't we?" Emily said.

"We do, indeed," Ethan said. "It's been a little while, however. Are we sure this is a protest we want to get involved in?"

Emily gazed across the green square at Xavier, trying to push his way into the mob in front of city hall. That told Ethan everything he needed to know. "OK, I guess we go in. But let's stick together. This is already starting to get a little bit ugly."

Emily grabbed his arm. "We're not going in here to amp this up, right?" she said. "I mean, we're going in here to make it *work*, not to make it *worse*."

Ethan nodded, but there wasn't time to do more than that, because now they were jogging across the grass toward the group of yelling, straining people in front of city hall. Facing them stood two uniformed policemen, and behind them was a man in a suit—a very nice suit, too, Emily thought—holding up his hands as if begging for quiet. She couldn't hear a word he was saying. The mob had begun to chant as one, "Save our homes! Save our homes!"

The policemen stood shoulder to shoulder, as if protecting the man behind them. Their faces had set like stone, and they were no longer seeing the mob as people they knew, people from town they would have to do business with tomorrow and see at town events for the rest of their lives.

That meant the mob was already on the point of doing something catastrophically stupid. Emily knew that if the mob got out of control and arrests had to be made—or worse, if someone got injured—there would be no peace and no forgiveness. Whatever they were trying to persuade the city to do, the city would have to go ahead and do, otherwise they would be seen as having given in to violent protests. There was no way that would work. Besides, if she and her brother were going to employ the resources they had—say, publicizing things with their Uncle Ben and his press contacts with his web series and broadcast—there couldn't be any violent stain on the group. It had to be as peaceful and calm as possible.

They reached Xavier. He had been trying to shove his way in between a beefy man and a thin reedy woman, but hadn't been having any success. Emily, being smaller and quicker than her brother, saw a gap she could slither through.

She tapped her brother on the arm and pointed. "I'm going in," she mouthed to him, because the shouting was now so loud he couldn't have heard her. His eyes got wide and he shook his head, but she knew that she needed to get to a different vantage point to be able to do something useful.

Now the mob was waving their placards at the policemen like hammers. At any moment, one of them

would hit them, and then there would be real trouble.
She wiggled her way in between two people, dodged a
third, and found herself in a quiet spot in the middle
of the mob. The front lines were screaming, people in
the rear were doing the same, but in the middle were a
couple of people who seemed to just be standing there.

One of them, a broad-shouldered fellow in jeans and
a baseball cap, had an odd little smile on his face, as if he
found something amusing that he didn't want to share
with others. Next to him was another man, shorter, but
with the same broad shoulders and, inexplicably, gloves.
He looked considerably more worried, his face drawn
and pinched, but he stood resolutely next to the first
man.

One of the policemen had stepped forward now
and dropped his hand to his holster. There was no more
time to waste. Emily threaded her way through the front
of the crowd until she was right in front. Next to her on
either side were placard-waving, red-faced townspeople,
shouting and spewing spittle just a few feet from the
policemen. Then the crowd began to advance, almost as
if choreographed. There was no time left. There was no
one to reason with. The only chance was to do something truly audacious.

So Emily stepped out into the front of the crowd,
crossed the three feet to the policeman with his hand on
his gun, and threw her arms around him.

The effect on the crowd was electric. Almost like turning off a faucet, the shouting stopped. The policeman at first stiffened, as if he were about to react violently. But when he realized he was only being hugged by a fifteen-year-old girl, a different expression came over his face.

Up close, Emily could begin to guess his age. He wasn't any older than her father, and possibly even had a daughter at home. The natural father's reactions kicked in, and one arm came off his holster and around her back.

"Are you hurt?" he said.

"Not at all," she said into his ear. "I just wanted to make sure that *you* didn't get hurt." She felt him drawing a quick breath, but then let it out slowly, apparently figuring he was not being made game of, or being set up for something else. The crowd had stopped in place and were now quizzically looking at each other, trying to figure out what had gone on. Emily turned back toward them, her back to the policemen.

"I'm sorry," she said, "I thought he was someone I knew." Now, with the crowd's anger melting away, there was room for her brother to work his way toward the front. Ethan stepped from the crowd to her side and turned to face the mob. Two were better than one.

"We're new in town ourselves," he said, "but you all know our grandmother who lives in the little pink house." That got another powerful reaction, as nearly

everybody broke into some kind of a smile. Good old
Grandma. Ethan said, "This fellow back here," and here
he tossed his thumb back over his shoulder, "is trying
to say something. I am sure that you all have legitimate
grievances, but I still want to hear what kind of hole he
will dig for himself." Putting himself on the side of the
mob gave him a small advantage and made the crowd
feel like he was on their side.

One of them, a tiny woman who had to be at least
two hundred years old, said, "There's nothing he can
possibly say that we haven't heard already. That snake
would say anything, and he's never meant a word of it."

At this there were howls of agreement from the
crowd, but it wasn't sustained and the man was able
to get a word in edgewise. "I know you all think there's
something terrible going on with me and the chemical
company," he said, pitching his voice so that it would
carry. Ethan recognized the technique. Sometime in the
past, this man had done some kind of public speaking
work, or been on the radio or something. The man went
on, "But when I moved to this town, I did it with the
best of intentions. I like the people here. I like this town.
All I want is to see it prosper."

The crowd broke into raucous booing. One man
shouted out from the back, "You'd like to see the town
rot and blow away, is what you'd like."

"If all you want is for the town to prosper, tell your
masters at the chemical company to start hiring people
from the town, instead of trying to steal their land!"

The speaker shook his head sadly, as if feeling hopelessly misunderstood.

"I don't work for the chemical company anymore," he said, "And even if I did, I never had a position where I would have been able to make such a call. But I know that the chemical company does hire people from this town, although probably not as many as you would like to see, and it really is trying to do the right thing by the people that live here. After all, aren't we trying to relocate a factory here?"

The old woman spoke up again. "Over our dead bodies!" This was met with shouts of agreement.

"The referendum is next week," the man said again. "And then we will see what it is that the people of this town really want. Until then, your protest is only going to make things worse." The crowd booed again, but much of the steam had gone out of them.

A woman shouted out, "That referendum is a sham, and you know it."

His face hardened. "This protest didn't get a permit. Now, I'm not interested in arresting anybody—"

At this he was interrupted by one of the men most red in the face. "Oh, so now you have control of the police department, too?" he shouted out.

"I repeat, *no one* wants to arrest anybody. Not these fellows here, not the mayor, not anyone on the city council, least of all me. But you can't hold an illegal protest. You have to go through the permitting process."

"Which you control!" someone shouted.

"Were any of you denied a permit for this protest?" he said. Ethan could tell he knew the answer to that question. The crowd also knew it. No one had applied for a permit.

"Had you applied for a permit, I'm sure you would have been granted one," he said. "No one will ever be denied a permit for a legitimate protest, not in this town, not while I sit on the city council."

Losing its impetus, the crowd seemed to evaporate in different directions—one group to the south, one to the north—melting away into the gathering summer dark. A few tentative fireflies began to wink over by the library.

Xavier hustled up to the twins. "Wow," he said, "when I invited you in to be a part of the protest I didn't expect you to take it over."

"Disappointed?" Emily said, as if she really wanted to know and was really worried that the answer might be yes.

Xavier's face broke into a huge grin. "No! What you did was wizard. I've never seen anybody take over a crowd like that. I just wish Mr Grayson hadn't been able to make his little speech."

"But you've heard that speech before, right?" Ethan said, "I mean, nothing he said was new?"

Xavier shook his head. "We've all heard it before. But he sounds so darn reasonable. It makes it really hard for us to explain to people what's really going on."

As if on cue, the policemen Emily had hugged dropped his hand on her shoulder. "That was some quick thinking, miss," he said. "Things were getting kinda ugly there for a second. I'm grateful to you."

Emily took his hand and shook it. "I think things would have been fine," she said. "We've seen some pretty ugly things ourselves, I just didn't want this one to get out of hand. We're all friends in the end."

The policeman beamed. "That's what I keep telling everybody," he said. "But sometimes I think folks get a little scared and can't remember that." He chuckled to himself and he and his partner trotted off around the edge of city hall to the police station.

That left the twins standing there in front of city hall. The city councilman—Grayson, according to Xavier—stood there with a grin on his face, his hands spread wide. "That was pretty quick work," he said. "I've seen a lot of public speaking in my time, but that was right up there with the best. How do you know what to do in a situation like that?"

Ethan said, "Let's just say we've had some experience. You weren't so bad yourself."

The man waved that away. "I'm just telling folks the truth. In fact, it sounds to me like there's a whole lot of lies mixed up in what's being said around here. No matter what you may have been told, and I mean no offense to anyone who may have told you different, there's nothing illegal happening here. No one's putting any undue pressure on anybody. If you'll give me a few minutes, I'd be happy to explain to you what we're trying to do, and why it might be better to be on our side in getting it done."

If you think they should listen, turn to page 464.

If you think they should go home, turn to page 494.

The next night, as dinner concluded, Brock pushed back from the table and said, "I'm spent. I think I'll turn in early."

"Before pie?" Grandma said. "That's not like you."

He patted his belly. "Had some leftover pie for lunch. I can do without it, anyway. Look at me."

Emily kicked Ethan under the table. He reached down and rubbed his shin, but said nothing as Brock rinsed his plate in the sink and racked it in the dishwasher. He stretched, rather too obviously, Emily thought, and said, "Good night, everyone." He departed through the kitchen door and down the hall to the stairs to the basement.

"And what are the two of you going to do tonight?" Grandma said.

"Um, Xavier invited us to come light fireworks over at his house," Emily said. It was Ethan's turn to kick Emily. She smiled sweetly at him.

"How late will you be?"

"Not sure. It doesn't get really dark until almost ten, and then we'll have to walk home. It's not very safe to ride bikes in the dark."

"Be sure to lock up when you come in, then," Grandma said. "I'm going to visit Mrs. Zefir around the corner, but I'll be home well before that."

"We will," Ethan said, picking up his plate.

He went to his room, and before too long Emily joined him. "Xavier did not invite us." Ethan said.

Emily might have been blushing, but she turned toward the bed so Ethan couldn't see her face. "I did promise we'd get together tomorrow. Stump for votes, that kind of thing. I think he might have to work, too."

"Suits me. Maybe he'll get us shakes." Ethan lay back on his bed. "I assume we're going to be engaged in other activity tonight, making it impossible for us to attend Xavier's party."

Emily sat down on her bed. "My thinking exactly. Brock can't go until Grandma is gone to her visit, but I wouldn't be shocked to see him roll out of here right afterward."

"Why doesn't he just tell her he's going out Monongy hunting?"

"Beats me. But it doesn't matter, because we're going to be onboard long before he gets there."

The two of them dressed in their darkest clothing and stuck flashlights in their belts.

"Now," Ethan said, "how do we get out of here without either Grandma or Brock seeing us?"

Emily opened the window that looked out on the side yard.

"We're punching out the screen?" Ethan said.

Emily shot him a look of withering scorn. "Of course not. I took the screen off earlier today."

Ethan raised his eyebrows. "Well, sister mine. Allow me to congratulate you on a level of deviousness I would not have expected."

"Shut up and crawl through," she said, but she was smiling.

Ethan did and made the drop four feet to the soft bed of flowers beneath the window. Emily plopped down beside him, then took the screen and put it back in place. "No sense getting mosquitoes in there. Besides, everyone knows the open window means you went out it."

"Unless the screen is in. Right. Clever, again. You're nailing the spy vibe tonight."

They hustled out to the shed and took their bikes out, replacing the lock. They wheeled them over behind the overgrown rose bushes next door and dumped them out of sight, to trick Grandma. It wasn't really dark yet, though the sun had gone down, leaving a trail of purple and orange in the sky above them. It smelled of honeysuckle with a hint of ripe peaches.

"Dang," Ethan whispered. "I should have had a slice of pie."

"Have one later. Remember, we have permission to be out."

They jogged down to the dock and across to Brock's boat. It lay dark in the water, the waves lapping gently at its side. They vaulted over the gunwale and let themselves into the cabin by the door.

"Now what?" Ethan said. "You seem to have the whole thing planned out."

"This is as far as I got."

"There's a moth-eaten blanket in the cupboard, but I don't think we could hide under it." Ethan pried up the cushion on the bench. Underneath was a long cabinet for storage. He lifted the lid. "No good here; it's filled up with gear."

Emily clicked on her flashlight just long enough to take a look. She rubbed her chin. "If you took a little bit of it out, some of the ropes and a couple of life-preservers, you could make it work."

"Won't he notice?"

"You think he comes down here enough to know where things are? Look at this place."

Grime coated every surface. On the floor, rattling loose, was a boat hook, a buoy of some kind, two plastic buckets, and an open-faced fishing reel, among other things.

"Okay, probably not. I'll put the stuff over here behind the desk." He pulled out the life preserver and gagged. "Augh! That stinks!" A rancid smell filled the cabin. "No wonder," he said, holding up a dead rat by the tail. It had partially decomposed.

Emily plugged her nose and waved him away. "Throw it overboard! What are you thinking!"

"I'm thinking I won't be using that compartment, that's for sure. Maybe try the other side."

Emily did while Ethan went up and tossed the rat. The compartment on the other side was cleaner but smaller. It might fit one of them but not both.

"Rat disposed of," Ethan said. "What did you find?"

"I found my hiding place. But I don't know what you're going to do."

Ethan shrugged. "I'll crouch down under the desk and hope. He probably won't throw us overboard if he catches us. Besides, we don't know what he's doing out there. It might be perfectly innocent."

"Yep, it might. And I might be the Queen of England."

"Your majesty should get ready. I saw Grandma's bedroom light go out while I was up there. Brock will be out here any minute."

They took their hiding places, such as they were, and waited. They didn't need to wait long.

Five minutes later, the boat rocked as someone climbed on board. Brock headed right for the cabin. Ethan sucked in a breath and held it.

Brock pushed the door open and threw a coat onto Emily's hiding compartment. He turned and went out, leaving the cabin door open. He never looked behind the door.

Shortly, the rumble of the engine rolled through the boat, and Ethan felt the propeller dig into the water, pulling the boat away from the dock. The engine rose in pitch and the boat thumped through the uneven water of the river.

Ethan wanted to talk to someone. He would have loved to hear what Emily thought about their direction, their potential destination, but he couldn't risk moving a muscle, not with the door open. Even with the thrumming of the engine and the crash of the boat against the water, he couldn't risk it. Brock was right at the top of the stairs.

But he could figure things out himself. They were headed upstream. If Ethan hadn't got that from the motion of the boat away from the dock, he knew it by the pitch of the engine. It was working hard to push them against the current. Therefore, south

And this was no Monongy expedition—at least not yet. The boat was moving so fast, and making so much noise, that it could have driven over his father's stereo and never heard anything, even with Brock's fancy equipment.

The pitch of the engine remained unchanged for at least ten minutes. Ethan could see the time elapse on the luminous dial of his watch. Emily stayed buried in her compartment. Undoubtedly, she was reaching the same conclusions he was. But it still would have been nice to talk it over with her.

At about eleven minutes, the pitch of the engine changed, and the bow of the boat pulled to the left. The way the boat rocked, Ethan believed they had turned broadside to the current and were now drifting back to the north, downstream. He tried to remember the geography of the bank of the river from his previous night's expedition. Ten minutes would have been about as long as they had spent getting to the chemical factory, but he didn't know if the speed tonight was greater or less.

He kept a close eye on his watch, counting as the second hand swept around. Three minutes. Four. Then something scraped against the side. The starboard side, which Ethan thought would be the east bank, the side where the little pink house was, and also the side by the chemical factory.

Whatever it was that scraped against the side was soft and yielding, not a hard metallic scraping, but more like plants. Perhaps cattails? And then the boat stopped.

Actually, Ethan could not be sure that the boat had actually stopped, but the motion was different somehow. Water still sloshed against the sides, and in Ethan's mind it passed from stern to bow, as if the boat were pointed downstream, and tied up to the shore.

Brock killed the engine. Then, for three or four minutes, nothing happened. He could hear Brock tromp to the stern of the boat, but then nothing happened. He did not think Brock had gotten off. He would love to have known what Brock was doing, but he dared not look.

A whistle sounded, someone whistling, shrill and harsh in the night air, and the boat shifted as Brock moved from his perch, went to the gunwale next to the bank, and slid himself off onto the land. Ethan's ears strained to hear anything else, but he couldn't.

He had never noticed before how much noise there was in the atmosphere along the river. Frogs, insects, even night birds, kept up a steady clamor. With that and the whisper of the river against the hull of the boat, he could hear nothing. Tentatively, he crawled over to Emily's hiding space and gave one quick knock on the side of the compartment. She pushed her lid up an inch.

"What?" she whispered.

"He's left the boat," Ethan whispered back.

"Are you sure?"

"Positive," Ethan said. "Someone whistled and he got off."

"Do you have a guess where we are?"

"I do," Ethan said. "I'm pretty sure we're drawn up on the bank next to the chemical plant."

"What's he doing?"

"No idea," Ethan said. "I couldn't even begin to guess."

But he didn't have to, because very shortly, the sound of voices carried down into the hold, and Emily shut herself back in. Ethan moved back to his perch under the table. The voices neared the boat, and he could make out what they said.

"Just like last time," one man said.

"I can't go back to that place," Brock said. "You know what they said the last time I was there."

"They always talk big. But when you show up with the cargo, they'll take it."

"I don't want to do this anymore. This is the last run."

"You'll do as many runs as we tell you, and take whatever we tell you, and you'll keep doing it as long as we want. We know where that cute little house of yours is, and it would be a terrible shame if someone were to light that on fire while your old mother was lying asleep in her bedroom. She uses the front north corner, doesn't she?"

Brock swore, a string of oaths that made Ethan raise his eyebrows. Some of those were words he had never heard before.

Something heavy was loaded onto the boat. There was a clanking as someone raised the ring of the smuggling hatch—Ethan knew now that's what it was for sure—and a low thud sounded through the hull of the boat as the goods were dropped down below. This kept up for several minutes, with more than one man carrying goods on to the boat, and someone, probably Brock, loading them into the hatch. No one bothered to come to the cabin. No one spoke.

"I'm full," Brock finally said.

"Aw, you can take some more," the other voice said.

"No, fellas, I have no more room. Besides, the water in the bilge is pretty high. I wouldn't want it soaking your precious cigarettes."

Cigarettes? Ethan thought. Why are they carrying cigarettes? Can't you just buy those at the grocery store if you want them?

The men on deck didn't have any more time to debate, because a completely new sound ended their conversations.

It was a pistol shot.

Turn to page 234.

In the end, Ethan went with the Wolfie burger, because it also had bacon. He'd leave the Diablo for another time.

The twins walked together back to the booth where their parents were sitting. Ethan seemed a little hang-dog, as if he were mildly ashamed of himself.

"Honestly," Emily said, "I'm actually kind of im-pressed that you even considered going for it."

This seemed to be the right thing to say, as Ethan brightened up a little bit. Along with teasing, some-times, it is the little sister's job to make her older brother feel better about himself.

"I take it he didn't actually order the El Diablo," Mom said, as they sat down.

"I was going to," Ethan said, "But it's probably a bad idea, my first day in town, to do something that might have gastrointestinal repercussions."

"Gastrointestinal repercussions?" Dad said, eye-brows raised. "Listen, dear, all that vocabulary time you spend with these kids is paying off."

"I'm glad to hear it," Mom said, munching on a fry. "We put a lot of work into it. I wasn't sure it was doing any good."

A few moments later, the burger guy came by their table to deliver a strawberry and a chocolate malt milkshake. Both of the shakes had ice cream way above the rim, as if they were souffles that had risen too high for their tins.

"These belong to you," the burger guy said. His name tag read "Xavier."

"Javier, thank you for bringing these to us," Mom said.

"Begging your pardon, ma'am, but it's Ex-a-vier. And you're welcome."

"How very polite. Dear, did you hear that? People in Gnarled Oak still beg your pardon when it's you that made the mistake. I love it here."

"You say that every time we come, Dear." Dad said. "Ex-a-vier, pleasure to meet you."

"The strawberry is mine," Mom said, "And the chocolate is my husband's."

"I put extra malt in that one," Xavier said. "I hope you don't mind."

"Mind?" Dad said, with a note in his voice as if he were impressed. He took a sample bite and smacked his lips. "On the contrary, I'd like to offer you my daughter's hand in marriage."

"Dad!" Emily said, feeling color rising into her cheeks.

"I'm only kidding," Dad said, licking a drip off the side. "Then again, this is good enough that perhaps I mean it after all."

"I think it will take something a little more impressive than extra malt in a shake to get us to give up our daughter," Mom said. She cocked her head at Xavier. "So maybe some onion rings, too?"

Emily wanted to crawl under the bench.

Instead, she said, "Excuse me, may I get by?"

And she headed for the bathroom.

A few minutes in the bathroom should give the guy time to go back to cleaning glasses behind the counter, Emily said to herself. She washed her hands, and made sure her hair was in the best possible shape. She frowned at herself in the mirror. Something nagged at her about the burger shop.

Ordinarily, when they had been here before, the place had been full of people, even in the dead time just after lunch. Teenagers chatting over their plans for the summer; adults sitting over a shake, talking about local politics, and so on. Today, though, Thusnelda's was more than half empty. Even the people who were there seemed considerably less interested in chatting with each other, much less loudly discussing things going on in town. It seemed like some of the light had gone out of the place.

Probably it was just her imagination, but it refused to go out of her mind. Making sure that her lip gloss was applied correctly, she made her way back to the table. As she expected, her family was alone. Unexpectedly, she wasn't entirely pleased about that.

She scanned the place for the burger guy and found him in the back corner of the restaurant, wiping down a table. Without exactly knowing why she did it, she wandered back in that direction.

Emily stood there and watched the guy for a moment. Taller than Emily or even Ethan, thin, with sandy blonde hair cut a bit too short. Jeans, Thusnelda's t-shirt, apron. Battered tennis shoes. He seemed conscientious enough, doing an excellent job cleaning the table—he got down underneath and retrieved a stray wrapper—even though there was no one standing over him to make sure he did.

"So what's with the town?" she said.

Without looking up from wiping the formica, Xavier said, "I'm not sure what you mean."

"You really don't? Ordinarily the place is packed with people and everyone's jabbering about cool things going on in the town. Today the place is half dead. It's probably nothing, it's not like I come here every day, but I just thought I would ask."

As a response, Xavier gave one stubborn spot an especially vigorous wipedown.

"I take it you don't really want to talk about it," Emily said.

"I don't."

"Will you overcome your reluctance, just for me?" Emily said, crossing her arms.

Xavier breathed an elaborate sigh. "OK, just for you. Mostly it's that chemical company."

"The one out south of town?" Emily said.

Xavier put his rag down and turned towards her. He leaned back on the table.

"You are new in town, aren't you?" he said, matching her folded arms. "Do you think there are several to choose from?"

"We only come here a couple times a year, if even that often."

He nodded. "Yours is a face I would remember." He cleared his throat and reached back for his rag, twisting it about in his hands as he talked. "The big chemical company in town is an outfit called Jaxton Chemical. They own pretty much everything to the south of town, and they are currently buying up everything else they can get their hands on. "

"Why would they be doing that?" Emily cast a glance back to her family's table, but they were munching happily on fries and staring out the window.

"It's something to do with building a new plant or something."

"That sounds like a good thing," Emily said.

Xavier laughed, but there was no mirth in it. "It does sound like it, doesn't it? But what it really means is that most of the local residents are selling and moving out. Not everyone, understand, just some people in some parts. There are some that don't want to sell. That's a whole 'nother problem."

"That does explain why it's a little quieter around here," Emily said.

The burger guy nodded. "Lotta drain on the town, having a hundred people move out."

"But if the rest won't sell, they won't sell. That sucks for the chemical company, but I don't see why it's a big problem for the residents. Shouldn't businesses be able to buy whatever they want?" she said.

"I don't know about *whatever* they want. But probably, yeah, They should be able to buy land if they want to expand. The problem is, this business seems to want to buy land that people don't want to sell them."

"What does that mean?"

"It means that some people don't want to sell, and the business wants their houses anyway. They'll do whatever it takes to get the house."

"Whatever it takes? Don't they just have to keep offering more money?" she said. "What else can they do?" This sounded alarmingly like something she and her brother had experienced in the battle over the road to Surfdom.

Xavier turned back to his table and began wiping with his rag again. "I shouldn't say any more," he said. "It's hard enough to find a job in this town, let alone keep it, if people know that you're not on the side of the big boys."

"Surely Thusnelda can see your work ethic."

He laughed. "Thusnelda is a legend, and sadly, no longer able to protect me."

"I'm Emily Tuttle," she said, offering her hand. He extended his hand, realized he was still holding his rag, and switched to the left. He wiped his right hand on his pants and tried again. His hand was cool and he didn't have one of those dead-fish handshakes, either. She liked the look of the spray of freckles across his nose. "We're going to be here for a couple weeks, so I hope that at some point over the holiday we get a chance to see you."

"Staying with family?"

Emily nodded, taking her hand back. "My grandmother. She lives by the river."

Xavier's eyes widened. Abruptly, he turned back to his table, as if his boss had just walked in. Emily scanned the place, but there was no one paying any attention to them.

"Well, nice to meet you," she said.

Xavier said, "You know where to find me." He didn't turn around as she walked back to her family's booth.

Turn to page 58.

It looked on the plate like a huge meal, but it *felt* like lifting the Titanic. El Diablo had to be at least six inches tall from the plate to the top of the bun, and Ethan had no idea how he was going to get even a small part of it into his mouth. He thought for a moment that he would use a knife and fork, but he knew as soon as he picked up utensils, his sister would start howling in laughter, and he couldn't have that. So as carefully as he could, Ethan reached out and squeezed the burger and bun and lettuce and tomato together, packing it down as tightly as he could to be able to get his mouth around part of it. The operation was only partly successful. He lifted the giant burger to his mouth and attempted to take a bite. What he mostly got was bun and a little bit of lettuce. Not too bad. The bun was soft and tasty and the lettuce was crisp. Maybe he could do this.

Then he got to the hunk of burger. He bit down.

Immediately he knew that this had been a spectacular mistake. It was so hot that sweat broke out on his forehead before he even had a chance to swallow. It made his teeth hurt. His tongue wanted to jump out of his mouth and run yelping down the street.

But in for a penny, in for a pound. He couldn't possibly back out after just one mouthful. He already knew that Emily was right that he would regret it, so now the only thing to do was to finish it. The second bite was larger, and there was a goodly amount of the burger in it. His mouth felt as if he were trying to eat molten lava. There was no beef taste to it at all, just hot sauce and jalapeño. Ethan thought he liked hot food; he was always the one who went for the biggest jalapeño on the plate, always got the hottest salsa, but this was another order of magnitude.

By now, he couldn't feel his tongue, or anything else in his mouth. All he could do was keep working his way, as far as he could, through the burger. Mechanically, sniffling and with tears running down his face, he put hand to mouth, bit, and chewed. The problem was that the burger itself was so large that even if he had only had the meat itself, he still wouldn't have been able to eat the whole thing in one sitting. It was just way too much food.

If you could call it food. Ethan wasn't entirely sure that it qualified, as the burger guy had said. It was more like a raging inferno stuffed in a burning log and rolled in a steel furnace. And every bite just made it worse. The flame reached down his esophagus all the way to his gut, and he knew that Emily had also been right about what would happen later on that night.

Halfway through, Ethan knew he was never going to make it. He was already in serious distress from what he had eaten so far, and he could feel the burger's flame eating through his innards. Even if it had been delicious, which it decidedly was *not*, he would never have been able to finish it. The soda jerk wandered by a couple of times to check on his progress, and the last time, mercifully, had brought back a shake to use to cool down the fire in his mouth.

Ethan was so full from the burger that he could hardly drink any of the shake. With the restaurant nearly empty, it seemed that everyone in the place was watching to see how he would handle the challenge, and it made him even sicker to his stomach to know he was going to disappoint everyone. But there was no help for it, the task was simply too large for him.

He sat back with an audible whine onto the bench and ran a napkin across his face. It came away dripping. "I can't do it," he said. "It's too big."

"I thought you did very well, son," Dad said.

"It's a lot better than most people do," the cashier said, perching himself on the table of the booth opposite. "I think that burger is manufactured by Satan just to torment people whose eyes are bigger than their head. I'll give you full marks for even getting this far. But I can't give you the t-shirt along with it." The burger guy picked up Ethan's plate and began to carry it away. "I'm assuming you don't want a doggy bag for this?" he said.

Ethan groaned as if in the pit of despair. He looked at Emily to see what her reaction would be, but there was nothing on her face but solemn admiration.

"You didn't laugh at me for throwing up every couple of miles," she said. "So I'm not laughing now. However, I make no promises for later on tonight."

Ethan sat slumped in the booth, nursing a Coke. Dad was mopping up the remains of his demolished chocolate malt when two men sat down in the opposite booth.

"Shame, really, having to eat here," one of them said. "This time next year we could be having lunch in the clubhouse."

"We gonna be done by then? Seems a little quick to me," the other one said. He wore a hat that had a little stylized shark on it.

"Whatever. The next year, then. Either way. Can't wait to get started on that beautiful par-5 going down toward the river."

"Clubhouse?" Dad said, rising and collecting trash from the table to take to the can. "Sorry, couldn't help overhearing."

Shark Hat said, "Yeah, the new golf course."

"Golf course? In this town?"

"Yeah. It'll be the only one in this part of the county. About time, too."

Mom ducked her head back in the door to the parking lot. "Dear, we need to get on the road," she said.

Dad handed the trash to Ethan. "Where are they going to build it?" he said to the guys in the booth.

Shark Hat looked at his friend, and something seemed to pass between them. "Well, you know, that's still being determined. It's, um, not really official yet. Lotta things have to be decided. We kinda spoke out of turn."

"Right," his friend said. "We don't really know anything anyway." He wouldn't meet Dad's eyes.

Ethan waited until they were outside before he said to Dad, "What's that all about?"

"I don't know. Heaven knows the town could use a golf course, or something like that. But did you see how they clammed up when I asked where they were going to build it?"

"Sure did."

Dad tossed Ethan a glance. "Maybe you should keep your eyes and ears open while you're here the next couple weeks."

"I'm on it," Ethan said. "Maybe a lot of people will come down to the rope swing and tell me secrets while I'm swimming."

Turn to page 99.

The library was well equipped with reading nooks, and since Shannon was just going to snarl at him anyway, Ethan figured he would go over to the young adult section, find a book, and plop down in a chair to wait for the top of the hour when she would be free.

The young adult section was fairly robust. Ethan was surprised to find that three whole shelves, at least twenty feet long, floor to ceiling, were filled with young adult books. It was possible that there were more young adult books in this library than there were adult books, something he had never seen. Maybe it was Shannon who was doing the book buying.

He found a dog-eared edition of *The Screwtape Letters* and settled into the brown leather chair to read through it. Not his first time. The familiar book was like putting on an old sweater. That hour flew by. Soon, he heard a tinkling bell from the front desk, apparently meant to signal something.

He looked at his watch. Five minutes to the hour. He closed the book, put it back on the shelf, and wandered out to the reception desk just as the last of the patrons was leaving the library.

"I'm available to help," Ethan said. "I don't know if there's anything I can do, or what. I just wanted you to know."

Shannon nodded. "Thank you. I'll let you know."
She wandered off toward the back, made a circuit of
the place, and came back up to the front door. "All set,"
she said. She drew a key from her pocket, held the door
open for Ethan to leave, and came out herself, locking it
behind her.

"Not a lot of people here Saturday night, " Ethan
said. He was just making conversation, feeling awkward,
and not knowing how to talk to this strange girl.

"That's about normal for a Saturday," she said. "A
couple of people is about what we get. Weekdays are
busier." They stood together on the porch of the library
for a moment.

"I brought my bike," Ethan said.

"It's not too terribly far," she said. The sun's rays still
beamed down from the west. "I can give you the address, if you want to ride on ahead."

"I'm okay to walk along with you, if you're walking."

Shannon nodded. "I don't have a car. My house is
only three or four blocks from here. This guy though, he
lives quite a ways out in the other direction." Shannon
bounded down the steps of the library and headed off
toward the northeast.

Ethan scurried around the back of the library,
retrieved his bike, and caught up with her. He was
going to walk along next to her, but that seemed weird,
because he couldn't figure out what to say.

There were no real plans to be made, nothing that they needed to talk about. They were going to do this thing together, and then they would probably never see each other again. So he found himself riding back and forth as she walked along. He'd ride in front fifty yards or so, turn the bike around, ride back past her fifty yards or so, make another u-turn, and come back. Ethan supposed it was kind of rude, but he didn't see what else he could do. He just wanted to get out, meet this guy, and get back in.

It took almost an hour to get out there. The sun was starting to get pretty low, and shadows stretched out long to the east when they came to the street the man lived on.

Emily pointed down the block. "It's that one," she said, indicating a single-story house in the middle of the block, with a vacant lot across the street. Odd heaps of earth lay all over the lot, as if it were a sandbox for giants.

"What's that in his backyard?" Ethan said, noting the poles sticking up over the roofline.

"It's his teepee. Built it himself," she said.

"Wow. This is some guy," Ethan said.

"You have no idea."

Shannon led him around to the back of the house, where a dingy lawn chair sat empty in front of the open flaps of the teepee. "Huh," Shannon said. "He's not here. He's always here."

"Is he maybe inside?" Ethan said.

Shannon laughed. "I've known him all my life, and I don't think I've ever seen him inside. Even in the winter."

She peeked into the tent, but there wasn't anyone there, either. "I suppose he might be across the street. That's where his dig is."

"His dig?"

"He's an archaeologist. He digs up ancient artifacts. Across the street, in that vacant lot, is a dig he's been working for the last several years. He's over there a lot."

"I didn't see him a minute ago."

Shannon headed back through the archway into the front. "You wouldn't, unless he wanted you to."

Ethan watched her go, then went to the teepee. Inside were dozens of artifacts, small, large, simple and ornate. Perfectly suited for exactly the kind of thing Ethan wanted to do—bury them and get the Native preservation people to come take a look. He knew it was a long shot. But it was the best he had. Everything else had failed.

The ones that were labeled, that had descriptions attached, obviously those were no good, but there was a bucket to one side at the end of the table that was different. It was filled with pieces of pottery of all kinds, some of them quite old. They would do nicely. Ethan dipped into the bucket and came up with half a dozen good shards of pottery. They bulged in his pockets, but who was looking at his pockets anyway?

Shannon met him in the middle of the street. "He's not over there. I don't know where he is. Sorry. Maybe we can catch him another time."

"That's okay," Ethan said, mounting his bike. "I gotta get home anyway. I'll see you around."

He rode back home. No one was outside when he got there. He went to the shed and got a shovel. Of course they wouldn't look like they'd been buried for centuries. But he meant to dig them up anyway, and say he found them. Where? Not on this property—that was too convenient. But close. Maybe right on the line between Grandma's property and old Mrs. Cowley's next door. Why was he digging there?

Wait. Why *was* he digging there?

Gophers? That was stupid.

Hunting buried treasure? Was he six years old now?

Back here, behind the shed, the old fencepost that once held up a wooden fence separating the river from Mrs. Cowley's yard had fallen over, and a ragged stump was left poking out of the ground. Good enough. Yard work.

He dug up the stump, dropped three of the artifacts into the hole, and put the stump back. About a yard farther along the property was another stump of the next post. He put the other three potsherds into that hole, and replaced the stump again. Tomorrow, he'd make a miraculous discovery.

So, so stupid. Of course they didn't believe him.

"Couldn't you at least come out and look?" Ethan said. They could not. They'd had a number of false alarms in that part of the county already. If he liked, they could send the resident expert, a Mr. St. Lawrence, out to take a look. He lived right in town, if they understood correctly.

Ethan knew right away who that expert would be, and he was pretty sure that expert would know just what he was looking at.

"Thanks, anyway," he said.

The referendum wasn't a total disaster. But they lost. Close, but they lost.

Mom and Dad came to get them a few days later. It wasn't a happy time. They spent most of their short visit walking around the house and talking about what would need to happen with the place, now that it was more or less certain that it would be sold.

"At least you'll get some money out of it," Dad said.

"That is the least I can get out of it. I don't want their money," Grandma said.

Ethan and Emily swam in the river and swung on the rope swing, for the last time. Shannon didn't come around, although Xavier did, once or twice. He would have been a good friend, if things had worked out differently. Now, when would they ever see him again?

"One more try on El Diablo before you go?" Xavier said, feet dangling in the water off the edge of the dock.

Emily lounged next to him, taking in the sun.

Ethan leaned back against a dock post. "Nah. I don't think so. Like everything else on this visit, it didn't quite work."

They stayed out there until the sun went down. Fireflies lit up the waterside, and a cool breeze wafted off the water. It was as beautiful a place as they could imagine.

They walked slowly back to the little pink house, one last time, and the door closed behind them.

THE END

The moon cast plenty of light onto the empty town square. Huddled in the shadow at the side of the library, the three conspirators surveyed the scene: Shannon, Ethan, and their new lockpick, Uncle Brock.

"I could wish for it to be a little bit darker," Brock said.

"It doesn't really matter, does it?" Ethan said. "We'll be through that door in no time."

"It has an alarm," Shannon said. "I think I have the code, but we'll have to be through very quickly, so I can enter it in."

Brock nodded. They were all dressed in black, their clothing blending in well with the wall in the lee of the library. Their faces shone out, and undoubtedly they would have been seen had anybody been looking. But it was a sleepy town, a holiday weekend, and no one was about. The square was empty, and their circuit of the police station showed just the one car. Just one some-one, no doubt on call in case something happened that needed an immediate response.

"More than likely it's Reggie. He usually draws the late shift. He'll be in there asleep, if I know him at all," Uncle Brock said.

Ethan decided he had waited long enough and wanted to lead out. He moved out, crouching and scur-rying, into the central area. A meaty hand clapped itself onto his shoulder. It was Uncle Brock. In the darkness, he shook his finger at him and hauled him upright.

"We're not doing anything wrong. At least not yet," he said. "Walk normally, look natural. It's when you do something that makes you look suspicious that you get caught."

Taking that advice, they strolled across the green court in between city buildings as if they owned the place. Shannon kept a little distance from Ethan, probably still not sure that he was on the square, although he was the one who had arranged for Uncle Brock to help.

Emily had begged off. "There's too many of you anyway," she said. I'll just get in the way. Besides, I'm not entirely sure this is a good idea." She had tried to go to bed before they left, but pronounced herself too nervous. So, she was sitting up in bed, reading, and no doubt checking the clock every thirty seconds or so.

Ethan promised her they would be home within an hour. If it took any longer than that, he thought, the chances of discovery were far too high. When they reached the front of city hall, the moon shone directly on them. Even in dark clothes, there was no way they could avoid being seen, if anyone were looking. But the police station was on the back side of the building, and as they had checked out before, there was only the one car on duty. And why not? Who would possibly be breaking into city hall?

"You two stand guard," Uncle Brock said, "And I'll get to work on the lock."

Shannon and Ethan stood next to each other, not quite touching, staring out over the courtyard.

"The library looks creepy," Shannon said, in a whisper. "Aren't there lots of horror stories about terrible things happening in libraries?"

"Not that I'm aware of," Ethan said. "Other than people having to be quiet in there."

Brock made a shushing noise behind them, and their conversation cut off. Even standing just a foot or so away, they could not hear any sound of Brock's manipulation of the lock. Whatever he was doing, assuming he was actually doing something, it was very quiet.

Crickets chirped all about them, keeping a rhythm. Ethan had heard that you could tell what the temperature was by counting cricket chirps in a minute and then doing some sort of math, but he couldn't remember the formula, and anyway, he was far too nervous to make an accurate count.

Ethan stood there, listening to the crickets, and thinking to himself, *Here we are again, one of the things my uncle tells me he can do, but he really can't. We're going to be standing out here until either we get tired and give up, or somebody comes around the building on night patrol and picks us up like a couple of stray dogs.*

Any minute now, I'm going to give up and go.

He started to consider how he would break that to Shannon and Emily after getting so far along in the process of this insane break-in idea.

He heard Uncle Brock say, "Open sesame."

Somewhat surprised, Ethan turned around and there was Uncle Brock with the door propped open an inch or two.

"Nothing to it," he said. Ethan raised his eyebrows. Could it be possible that Uncle Brock was actually good for something?

Shannon gave a glance to Ethan that said, "Wow, you guys got something right." It wasn't too encouraging, but Ethan would take it.

Besides, now was the time to move. They were through the door in a flash, and Shannon located the security pad on the left-hand wall. She consulted a piece of paper that she pulled from the back pocket of her jeans and typed in five numbers. The pad chirruped. Lights on the pad that had been blinking softly, pink and red, turned green before going out.

"The place is ours," she said.

That wasn't quite true. Down the hallway, there were the doors on the left to the city recorder's office, the doors on the right to the city council chambers, and the door at the end of the hall that presumably led back into the city offices.

"Is there an alarm on those doors?" Ethan said.

Shannon started to say something but thought better of it. "I don't know," she said.

Brock was already moving past them, selecting another pick and loading it up. "I'll get us through that door, too," he said. "Once we're inside, we'll have to choose the filing cabinets and desk drawers to try. I hope we don't intend to spend too much time going through those. But they're better than the computer systems. I don't know what to do with those at all."

Moments later, another click, and the door popped open. Brock was really on a roll.

"It's like riding a bike," he said. "Once I get the hang of it, it's easy."

They went through that door as well, and finally Ethan began to breathe a little easier. They were deep in the interior of the building. Anyone who came by on a routine patrol would not be able to see them.

This office was not large, but there were two desks, one for a receptionist and another one that looked like it was used for whoever was visiting from the city council. Back behind it, another door led to the mayor's office. File cabinets lined the right hand wall, ugly gray metal things.

One of them was locked up, but the other three were open, and Shannon immediately clicked the latches to open the drawers and pull them out where she could take a look at the file tabs.

Her black gloves ran over the files, running a 5K across the top of the folders.

She finished one row and started on another. Ethan sat down at the receptionist desk and wiggled the mouse.

The computer monitor came on, glowing softly. He turned the brightness down as far as he could to minimize anything that could be seen from outside. The office itself did have an exterior window, all the way at the left-hand wall, and Ethan checked to make sure the blinds were twisted shut.

Shannon kept the flashlight in her mouth, pointed at file folders, but so far didn't appear to be having any luck. Brock was working on the door to the mayor's office.

As Ethan expected, when the monitor came up and the desktop finished its boot cycle, it came to the window screen with the password. He tried a couple of things, the usual stuff like password 1 2 3, and ABC 1 2 3, but those didn't seem to work. "Any ideas on a password?" he said.

"That's Mabel's desk," Shannon said. "I think she has a dog named Peaches."

"Her dog's name is Peaches?" Ethan said, but he typed it in along with one two three, in a couple of different combinations. No luck.

"There has to be a way into this," Ethan said.

"That's the problem with passwords," Shannon said. "If they're so complicated that they're really secure, they're too complicated to remember. I bet she has it written down somewhere. Check through the desk."

None of the desk drawers were locked. Ethan went through them without success. Frustrated, he shoved the keyboard away from him, and underneath it, taped to the desktop, was a list of passwords. "Bingo," he said.

"Same here," Uncle Brock said, opening the door to the mayor's office. "I'll see you kids in a minute."

Turn to page 378.

When Emily got home, a familiar car was in the driveway. She put her bike away in the shed and came in through the back door. Before she even got to the dining room, she heard the voices.

"You guys put all this together?"

"Well," Ethan said, trying to be modest, "we just used the stuff that Penelope Burns gave us. But, yeah, we had to connect the dots."

Emily swooped into the dining room and threw her arms around Uncle Ben.

"Whoa, there, Millie. That's quite a welcome."

"You're *so* welcome, Uncle Ben. We need you," she said, letting go and stepping back, knocking over a pile of papers.

"Careful!" Ethan said. "That's the noose we're hanging the city council with."

"Not all of it. Just Osterhout. He's a big enough target," Uncle Ben said. "I'm glad I brought my equipment with me. I want to get all this recorded tonight and get it on the web tomorrow."

Emily departed for a second and came back with a cookie. "What are you doing here?" she said. "We tried to get hold of you for days with no luck."

"Mom is much more persuasive. I was really busy, sorry, and your calls I can ignore, no offense. Mom's, though? No. One does not ignore a call from one's mama." He pored over more material, absorbing in minutes what the twins and Xavier had teased out over hours. "Brilliant. This is great work. And it's going to have an impact. But I want to warn you, it's not going to be enough. Osterhout is a class-A jerk and a plant for the chemical company and he probably picks his nose, too, but you're going to need more. He's not actually doing anything illegal."

"Just unethical and evil," Ethan said.

"By our lights, yes. But he'd probably argue that he's bringing business to the town."

"He does argue that."

"All right, then. Isn't that good for the town? Isn't he a benefactor? He's trying to save the town, and *you're* the ones trying to murder it."

Emily thought for a second. "Force," she said.

"What?" Ethan said.

"That's why it's wrong. He's using force. And, yeah, being sneaky and dirty about it, but he's using force to deprive Grandma of her property rights."

"Brings in money, though," Uncle Ben said, with a twinkle in his eye.

"Doesn't matter. Look, the money is great. Business is great. But it's just like what we were talking about before. Grandma has the right to this property. She owns it. The city shouldn't be able to take it, not for a hundred thousand, not for a couple million."

Ethan said, "Oh. I get it. I go into a store, and I take a radio. I give the clerk five bucks. But the store wants to sell it for fifty. I walk out, but I'm stealing. I'm taking what I want by force. It doesn't matter how much I paid for it if the person that owns it doesn't want to sell."

"You got it," Uncle Ben said. "And that's what's going to lead off my show tonight. You guys want to be rockstars in an obscure but important way?"

The show was in the can, and half a dozen of Grandma's cookies in their bellies.

"That was great, guys," Uncle Ben said. "You're naturals in front of the camera."

"But?" Ethan said, patting his stomach and leaning back on the couch.

"But like I said, this will help. The word will get out. It's kind of like planting seeds. You're going to have to do much more if you're going to make those seeds grow."

Emily drank half her milk and put the glass down on the coffee table. "It actually makes the problem worse if the city can't get the money, because some businesses are bleeding cash, too. The town is having trouble all around."

Uncle Ben said, "There are always ways to generate business. People like to think the salvation is tax money, or some grant from the government, but that just moves money around. The only thing that *makes* money is people adding value to products."

"Like assembling a car."

"Yes, but not just that. People can add value by being themselves, too. Community is value. Sometimes, in the world of the Internet, people lose sight of that. There's a ton of value added when you just smile at people." He finished his milk and stood up. "Well, I better go. Long drive ahead of me tonight. But you guys did well. I don't think Osterhout is going to win re-election."

"I don't think he'll even try," Emily said. They walked Uncle Ben out to his car and watched him drive away.

Uncle Ben's show did make a difference, the twins thought. Grandma reported that a number of people stopped her and said they'd seen the show, and it had made them mad. Osterhout, Grandma said, had decided to take a vacation, and his voicemail was full.

In the end, the vote was very close—fewer than fifty votes separated the winning side from the losing side. But Grandma was on the losing side. The broadcast hadn't been quite enough.

A curious thing happened, though. As the disappointed crowd filed out of city hall after the vote results, one of the city councilmen tapped Grandma on the shoulder and asked to speak with her for a moment. They went off to a corner and the man talked for a while, his hands pointing and making shapes in the air. Grandma nodded a bit, shook her head, nodded again, and shrugged. Eventually they shook hands and Grandma rejoined the twins.

"What was that all about?" Ethan said.

"Councilman Willoughby and some other council members saw the news you dug up for Ben's video. So despite the referendum, I'm not sure they would want to force me to sell my property. Political suicide."

"Wait," Emily said, "does that mean we might win even though we just lost?" She and Ethan exchanged a hopeful glance.

"We'll have to see," Grandma said, but her face was calm and a small smile showed there. "Politics is funny."

Ethan whispered to Emily for a second, and Emily nodded enthusiasically. "Grandma," Emily said. "We haven't been fishing for a while. Do you think Uncle Brock would take us out?"

Grandma cocked an eyebrow. "He's not much of a fisherman," she said.

Emily's smile got a little bigger, with a hint of mischief lurking in it. "That's why we thought it might be a good idea to have someone else along, someone with experience. Like, oh, maybe Art Willoughby."

Grandma stopped dead in her tracks, turned, and let her gaze fall on her grandchildren. "You know," she said, "I think he'd be very pleased to be invited. And you two are starting to scare me just a bit."

"In a good way?" Ethan said.

"Very good," Grandma said. "Very good indeed."

THE END

"It's stupid and you know it," Ethan said.

Emily had to admit he was right. There was nothing to be gained by going through this little gap in the fence, even if they could take their bicycles with them, which seemed risky. Plus, there was nothing to gain from going in anyway. They probably had security cameras and guards, not to mention big, ugly dogs.

"On we go then," Ethan said. "I want to get to the front entrance anyway. We can ride home from there."

Past the downed section, there was a good deal more room between the fence and the forest, and that allowed them to roll their bikes a little more easily. Another three or four hundred yards farther along, they came to a much larger road leading to a blacktopped entryway where the guard house was flanked by two uniformed guardsmen. Deep in the shadow of the trees, they watched the guards for a few moments. Two cars came through, long black sedans, rolling down their windows just long enough to have a chat with the guard and show some form of ID. The guard would take the identification to the shack and return a few moments later to hand it back to them. The huge iron gate would roll up, and the car would drift inside and down the long black pathway toward the main building. From what they could see, it was a glass-fronted structure, probably right against the river, with a row of flags in front as if it were an important government building of some kind.

No one came out. After a while it became obvious they weren't going to get any information from this, and it was just as likely that the other side of the fence, around the other end of the property, would yield them the same lack of information. Ethan crooked a finger at Emily, and they slunk back about thirty yards into the woods.

There they held a whispered conversation. "Not very enlightening, is it?" Ethan said.

Emily shook her head. "All we know is they are very intent on making sure nobody gets inside."

"I'm assuming that nobody includes us," Ethan said.

"It does today," Emily said. "Let's go back to the last road and take it out to the east as far as we can go. It has to connect to a main road up there somewhere."

This they did, wheeling their bicycles as best they could, but mostly having to carry them through the forest.

Ethan's arms grew achy from holding the bicycle up over the tangled undergrowth. Emily was having a worse time yet, getting her bike tangled in ivy and having to skirt around the poisoned variety. It seemed like an hour before they were able to reach the previous road, where their bikes would roll again. Twice they very nearly rolled over broken beer bottles, which would have slashed their tires to ribbons.

"How involved are we going to get in this thing anyway?" Emily said.

"I've been thinking about that," Ethan said, "And I don't really have any good answers. I want to save Grandma's house, but if the chemical company is just buying up the land, I don't know what we can do about it."

Emily was very quiet, wheeling her bike along on the dirt road. "It's just a horrible situation," she said. "I know I should be rooting for Grandma, and I am, but I don't see that the chemical company is doing anything wrong."

"It all hinges on the referendum," Ethan said. "If the referendum passes, and they get the rezoning, then there won't be very much we can do. Those derelict houses will stay that way, no one will take care of them, and Grandma's property value will decline to the point where she wouldn't even be able to sell it for the price they're offering her now. It might just be better to sell out, take as much money as possible, and get free of the whole situation."

Emily kicked a rock. It went skittering down the path and danced into the underbrush; a pair of birds, startled, erupted from the bush and flew toward the canopy above. "All I know is, the whole thing stinks."

Turn to page 179.

Brock said, "What time is it?"

Emily looked at the panel on the dashboard. "It's almost ten," she said.

Brock shook his head. "The watch comes by at about 10:15," he said. "If we're here in the middle of the river, they will definitely see us, not to mention hear us. We can't be caught here. We'll have to tie up on the far bank anyway, so we might as well listen to the phone call."

Brock took the wheel from Emily, put the boat into slow, and guided it to the far bank, where a tree over-hung the water.

When they had positioned the boat underneath the foliage, Brock tossed a rope up to a branch above them and secured it to a cleat at the stern of the boat. "That will hold us," Brock said. "But we'll have to be very quiet for about the next twenty minutes."

Ethan took the sonic device and aimed it at the building. It was much easier to hold it steady with the boat braced against the tree. He craned his neck around to look at Brock. "Do we have headphones for this thing?" he said.

Brock nodded and went down below.

"I don't know if this is a good idea," Emily said. "Isn't this kind of eavesdropping illegal?"

"Weren't you the one who a couple of minutes ago wanted to go trespass on Jaxton Chemical property to snoop on a document through the window? What kind of legality do you think that is? Besides which, you need to keep those binoculars fixed on the other bank. We need to know when the watch comes by."

Brock popped his head up from below and tossed a pair of headphones to Ethan.

"You plug them in on the right side of the box," he said. The headphones were foamy and black, covering the entire ear. Ethan put them on and all the nighttime noises of the river disappeared. He plugged in the jack where Brock indicated and immediately the vacuum cleaner sound came through loud and clear.

Inch by inch he changed the aim of the box until it pointed exactly at the window where they had heard the conversation before. Unfortunately, the conversation was not particularly interesting. Apparently, the man in the office needed to call his mother. Disgusted, he reached over and switched off the recording device.

"Well, that was a waste of time," he said. "I was really hoping for something better than that."

An audible click came from speaker as it shut off. Along the riverbank, a rotund man in an ill-fitting uniform strolled north. Occasionally, he would hold his cellphone to his ear, tap on it a couple of times, and start walking again. From across the water, the tinny sound of music reached them.

"He's playing his Spotify playlist," Emily said. "I suppose there's something less cloak-and-dagger than that, but I'm not sure what it would be."

It took the man five minutes or so to come into view, walk all the way up the riverbank, turn around, and stroll back. He disappeared into the pools of darkness to the north. "And so concludes an uneventful evening," Emily said.

But she was wrong.

As soon as she finished, a metallic click came from the foliage behind her, from the solid ground under the tree.

Brock, sitting on the port gunwale with his back to the tree, froze solid. From behind him, a voice said, "I think it would be best if nobody moved. At least long enough for me to figure out what y'all are doing here. "

It was like a scene from a movie. All three of them let their hands drift slowly upward, even though they could not see the source of the voice.

"Now I think, one at a time, you should step out of the boat." This was a woman's voice.

Brock was closest to the bank, so he slid his legs up and over the gunwale. The bank on the other side was a convenient height for debarking; at least he didn't have to scramble. Using tree branches for leverage, he hauled himself up to land. When he did so, he almost disappeared.

Ethan motioned for Emily to go next. She cast a longing look at the cabin underneath, which she was pretty sure she could reach if she dashed. But then what good would that do? It wasn't as if the gunman—gunwoman—wouldn't know where she was, and she had no way to get back up, start the boat, and cast off the line without getting shot. There was nothing for it but to comply. A moment later, Ethan joined the other two on the bank.

Now Emily could make out a dim outline. It was a woman for sure, dressed in black, her hair tied back in a ponytail. The reflected light off the water glinted on the barrel of a very businesslike gun.

"I didn't really expect to catch you out here on the river in the middle of the night so close to the Fourth of July parade. You have to know the police presence is beefed up around the holidays." She spoke to Brock, almost as if she knew who he was.

"I'm sorry," Brock said, "I have no idea what you're talking about."

"Oh, come on," the woman said. "Are we really going to stand here all night and do this?"

"Maybe," Brock said. "Because I'm not the one with the gun. But in your place, I would say let's just forget this whole thing and everyone go their separate ways."

"You'd like that, wouldn't you? But I think before any of that happens, I'll be searching your boat." The woman motioned with her gun for Brock to step farther away from the side of the craft. The bank sloped steeply here, and Brock had to scramble a little bit to get higher up the hill.

"Just a little farther," the woman said.

Brock stumbled up another tree line and paused. The woman took a step forward toward the twins. Her face came a little bit more into the light. She was young, but there was a hard line to her mouth that said she meant business.

"Kids?" the woman said, arching an eyebrow at Brock. "You're bringing kids into this now?"

"We were the ones that suggested it to *him*," Emily said. "He's just the guy with the boat."

The woman's face went blank. "You *have* to be kidding me. There's no way *you're* behind this."

Ethan said, "I'm afraid we are. We haven't really done anything wrong, though. All we did was listen."

The woman's face went from blank to surprised. "Listen? What on earth would you be listening to?"

Now it was the twins' turn to be surprised.

"Nothing," Ethan said. "I mean, we were mostly listening for the river monster."

The woman scratched her head a second. "This is getting a little too weird for me. What on earth are you talking about?"

"I know it sounds crazy," Emily said. "I'm sure you're going to think we're nuts. But we actually came out here to try and catch the Monongy, or at least prove that it's out here somewhere."

"Yeah," Ethan added, "We just happened to be here by the chemical factory and testing out some of our equipment. "

"That's the most insane thing I've ever heard, and I hear a lot of crazy stuff on this river."

"I knew you'd think it was nuts," Emily said, "But it's the truth. We're only in town for a little while, and our uncle here told us that he sometimes goes out looking for evidence of the river monster."

"Oh, that's what he said, did he?" She arched an eyebrow at Brock again. "That's very clever, I give you full marks for creativity."

Brock shrugged, a small smile on his face. "You can believe whatever you like. The truth will do as well as anything else. But since you're not going to be satisfied with that, you should probably check the boat."

"Oh, I will." She unclipped a walkie talkie from her belt, thumbed the button, and spoke slowly, quietly. "One boat, three suspects. Directly opposite the chemical plant. Subjects in custody, need backup."

The set crackled and a moment later came a low, breathy response. "On the way." A male voice this time.

"What you're going to find on the boat is a lot of sonar equipment and scientific notations, except for the conversation we overheard a couple minutes ago over at the chemical factory," Ethan said.

The woman was unimpressed. "I'm sure that's what it looks like," she said, "But in a minute, I bet we can find other interesting things on this boat that maybe you weren't aware of."

Ethan pointedly did not look at Emily, and Emily made sure that she kept her face as blank as possible. How did this woman possibly know about the secret hold? And was it really empty, or were there things in it that Brock hadn't told them about?

They stood there in the dark, listening to the river gurgle by, until there was a crashing in the underbrush, and a huge man, at least six-foot-three and two hundred fifty pounds, came stumbling through the undergrowth toward them.

"Hank," the woman called out, "I need you to search this boat."

"You got it," the giant said.

His enormous size made it a very difficult operation for him even to get onto the boat, but eventually he managed it. He stumbled about on deck, looking for Heaven knew what.

Then he held up a rod and tackle.

"You have to be kidding me," the woman said.

"I wanted to fish," Ethan said. "Those are mine."

She looked disgusted. "That's the lamest attempt at a cover story... *Everyone* tries that one. At least the river monster was original."

Turning back to Hank, she said, "You can put that stuff down. I think there's a hold underneath. You'll have to find the hatch, probably toward the back of the boat."

Ethan and Emily exchanged a glance. Moments later, there was a shout of triumph, as Hank found the hatch in question. At first, Emily hoped he wouldn't be able to get it up, his fingers being so big they wouldn't fit through the ring. But eventually he apparently managed it, lifting up the tiny hatch with an audible groan. He reached into his belt, unclipped the flashlight, and shined it downward.

"I found the hold," he said, unnecessarily, "but there is nothing in it."

As they waited, Emily kept her eyes on Uncle Brock. He did not seem flustered in the least.

Of course he knew the hatch was there, and of course he knew they would find it, but he didn't seem to care about that one way or the other. Emily wasn't sure what it was they suspected him of, but she was sure that whatever it was, he wasn't guilty. Or, the other possibility, that he was very guilty indeed and too smart to get caught.

The woman seemed distressed, or at least annoyed, by the fact that their investigation hadn't turned anything up. "Seriously?" she said. "There is nothing in the hold at all?"

"I'm looking at it right now," Hank said. "There's nothing there. I can see right down to the keel, and there is nothing but bilge water there."

The woman turned her attention back to Uncle Brock. "OK, smart guy, where is the stuff?"

Without missing a beat, Uncle Brock said, "What stuff are you talking about?"

"Do we really have to do this?" she said, sounding exasperated. "You know exactly what I'm talking about. It's a cute story you told the kids about searching for a river monster, but that story won't wash with me. I know all about the stuff you guys are running up and down this river, and it's my job to put a stop to it."

Now Emily was getting intrigued, and she could tell by her brother's face that he was, as well. What on earth were they talking about, running up and down the river? Surely in this day and age there was no smuggling going on.

But Brock, if he knew what the woman was talking about, kept his opinions entirely to himself. He shook his head sadly, and said, "I'm sorry, I'm afraid I have no idea what you're talking about."

"Well," the woman said, "I suppose we'll have to discuss this at the station."

Brock kept shaking his head, still not rising to debate whatsoever. "I don't think so. We have done nothing wrong."

"What about trespassing?" the woman said, a note of triumph in her voice.

"Trespassing how?" Brock said. "On what? Government land? This over here is administered by the Bureau of Land Management. I don't think we can trespass there. We have as much right to be on this land as anyone else. Yes, it's the middle of the night, and yes, you could describe our activities as suspicious. I get that a lot, chasing down a river monster nobody seems to believe in. But in point of fact, we haven't done anything wrong, and we aren't going to go down to the station to answer questions about it. What we're going to do is get back on our boat, sail back home, tie up, and go to bed. I don't know what you are going to do," he said, with a calm patient smile, "but I recommend the same course of action to you and your men, however many of you there are." And with that, Brock put his hands down and marched over toward his boat.

Honestly, it was probably that the woman looked so crestfallen that Ethan said what he did.

"We really are looking for a river monster," Ethan said. "I know it sounds hard to believe, but I also don't know what you're looking for, and I don't think you're going to find it on this boat. This is our uncle. We've known him a long time. He's kind of a weird dude in many ways, but he's no liar." Which was, itself, a bit of a lie, but Ethan kept a straight face. It was plausible.

The woman snorted, clearly in disbelief. "I don't know what he's told you, but I've never heard about any kind of river monster."

"You should get out more," Emily said. "What are you looking for out here anyway?"

The woman just shook her head.

"Okay, Hank," she said, "you can go back to your area. I guess there really isn't anything here." Hank shrugged his enormous form over the side of the boat and scrambled up into the forest again. They could hear him, smashing through the undergrowth, for another thirty seconds or so.

It seemed to make the woman even more embarrassed.

"Seriously," Ethan said, "What is it that you're looking for? You can't tell me that in the twenty-first century you actually have smugglers on the river."

At the word 'smugglers,' the woman seemed to stiffen and then take possession of herself, relaxing back into her previous state. She holstered her gun, snapping the holster closed. "There are smugglers on this river," she said. "I suppose there have been smugglers here since the early 1800s."

"What on earth are they smuggling?" Emily said.

They had all dropped their hands, and Emily leaned on the boat, not paying attention to Uncle Brock, who was making 'hurry up' motions with his hands.

"They smuggle the same things they always have smuggled," she said. "Alcohol, cigarettes, drugs of various kinds."

Ethan supposed that made sense. "So, before the government outlawed alcohol during Prohibition, was there smuggling?"

"Sure, they did," Emily said. "You remember our Revolutionary War lessons? You can argue that the entire Revolutionary War was started because of smuggling."

The woman looked incredulous. "You're seriously going to talk to me about the Revolutionary War now?"

"Well, it is the Fourth of July. It seems appropriate. The colonists really didn't like the idea that the British were telling them what they could and could not bring into the country, and whom they had to pay in order to get the right to do it. So they smuggled. A lot. The smugglers made the British angry, so they cracked down. When they did that, the colonists responded by throwing British goods into the Boston Harbor.

"And a number of other things," Emily said, hurrying things up. She swung one leg over the gunwale of the boat. "But every time the government does something like that, you get smuggling. That's probably why you still have it. If you would just leave people alone, you'd get a lot less of it."

The woman's mouth hardened into a line. "Sure," she said, "If you repeal all the laws, you don't have any criminals at all. But that's no way to run a society."

Ethan shrugged, climbing over the side of the boat himself. "I don't want to run society," he said. "I just want to be left alone to make my way the best I can. And if I want to go boating on the Monongahela River in the middle of the night, well, I suppose I can do that."

The woman stared at the three of them for a moment and then burst into laughter. "I swear, if I go back to the station and write this up in my report, people will think I'm completely nuts. Here I am being lectured on governmental policy and economic theory by a pair of fifteen-year-olds, and on Fourth of July week, as well. Aren't you guys supposed to be off at a party or something?"

Ethan found he really liked this lady. At least she had a sense of humor. "We're not really much for parties," he said. "But let me ask you a question. Why did you join the police force? If you are even police, which, you know, you never showed any identification or anything."

At this, the woman reached up and grabbed a tab on her uniform, and pulled downward. Velcro tore, and there was a shiny badge underneath. "For reasons that should be obvious, I don't wear this out where people can see it glinting off lights in the middle of the night. But yes," she said, "I am a police officer. Actually, I'm part of a special federal task force assigned to shut down smuggling on this river."

"That didn't answer my question," Ethan said.

"OK, in the interest of prolonging this surreal conversation, I got involved in a police force to help make lives better. A peaceful society is a happy society," she said.

"And was there anything unpeaceful about the way we were going about our business tonight?" Ethan said.

"Not particularly," she said, "But that doesn't mean you weren't planning some sort of mayhem for later."

That being uncomfortably close to the truth, with protests and referenda and all, Ethan thought it was better to move along.

"I don't see how stopping us in the middle of the night and searching our boat is doing that. I mean," he said, "look. The smugglers aren't doing much harm. All they're doing is evading taxes." He saw her body stiffen and her mouth open, clearly in response, so he held up a hand. "No, no, wait a second. Let me finish. You need to make sure that you keep the peace," he said. "But you can do that without stopping people from smuggling relatively harmless material like alcohol and cigarettes."

"Relatively harmless?" the woman said, arching an eyebrow.

"I said *relatively* harmless. Cigarettes are not going to do anyone harm sitting in a box. No one is going around at gunpoint forcing people to smoke. All you're doing is stopping people from engaging in an activity people have been engaged in for a thousand years. Yes, it's bad for them. Personally, I wouldn't smoke for all the money in the world, but that's not the point. I don't drink either, in case you were thinking of asking, but that doesn't mean that I think other people shouldn't be able to."

"I'm not saying they shouldn't be able to," the woman said, taking a couple of steps forward. Leaves crunched under her feet, leftover from last year's fall. "If people want to have a drink, then I think they should go ahead and do it. But there are rules about this kind of thing. The services provided by people who protect their liquor shipments cost money. Those shipments need to be taxed, in order to be able to provide the services. That's all I'm saying. When people evade those taxes, they're essentially saying they want those services for free."

Brock, clearly interested by now in this conversation, as odd as it was, stepped away from the wheel and stopped trying to get the twins on board. He leaned two hands down on the gunwale of the boat. "That sounds perfectly reasonable," he said. "That was exactly how I thought for a long time. And it is certainly true that if you want services, you should pay for them. But none of the people who are being provided these services have been asked if they want to pay for them, or how *much* they want to pay for them. The government simply decides that there will be such and such a tax. Then the taxes are imposed. In fact, as long as we're talking about the American Revolution—"

"I thought we stopped talking about that five minutes ago," the woman said. But she was clearly teasing, and kept her eyes locked on Uncle Brock.

"Never mind that," Brock said, waving the objection away. "One of the very first acts of the new Congress in 1787 was to pass a tax on whiskey. In fact," he said, "this exact area of the country rose up in rebellion when they did it."

"The Whiskey Rebellion, I remember," the woman said. Now she was close enough to sit down on the gunwale, and Ethan moved aside so she could.

"That's right," Brock said. "River smuggling is just a kind of whiskey rebellion. People in D.C. are the ones who make the rules, pass a law that says certain products have to be taxed at such and such an amount. Does it have anything to do with the cost of providing services to those people? Not a thing. It's a number they make up in their deliberations, and then they impose them on the people."

"The people do get to vote, though," the woman said. "By the way, if we're going to have this conversation, you should probably know my name is Eve."

Brock held out a hand. "Brock," he said. "The point is, that although it may look as if the people get to make the decision, the truth is that the government makes the decision, often without consulting the people in the first place. I'll bet, for instance, that this particular tax on alcohol and cigarettes was decided on by a regulatory agency, not by a legislature."

The woman gave a little half-shrug. "I'm actually not sure."

"Yet here you are enforcing a law, and you don't even know where it came from. Now don't get excited," Brock said, holding up his hands to keep her from vaulting off the side of the boat and coming after him. "It's only an illustration. The point is, none of us know where that law came from. And yet we treat that law like we treat any other."

"Wait," Ethan said. "Em and I were talking about this just the other day. There's a referendum going on in town right now, and that looks like it's going to tell us the will of the people. But it isn't."

"Not even close," Emily cut in. "It's only a couple of thousand people in the whole town who even bother to vote. Maybe even less, on something like this, in the middle of the summer. What that means is that a very small number of people are going to make the call on what the rules are for a whole lot of other people."

"But that's the way government works," the woman said. "That's how all government works. The people who know best are the ones to make the rules for the people who are too lazy to get involved."

Eve looked at each of the three passengers on the boat in turn. "So I take it this means that if I asked you for help in apprehending the smugglers, I wouldn't get very far, would I?"

Brock looked a little sheepish, but said, "Sorry. I'm not into that sort of thing. Police work gives me a rash."

Emily joined her brother sitting on the stern of the boat. "Don't look at me," she said. "I'm just fifteen years old."

The woman said, "These two are the least fifteen-year-old fifteen-year-olds I've ever seen. I suspect if I needed help with something along these lines, there aren't a whole lot of people I could get a hold of that could do a better job than you two." She blew out a long breath and stared over the water toward the chemical plant. "I can't have you listening in on conversations over there," she said. "That *is* illegal, and probably immoral, and definitely unethical. Or do you have some sort of fancy argument about how information wants to be free, and stealing it with electronic listening devices strapped to the side of your boat is somehow an advance for the free market?"

It was Emily and Ethan's turn to look sheepish.

"Nope, Ethan said. "I got nothing."

Emily said, "I could say something here about the ends justify the means, but I don't really believe that, so I think I'll just keep my mouth shut."

The woman looked at Brock. Brock smiled blithely back. "Don't look at me," he said. "I'm here listening for river monsters."

Now the woman laughed, tension leaking out of her. It was surprisingly musical, charming, and it made her very human all of a sudden. "Someday you're going to have to tell me about this river monster thing. It's got to be the flimsiest excuse I've ever heard of."

Brock stood up straight. "Listen, Officer," he said, and bent down to take a look at her badge, "Eve Hamilton, there really is a monster out here. I know people say I'm crazy, but there's an awful lot of evidence to support the idea that there's something going on in this river that people just don't know about."

"Oh, there's plenty going on on the river that people don't know about," Officer Hamilton said. "And I do need your help with one thing in particular. I know you're maybe not terribly opposed on principle to the idea of smuggling, but I bet you're opposed to the idea of extorting river traffic, threatening the boats that go up and down the river to carry contraband under the noses of the authorities."

"If you strike the authorities part," Ethan said, "You have my attention. We're not big fans of force of any kind… unless it's to defend against an aggressor."

Officer Hamilton flicked a glance down to her holster. "That was probably a bad way to introduce myself, wasn't it?"

"We forgive you," Emily said. "We've been blessed with terribly faulty memories anyway."

An interesting change had come over Brock. Where he had been open and friendly up until a couple of moments ago, the mention of extortion on the river had him backing away from the officer and starting up the engine of the boat. "We'll keep an eye out for you," he said, but it was obvious from his tone that he would do no such thing.

Eve took her hands off the boat, untied the rope from the branch above, and tossed it onboard. "I'm sure you will," she said, obviously disappointed. "I do hope we have a chance to meet each other again, under a little bit better circumstances."

"Yeah, that would be great," Brock said, engaging the throttle and pulling the boat smoothly away from the riverbank.

The engine had almost no work to do heading downstream toward the house, so its growl was a lower pitch, the kind that masks talking very well. Ethan and Emily kept to themselves at the stern of the boat and had a short private conversation.

"What was that about?" Emily said.

Ethan shrugged. "It sure as heck was *something*. He and the officer seemed to get along real well until she said something about extorting people on the river. I wonder if he knows something about that."

"And he seemed just fine with the big officer investigating the hold on the boat, but he didn't go into the cabin, and he sure couldn't see very much of the hold of the boat from the little hatch here in the back." She thumped her heel on it a couple times. "I'll bet that hold only goes forward a few feet. I'll bet you the real cargo area on this boat is forward."

"But there's no way into it," Ethan said. "We both looked."

"We looked," Emily said, keeping her eyes fixed on Brock's head. She was pretty sure he couldn't hear them, but she still didn't want him to turn around. "I think we'd better find a way to take a closer look at that cabin."

Turn to page 276.

The restaurant was only four blocks up and two over from the center of town. The twins had bikes, but the other two had walked, so the twins left their bikes on the rack by the library and set out with their two friends. Xavier wanted to talk to Emily, and Ethan wanted to talk to Shannon, but with one thing and another they ended up walking four abreast down the middle of the road.

"We could never do this in our town," Emily said.

"What's your town like?" Xavier said, kicking at a loose rock and sending it skittering down the road.

"Not much to tell. It's not really a town, like this one. We don't have a Main Street, and our town doesn't do parades. I think it's because we're a suburb, and not a town in our own right. We didn't even exist before the city exploded in size and people needed a place to live close enough to the city that they could commute."

"Nobody commutes from here."

Shannon coughed. "Some people do. The ones that work for Jaxton."

"Not many of those," Xavier said. To his left a dog barked furiously behind a fence. Emily smelled fries on the wind.

"Why not? I'd think most of the workforce for the place would come from the town," Ethan said.

"But it doesn't. I don't think the town has a lot of chemical engineers in residence." Xavier walked backward for a bit so he could see everyone. "Most of them commute the thirty miles or so to Hipping. They have a Sammy's there."

Emily waved at him to pause a second. "What does that mean?"

"It's sort of the marker of civilization."

"You have a MegaMart out at the crossroads."

"Yeah, out at the crossroads. They have to drive right past it to get to work every day. So they might as well live in Hipping. And they do." Xavier reached the rear door of Thusnelda's and cracked it open. "I'll go in and get shakes started. Who wants what?"

Emily said she'd have cookies and cream. Ethan wanted raspberry, and Shannon settled on peach cobbler. Xavier disappeared inside.

"How long have you known Xavier?" Ethan said. They skirted the back of the building and came to the glass side door. He held it open for the ladies.

Shannon tried to think. "Long time. All my life, I guess. We're in the same grade, and here that means we're in the same class every single year. Right back to kindergarten."

"You must have done a bunch of things together." Ethan sounded jealous. Emily staked out a place at the back corner in a circular booth and slid around to the middle. Ethan grabbed napkins and headed back.

Shannon stood there by the side of the booth until Ethan got in and slid around to his sister. Then she climbed in on the opposite side. Some of the fun went out of the evening for Ethan.

"I don't know the two of you at all, so it's only because Xavier wants me to that I'm even talking to you about any of this. I don't tell my business to strangers."

"We're not really strangers," Ethan protested. "You must know Patty Tuttle."

"I do," Shannon said, pouring some salt in a thick layer onto the orange tabletop. "But I don't know you. And I don't run in the same circles as Mrs. Tuttle."

Xavier appeared with two shakes as if he popped out of the floor. "You don't have to," he said, setting one each in front of Shannon and Emily. "They're good people, Shannon. I can tell you that. I think they might be able to help us. Anyway, I need the help and I want to have two new friends, so if I can put those two things together I'm going to do it." He headed back for the counter.

Shannon watched him go, and then said, "Xavier likes everyone. I don't. But this is mostly his deal, so I'll let him make the call." The shakes were too thick to drink, so Shannon spooned some out and ate it with the spoon flipped, using her tongue to scrape the spoon clean. Then she began drawing pictures in the salt.

Xavier returned, took in the seating arrangements, and slid in by Ethan. "Now, let me tell you all why we're here. Take a look around the place and tell me what you see."

They looked and Emily finally said, "It's been here a while. I can see the marks on the tile where the benches used to be."

"When there were more of them, yeah. What else?"

"There's nobody here," Ethan said. "It's just us and that one other couple over in the other corner."

"Bingo," Ethan said. "Tonight the place should have been hopping. And there's no one here."

"Maybe the protest put them off. They all went home to be angry," Emily said. "And this shake is really good."

"Thank you," Xavier said. "I take pride in doing a good job, even when it isn't my job I'm doing. There should be people here. We're one of the oldest, most established burger joints in town."

"You are the *only* burger joint in town," Ethan said. "Unless I missed one back by the library."

"You didn't," Xavier said, shoveling in a giant spoon-ful of shake. "But you did miss that there's a MacBurger out by the MegaMart, which is where everyone is. If we went out there, we wouldn't be the only people in the place. There are more kids in the playland out there than there are customers here."

"We can't go there," Emily said. "We don't have a car."

"Correct. But we are the only people in town that don't."

"Not quite."

"Close enough. Anyway, the point is that Thusnelda's can't survive like this. We have inventory going bad in the back. We have payroll. We have, well, we have me. There needs to be people coming in or Thusnelda's is going away."

"This is about your job," Emily said, incredulous.

Xavier waved his long plastic spoon. "Not just about my job, but yes. That's part of it."

Emily stared.

"Look," Xavier said. "There aren't a lot of jobs for kids my age, as I'm sure you know. The people here are good to me, and I like the job okay. I need money, same as anyone, so when I see a pretty girl I can take her to the movies." He stopped for a second and concentrated on his shake, but Emily kept her eyes on him, in case he meant her. "Besides, Thusnelda's is an institution in this town. This joint has been here since before my father was born. It would be a shame to lose it to a MacBurger."

"What's the game plan, then?" Ethan said.

"Just like that?" Shannon said. "You're all in on this?"

"Yep," Ethan said. "This shake all by itself is worth many hours of my time. So what do we do?"

"Uh," Xavier said, "that's still to be determined."

"You don't have a plan? Jeesh, you brought us out here and fed us shakes to get our sympathy?"

"Well, no, I was hoping you'd have something constructive to offer."

"It seems to me," Emily said, "that your problem isn't MacBurger. Yes, competition is hard, but it should make everyone better. Yes, the zoning laws are giving people incentive to drive out to the freeway to find their shopping options, instead of finding them in town—"

"This is what I've been saying," Shannon said. "Maybe you'll listen to her, when you wouldn't to me."

Emily glanced at Shannon. "What? He doesn't get zoning?"

"Oh, he understands what it is. He knows it's how the city council puts one business here and another there," she said, drawing boxes in the salt layer in front of her, "But he doesn't appreciate what that can mean in this case."

Emily turned a rather different glance on Xavier. "You do know that the zoning is part of the problem here, don't you?"

Xavier scraped the bottom of his cup. "Explain that to me. I don't see how it makes any difference."

"But you must," she said, leaning forward to catch his eyes. "Think about how it works. The zoning makes islands of certain kinds of businesses. The big box stores locate in a group, and to go to them you have to drive. Around them other businesses pop up, but again, driving is key. So your restaurant, which is a walk-to place, nobody goes to because they're already in their cars. Then, because all those businesses are out there, beyond the borders of town, the businesses *in* town dry up.

They can't compete, because their potential customers forget they even exist, or can't be bothered."

"But they could," Ethan said, idly tapping the table. His eyes were far away.

"What do you mean, 'they could'?" Shannon said, glaring darts.

"I mean they could, if they did the right sorts of things," Ethan said, not backing down. "It's true that the zoning pushes a lot of the retail outside of town. And it's true that those big box stores make more sense in that location than building small shops. But it's not true that they have all the advantages, especially with a shop like Thusnelda's that's had such a long tradition. I think there are things that Thusnelda's could do that would capitalize on the advantages they have that the big box stores don't."

Xavier's face broke into a slow smile. "Now that is worth a shake."

"If it were true," Shannon said.

"I think it is," Emily said, leaning over the table to catch Xavier's eye. It wasn't hard. He seemed to be watching her a lot.

"I mean, look. Is there anyone in town that hasn't eaten here at some point?" Emily said.

Xavier shook his head slowly. "I don't know, but I don't think so. Not if they've lived here any length of time."

"Okay. Do most people like the food?"

"I think so. Some people love it. It's sure better than the crap you get over at MacBurger."

"They have salads now," put in Ethan.

"Very funny," Emily said. "I'm serious about this. If the food is good, then you're going to have people who will be excited to come eat it. You just have to remind them to do that."

"Or do things that will help them remind themselves," Ethan said, getting excited.

"Like what? I still don't see it," Xavier said, tapping his teeth with his long red spoon.

Shannon stirred her shake. "I don't see it, either. They've tried lots of stuff, and it hasn't worked."

"You haven't tried this," Ethan said. He pointed at the wide, blank walls, one at a time. "It's a small town. Everyone knows everyone. You could use the power of herd mentality."

"Explain."

"Take a photo every time someone comes in to eat. Put it on the wall. In no time you'd have a lot of proof that this is the place people want to come and eat."

Emily pulled a napkin and wiped the side of her cup. "Not to mention that people love to see pictures of themselves."

Xavier made a note on a napkin. "We haven't done that. Haven't even thought of it. What else could we do?"

"Who designed your menu?" Emily said.

"I, um, I'm pretty sure it was placed there by Moses when he came down from the mount." He craned his neck, trying to see the board. "Forget it. Come with me." He popped out of the booth and started for the counter, not waiting to see if anyone was following him.

"We going to follow him?" Ethan said.

"I have to wait for one of you," Emily said, shoving Ethan.

"We better. He gets cranky when he gets excited and nobody gets lit up because of it."

Ethan slid out and Emily, who had been prepared to climb under the table, if necessary, followed him. After a minute, Shannon brought up the rear.

Xavier stood before the counter, looking up at the board. "Okay. What am I supposed to be looking at?" The plastic board was lined with little plastic letters and numbers. Some of them, when you looked closely, had been there a while.

"Well," Emily said, "That first one. Jack's Dog. What's that?"

Xavier said, "It's a hot dog with relish, mustard, and ketchup."

"Why is that Jack's Dog?"

"I don't know."

"Anyone in town named Jack that you know of?"

"Nope."

"Why is his dog such a big deal, then?"

"That I couldn't say. And before you ask, I don't know who Peter is, or why his BLT should be honored with an entire line on the board."

"If you could have these people name their dishes, why not people that actually live here?"

Xavier toed a line in the tile. "You're messing with tradition here."

"I'm trying to keep a larger tradition alive," Emily said, and put her hand on his arm.

The smile came out. "I know. It's a good idea."

They stood there, the four of them, for another half an hour, throwing ideas back and forth, as much because no one wanted to go home as that they really thought they would work. But Xavier promised to talk to the boss and see if some of those ideas could be implemented.

"It's just a chance to make sure the restaurant has the best chance to survive. I've never eaten anywhere else in this town—except at Grandma's," Emily said. She had inched closer to Xavier all through the discussion.

Only Shannon didn't seem to be impressed by the brainstorm session. "It's tough to reverse the momentum. Once a place starts to die, there's a kind of aura about it. People can tell. I don't think putting people's pictures on the wall is going to change any of that."

Ethan couldn't understand her. She seemed a perfectly nice girl, great teeth, incredible hair, and clearly she read widely and had a solid grasp on the world. She was just negative, snarky, and cranky. Was she like this all the time? Because it would surely be convenient if she were nice and interested in him, because he was pretty sure his sister and Xavier were interested in each other, and that could make for a long couple of weeks.

"Well, we have to try. Let's see what the owner says. He's got to have some ideas about how the town would respond," Ethan said. "You never know. And it's not like any of this is going to make things *worse.*"

"We can't put it in the paper. The paper isn't going to be coming out for two weeks, because Ms. Burns is out of town. We went and knocked on her door, and there was a note. She's left town until after the referendum," Emily said.

Richard Hanks, owner of Thusnelda's, rubbed his chin and sighed. "That means we have to tell everyone ourselves."

"Flyers," Xavier said. "We can distribute them during the parade. That will work—everyone in town comes to the parade."

"You'll need four or five people, I think, to get enough out to make a difference."

"No problem. Ethan will help us, and I'm sure Xavier can talk Shannon into it," Emily said. She set the remains of her shake in the trash and rubbed her belly. "I better get this place back on its feet, or I'll weigh a thousand pounds, and every bit of it shake."

"We do make good shakes. Maybe we can name one the Emily," Hanks said. "I am grateful for your help on this. I had started to think that we were never going to make it."

"You haven't made it yet," Emily said, but she was smiling. "There are still a few hundred people we need to persuade to come and get onion rings."

"Soda," Hanks said, rounding the counter and heading back to the big, flat fry burners. "We make a ton on soda. A couple hundred large Pepsis and we'll be back in business."

"I'll walk you home," Xavier said.

"I didn't expect you'd have talked to your boss quite so fast," Emily said. "We just brainstormed last night. You work pretty quickly."

"When it's something I want, yes, I do," Xavier said, holding open the door.

Emily kept her eyes on his face. He felt it, and gave her an innocent smile. "What? I do."

"Apparently."

"What's that supposed to mean?"

She sashayed across the parking lot, tossing her hair over her shoulder. "Nothing," she said. "But I will allow you to walk me home."

The Fourth dawned clear and warm, trending toward hot. It would have been a prime day to use the rope swing, but there was work to do, both for the referendum, which was only a few days away, and Thusnelda's, which had decided to do a Fourth of July weekend promotion to call attention to their rebranding. Both causes had fliers ready, and the twins and Xavier, along with Shannon, if she showed up, had given their word they would walk the parade route handing out leaflets.

Emily wore her best parade outfit—dark blue jean shorts with white stars, and a fire-engine red shirt—and Ethan went for his signature royal blue polo with white and red stripes across the chest, and khaki shorts.

Grandma said over breakfast that she was proud of the twins and wanted to do something to help. "I can't walk that route any more, not fast enough to get to the end of it before the parade passes by, but I can make cookies. I'll go to the park and sit in my chair, and after the parade I can hand out cookies to anyone that takes a flier and agrees to vote no on the referendum."

"Grandma! That's bribery!" Ethan said.

"For all I know, the other side is being bribed to the tune of millions of dollars. All I have is cookies. I think that's a fair fight."

"Sounds fair to me," Ethan said. "I think your cookies are worth a million bucks."

They kissed Grandma and went flying out, down to Main and over to city hall. Xavier was already there and Shannon came running up a minute later.

"We're all here," Xavier said, reaching into an old canvas satchel and retrieving a thick sheaf of papers. "That's terrific. Since there are two different kinds of flyers, it would probably be best for us to divide up two by two. Also, I've been giving this some thought, and I think it would be most effective if we had one town native with one from out of town in each pair. That should let us have the greatest, um, impact."

Shannon looked at Ethan. "I'm impressed you showed."

"Why wouldn't I?" he said. "I told you, I'm in this all the way. I want my grandmother to stay in her house. I wouldn't mind if Thusnelda's stayed, too."

"I just… I think maybe I owe you an apology. Both of you," she said.

Xavier said, "We don't have a lot of time. Once the parade starts," he checked the time on his phone, "in an hour and ten minutes, nobody is going to pay much attention to us. They'll tuck our flyer in a bag, cover it with candy, and that will be that. We have to get to people while there's still some attention span left."

"Fine." Ethan said. "Shannon wants to apologize and I want to hear it. We'll go together."

"Suits me," Xavier said, looking relieved. "Emily, you want to come with me?"

"It looks like I do," she said. "Let's get rolling."

When they were alone, Shannon and Ethan split the flyers and started up Main, stopping every few yards to hand a flyer—one of each—to the people sitting there waiting. Thusnelda's flyer was on bright orange paper, and it contrasted with everything. The referendum flyer was printed on a light blue, and Ethan thought that was hard to read, but there was nothing to be done about it now. Together they went a couple of blocks, calling out, "Vote No on Tuesday! Save Thusnelda's!" Trying to link the two things together in people's minds, even though they weren't actually related.

In a dead patch, Shannon said, "I especially owe you an apology. When I met you I thought you were just going to pass through, get people riled up, and leave. Like it was a kind of practical joke. But here you are, doing actual work, and, well, I'm sorry. I misjudged you."

"If it's any consolation," Ethan said, handing a flyer to a middle-aged woman with three children, "I probably owe you an apology, too. I thought you were pretty negative and hateful. Especially because Xavier was being so nice—"

"That's about your sister. You know that, right?"

"Sure, I know. But still, he's a nice guy. You were kind of prickly. I couldn't tell what your problem was, or if maybe you were just always like that, but anyway, I'm glad to know the real you after all. I like this person a lot better."

They worked hard, all four of them. By 9:00am, when the parade officially began, they were sweating hard and running low on flyers with only a block to go.

But even though lots of people had taken them, they didn't feel much like they'd had success. Most people had shrugged when they read the top part of the flyer about the referendum, which a lot of people seemed not to have even known about. For Thusnelda's, they'd had better success. Lots of people recognized Xavier, and he could put a good word in. That personal touch mattered.

"How can they not know about the referendum?" Emily said. "It's one of the most important issues in town."

355

"Most of them, it doesn't affect. People are really good at ignoring things that aren't directed at them. So what if someone gets evicted, as long as it isn't them?"

Emily stopped dead. "Wait. I've been thinking about this all wrong. We need to get the others."

"What? We're almost at the end of the route here."

"Doesn't matter. I'm so stupid. Of course people think they don't care. Look at the flyer," she said, holding one up.

"I've been looking at that thing all day."

"No, you haven't. Neither have I. Compare it to this," she said, and held up one of the Thusnelda flyers.

"They're pretty close to the same. We designed both of them, remember?"

"Yeah, but think about what they say. Think about what each flyer is trying to do." The parade was still a block or so behind them, the American flag marching slowly in front. She dashed across the street and grabbed Ethan.

"You need to meet us at the end of the route. I need to talk to everyone. We're blowing this thing with the referendum."

Ethan grimaced. "Don't I know it. No one cares about it. We haven't talked to a single person all morning that gives a rip about the referendum. They just don't seem very engaged about it."

"Right," Emily said. "But I know why. Meet us in the parking lot two blocks down." She sprinted back across, coming to a halt next to Xavier as they waited for the procession to pass.

It took some time, now that the parade was in full swing, for the kids to make it to the parking lot where the parade participants gathered to disband. Xavier stopped to chat with several of the float participants, especially, Emily noticed, the ones carrying beauty pageant winners. He came over to the group with a bag of candy, a sucker already in his mouth.

Ethan was testy. "What did you want to talk to us about? What's so important?"

Instead of answering, Emily said, "Why would people want to vote no on the referendum?"

"Because we ask them to," Xavier said, or at least it sounded like he said that, his words were blurred by a Tootsie Roll Pop.

"Not good enough, obviously," Emily said. "Seriously. Why?"

Ethan thought for a second. "Because it's bad for the town."

"Is it?"

"Well, sure it is," Ethan said, flailing, and looking to Shannon for assistance.

Shannon shrugged. "This is mostly your fight. I don't want to see the chemical factory here because I hate those people, but that's not going to cut ice with the majority."

Emily pointed at Shannon. "And yet, that's exactly what we're doing wrong. Shannon wants a no vote for personal reasons. But personal reasons are why *everyone* votes the way they do. Like she said, this is mostly our fight. Why?"

"Because it's our grandmother," Ethan said, light dawning.

"Right. But Patty Tuttle is a lot more than just our grandmother. She's lived in this town all her life. People *know* her. They like her. She's a town tradition. That house, *her* house, is a part of the town of Gnarled Oak just like Thusnelda's is."

"And if we're using the personal touch to save Thusnelda's, why aren't we doing it with the referendum, too?" Ethan said. His eyes were wide in understanding. "That's good thinking, Em."

"We need to get these flyers remade, and fast. We still have a whole day of picnicking and booths and fairs where we have a chance to get the word out."

They ran to Xavier's house—it was closest, and he had a printer—and in an hour they had a completely reworked flyer. On it was a large photo of Grandma's house, in color, and above it the title read "Save This House." Below, the flyer asked people to vote no on the referendum to make sure that the Ancestral Home of Patty Tuttle would not be reduced to rubble.

"A little on the melodramatic side, don't you think?" Ethan said.

Xavier held one up and beamed. "Heck, no. This is perfect. You want to grab people by the heart, and this is definitely the way to do it."

They printed up all they could before Xavier's printer ran out of ink. By this time the parade had ended, and most of the town queued up at the park across from city hall for dunking booths, magic shows, rock bands, and hot dogs—the perfect small-town Fourth of July. Everyone's spirits were high and few people were willing to think about politics.

But they were willing to think about Patty Tuttle. She had a booth herself, a charity booth for the Rotary Club of Gnarled Oak, of which she'd been a member for forty years. Heaps of cookies graced the bar across the booth's front, and the line to get one of those cookies stretched back twenty yards. The twins and their friends took advantage of that all the way, making sure that for every cookie that went into someone's mouth, a flyer went into their hand.

"Wait… It's *your* house they'll be bulldozing to get the chemical factory built?" more than one person said.

Grandma would grimace and say, "That's right. I might be the only one left on Riverfront Road, but I'm still there and I aim to stay, if I can. I sure could use your help."

And that worked. Everyone who knew her—and that was a lot of people—promised that come Tuesday, they'd be voting with her, to save her house and to keep her in Gnarled Oak. "It wouldn't be home here without you," they said, and a dozen or more leaned over the bar to give her a warm hug.

Shannon and Ethan went away for hot dogs and churros and came back laughing. "We're over by the dogs, and there's a woman over there telling everyone to vote no on the referendum, because if they don't, and Patty Tuttle has to leave town, she's going to have the bulldozers knock every one of their houses down to see how they like it.

"Sounds like Constance Bramwell," Grandma said. "Tall, thin woman with a face like the Wicked Witch of the West?"

Shannon choked and spat out a mouthful of soda. "Yep, that's her all right."

"Great. She's got the biggest mouth in town, bless her heart. Everyone's going to hear about it now. This was a great idea, kids. I'm very grateful."

Xavier said, "I will expect to be repaid handsomely. In cookies, of course."

"There will always be a jar filled and waiting," Grandma said, and patted him on the cheek. "Now take my granddaughter out and show her a good time."

The flyers were nearly gone anyway. The day blazed ahead, perfect and clear, the summer day of all their dreams. They had cotton candy and sodas, played games—Shannon proved to have a very strong and accurate arm, especially when it came to dunking

Ethan at the dunking booth—and sat on the dock as the fireworks boomed over the river. In the flickering light of the rockets' red glare, Ethan thought he saw Emily and Xavier holding hands. But it might have been his imagination. He was concentrating pretty hard on someone else's hand at the time.

Sunday in Gnarled Oak wasn't a particularly useful day. Most everyone went either to the Gnarled Oak Church of Christ or up the highway to the Annendale Methodist Church. Businesses were mostly closed and Grandma would allow no rope swinging or bike riding until after everyone had been to service and come back for a little Bible study. It was simply the way things were done.

In the afternoon, they all three took a walk through the town, and here the twins began to see some results from their work of the past Friday. Passing one trim little house, they were stopped by a young couple who introduced themselves to the twins as Jeff and Nicole.

"Your grandma was the first one to greet us when we moved into town. We didn't know a soul. And there she was with a plate of cookies," Nicole said, and turned her gaze on Grandma. "Please tell me you're not being run out of town."

"I'm afraid that's exactly what's happening," Grandma said, and told about the referendum and the zoning change that would leave her house condemned.

"You can count on a couple of no votes from this house," Nicole said, her jaw jutting forward. "We won't be snookered by any fancy talk, either. We'll tell our friends. You keep fighting."

Grandma said she would, and they walked on. The twins exchanged an excited glance. "You remember them from Friday?" Emily said.

"No," Ethan said. "I think I would, too. But I don't think they got a flyer from us. That could mean word is spreading without our having to push it."

Grandma laughed. "You young people think you invented the idea of a 'viral' message. That's a fine joke. Little towns like this were spreading news a whale of a lot faster than your Internet long before you were born. Before I was born, come to that. You just have to find the right message—and that, it looks like, you managed to do."

Sunday night Shannon came over for a quick consultation. "Xavier won't make it. His mom wants him home this evening. But he's not working tomorrow, he tells me. So what are we doing?"

Ethan sat on the couch next to her, and Emily sat to one side in the loveseat.

Emily swiveled and put her head on the armrest, blew out a long breath, and studied the ceiling. "We think the flyers are working." She told the story of the couple out on their walk. "So people are talking. Is there some way we can pump that up?"

"No parades Monday. Business as usual," Ethan said, leaning back against the cushions.

"But there's always Thusnelda's," Shannon said.

"What do you mean?" Emily turned to look at her.

"Isn't this week the start of the big Thusnelda's deal? So there should be traffic there, right? And the traffic will be coming from people that care about the town, or they wouldn't be there in the first place. So that's the target market, right?"

Ethan smiled. "That's right. There might not be a lot of traffic, but there will be some. I guess we could stake out a place on Main Street, too, maybe with a sign?" He looked to Shannon for some idea if that would work.

Shannon screwed up her face. "I don't know. I mean, most of the town does have to go down Main Street if they're going to go anywhere. But that's early... So, we could hit a corner in the morning, then go to Thusnelda's, then back to the corner, I guess."

"Anything to get one more vote. Do you think it's going to be close?" Ethan said.

Nobody knew. How could they know such a thing?

They spent all of Monday standing out on the street corner or chatting with people as they came into Thusnelda's. According to Xavier, not many people usually came to the shop on Monday. Outside, the perfect summer continued—not too humid, and not so hot that it was impossible to be outside. Emily mopped her brow, standing out on the corner by the restaurant, where most of the people seemed to pass on their way in.

It wasn't busy. But there weren't long gaps between visitors, either, and that was unusual, Xavier said. "Monday, I hate to work. Nobody comes in on Monday. I'm not allowed to read a book or anything because it's a bad visual for people who do come in, so I end up cleaning everything in the place and then standing around counting tiles."

"You count tiles?" Emily said. "Hi, welcome to Thusnelda's. Have you heard about the referendum tomorrow?"

"Been hearing about it all weekend. I'm not registered to vote, though," said the man walking by.

Xavier stepped in front of him with a huge smile on his face. "Well, it's your lucky day," he said, "Because you can register at the polls before you vote. We sure would appreciate you doing that."

"What's in it for you?" the man said, peering at the flyer Emily had just handed him.

"My grandmother doesn't get her house pushed into the river," Emily said levelly, and waited. As she knew he would, the man raised his eyebrows and regarded her over the paper.

"Your grandma? You're a Tuttle?"

"I am. Patty's granddaughter."

The man shook his head. "I thought she was nuts when she had Marv paint that house pink, but now, I can't even imagine this town without it. I haven't voted since my Jerri died. She was the political one. But for Patty Tuttle, I'll do it. And you, missy."

"Thank you," Emily said.

"You're a great citizen," Xavier said.

The man humphed at that and shouldered his way past into the restaurant.

"Do you know that guy?" Emily said.

"No. Seen him around some. He doesn't strike me as the social type. But if the news is getting to people like that, we're in great shape."

"Both ways," Emily said, turning toward the parking lot, where a green minivan was pulling in to park. "Meaning both the referendum and Thusnelda's."

By the end of the day, the four of them were beat. They'd put a lot of miles on their tennis shoes and burned through two printer cartridges at Xavier's. The paper store had learned their first names. At Thusnelda's, the boss told them they never needed to pay for a meal again the rest of their lives, and asked the twins if they didn't want to move in down the street.

Ethan was so tired he didn't even want a cookie when he got home that evening. "I don't think I can sleep, though," he said, peeling off his socks. "Tomorrow is too big."

"I can sleep." Emily ran a hand through her hair and winced. "After I put some aloe on my face. I'm burned like overdone toast."

Despite his contention, Ethan was snoring when Emily got back to the room.

And then Tuesday dawned.

Grandma had to shake them awake. "Come on, warriors, today's the day," she said. Ethan groaned and rolled over. She smoothed Emily's hair back from her face. "You two are the best grandkids in the world. I can't believe all the work you're putting in to this. But it's almost over, and then you can relax for a couple of days. All the rope swing time you ever wanted. I won't even make you do any chores."

"No chores?" Emily said, her eyes still closed but a faint smile on her face. "That doesn't sound like my Grandma talking."

"That's because it's not. It's Patty Tuttle right now. The same Patty Tuttle that can't get out of her door or off her phone because of the deluge of people that want to talk to her about how she can stay in town." She stood up and pulled Ethan's covers off his bed. "You've worked very hard. But there's still more to do. One more day."

Emily leaped to her feet and started singing "One Day More" from *Les Miserables*. Grandma joined in, waving Ethan's sheet. Ethan groaned and put his hands over his head.

But he was up a few minutes later and wolfing down a plate of eggs.

"Where are the two of you going to be today?"

"Amm f yefrdy," Ethan said, trying not to spit egg all over the table, because neither Patty Tuttle nor Grandma would let that go, and he'd end up cleaning the kitchen.

"I think he means 'same as yesterday,'" Emily said.

"Yes, I'm sure he did," Grandma said, waving the spatula in his direction. "Don't talk with your mouth full."

"Thusnelda's was a little busier yesterday, so we think our flyer campaign did some good," Emily said, putting her plate in the sink. "Most of those people were interested in the referendum, too. Maybe they won't all vote our way, but a lot of them will. People really like you in this town."

"That's because it's a nice town," Grandma said. She opened a cupboard and got down a large white canister dusted with flour. "Tonight calls for something more than cookies, I think." She opened the container and a mouthwatering aroma filled the kitchen.

Ethan shoved the last of the eggs in his mouth and sniffed. "I know that smell," he said. "You're not making cinnamon rolls, are you?"

Grandma drew a large mixing bowl out from under the counter. "You worry about my house. I'll worry about the celebration. Be careful out on the streets. And keep an eye on the sky—I think it might rain later."

All day the twins and Shannon kept up a steady pressure on the Main Street crowd while Xavier worked his shift at the restaurant. Dozens of people cruised by, honking and waving at Shannon's homemade signs. Emily kept an eye on the polling place at city hall.

"Not real busy," she said, a note of disappointment in her voice. "I expected better."

"Most people will vote tonight," Ethan said, waving at a red car with kids hanging out the window.

"And remember, this isn't a big town like you two are used to. Everyone in town could vote in a couple of hours and the lines would still not be real long." Shannon put her sign down for a moment and rubbed her shoulders. The sun peeked through the cloud for a second and a strand of sunlight lit her face. A drop of sweat rolled down behind her ear along the curve of her neck.

Thusnelda's was busy. Not packed, but at lunchtime the lines for fries and onion rings snaked along the front counter. The boss had one of his children at the end of the counter with a camera—how he'd found an old polaroid, Emily couldn't imagine—and as soon as the order was complete, she asked the customer for a photo. On one wall they'd painted "Our Friends," and a smattering of pictures decorated the wall.

"Look, Mommy!" one kid said, running in from the parking lot, "There's our picture! Can we take another?"

It turned out they could.

Grandma came walking by at about noon with ham and cheese sandwiches and big Thermoses of milk. Xavier joined them as they were finishing, carrying a cardboard box with shakes in it. "We're so busy they asked me to stay for the afternoon. I told them I couldn't, but I think they'll need me. I'll get off tonight, though, for when the polls close."

They sat companionably in the shade of the overhang of Shoemaker's Elves Boot Shop and munched their ice cream. Darker clouds assembled to the south.

"Grandma might be right about the rain," Ethan said.

"Cool things off a bit," Shannon said, her shoulder and arm lying along Ethan's. She made no effort to separate them. "It's a sauna out today."

Emily shared her shake with Xavier, who never seemed to have a bottom to his stomach. Honeysuckle perfumed the air. She reached up and ran her fingers along the rough brick of the shop. "It seems so weird that we might never be back here again. I feel like we just figured out how wonderful this place is."

"I myself admit that at the beginning of this summer, I had no idea how delightful my hometown could be. But now I have another shift to work." Xavier dusted off his jeans and offered his hand to Emily. She took it and they stood together, watching the lazy traffic drift slowly by.

"I'll go with you and wait in the parking lot," Emily said. "We'll come back at seven. Polls close at seven."

The last hour at the polls, Shannon and Ethan abandoned their post on Main and sat on the library steps watching people go in and out of the city building. Not a lot of people, no major rush, but a steady trickle. Shannon tried identifying them for Ethan, but gave up after a bit. "I'm not Xavier. I don't know everyone in town by haircut and model of car."

She rested her head on Ethan's shoulder. "You're tired," he said, unnecessarily, but the smell of her hair was making him a little woozy.

"Of course I am. And I'm thinking how weird this all is. This is my town, but you and your sister were the ones that wanted to work for it. Honestly, I don't like this place all that much. I can't wait to get out of here and go someplace where things happen once in a while. But the last couple days, I'm starting to feel like, well, like this place is more like home." She picked her head up. "Why did someone have to come in from outside to show me that there were things here to appreciate?"

"Maybe if you worked at Thusnelda's instead of the library," Ethan began, then stopped. "No. You'd be like a fish out of water at Thusnelda's."

Shannon stared at him for a moment, then one corner of her mouth turned up. "Well, Ethan Tuttle. It's like you know me a little."

Ethan really, really wished he didn't blush so easily.

At a quarter to seven the rain began. Just a wetting, a drifting mist, coming in over the river and cooling things down. But the clouds to the west were ominous, and every so often a rumble rolled off the hills and down into town.

Emily and Xavier came running into the town square a few minutes later.

"Did we miss the glorious victory?" Xavier said.

"Yes," said Ethan. "Shannon and I were just about to go home and celebrate with Cherry Cokes."

"We must have lost, then," Xavier said. "Everyone knows the victory drink is Pepsi."

The seven o'clock close was a mite anticlimactic, after all the buildup. In fact, nothing whatever happened. Grandma marched into the square with fifteen or so other women, looking determined. Emily swapped glances with Xavier, and they both broke into "Sisters Suffragette" from *Mary Poppins*. Halfway across the square, Grandma halted, hearing the singing, and joined in. Then they were all belting it out in the strengthening rain, laughing and letting the tension run off them. Nothing to do now. No more work could change the outcome.

"It will take them some time to count," Grandma said. "Usually a couple of hours. The turnout is the thing—if it was heavy, it will take longer."

"I wish they had those electronic voting machines," Ethan said, wiping water from his hair. They crowded into the covered area by the door of city hall. The rain strengthened and the wind began to gust.

"You think you do," Shannon said, "But they have their own problems. What happens if they get hacked? Are there paper copies? If you have to use the paper, how is that an improvement?" She shook her head. "Most of the time, if the results get jiggered, you don't even have any way to know. As long as they're within the realm of what people expect, it's almost impossible to catch someone fiddling with the numbers."

A clerk came out of the building, took a look at the rain and the people huddled under the overhang, and said, "We'll be counting a while. You can wait in the council chambers, if you want. It'll be drier."

"No thanks, Haley," Grandma said. "We'll be along in a bit, but for now, it's kind of nice to be outside, even if it is a little damp."

"How long do you think it will take?" one of Grandma's friends asked.

"Not too long. A little over an hour, I think. The turnout was good, but not real heavy."

The twins exchanged a glance. Not heavy? Hadn't they given flyers to just about everyone in town? Hadn't they said they would come, no matter what? Didn't people care?

It got dark fast, the sun hidden by massive black clouds. When the thunder began to peal and flashes of light showed over the mountains across the river, the party had had enough and went inside, all but Xavier and Emily.

"You think they've had anything to eat in there? I mean, the counting clerks?" Xavier said, snugged up against Emily and not showing any signs of wanting to move.

"Probably not," Emily said. "But we can't bribe them. Illegal and unethical."

"Not talking about bribing anybody," Xavier said. He took her hand and led her out into the rain. "I'm talking about being neighborly. Those people probably want this thing to pass. If it does, I'm going to want them to like me. If it doesn't, I'm still going to want them to like me. Besides, it's *decent*. It's the sort of thing good people do."

"Hang on," Emily said, breaking contact and heading for the door. "If we're going to do this, we should probably know how many to get food for." She came back a moment later. "Five. Three men, two women. And if they've already eaten, they did a really good job of hiding the evidence."

So they went and did the good thing. Xavier went in back and found food that was already made. Someone had ordered and then left without picking it up. He put it all in a huge sack that they carried back to city hall and in to the clerks around their table with the massive pile of paper ballots.

"You're not supposed to be in here," one of the women said—*Haley*, Emily remembered—then stopped when she smelled the burgers and just said, "Ohhhhh." Her eyes rolled back in her head.

"Compliments of Thusnelda's and the League of the Little Pink House," Xavier said. He and Emily drew out the fries and burgers and set them up prettily on the side table.

"The League of the Little Pink House?" Emily whispered through the side of her mouth.

"Just go with it," Xavier whispered back.

She went with it. They were shortly ushered from the room, but by smiles, not frowns, and grateful people were kind people. It might make no difference, not tonight, but tomorrow would be another day, no matter what.

People don't like waiting. They are very bad at it. Grandma, apparently, was the exception to the rule, because she kept up a steady, polite, warm chatter with the growing group of people who came to the building for the results. By 8:20 there were no empty chairs left in the council chambers, and Xavier and Ethan went out to scrounge the chairs from the lobby. By 8:30, those were gone, too, and people had to stand. One of the vote counters stuck a head in, appeared to count the people, swallowed loudly, turned a shade of green, and left.

Ten minutes later, the five came in, looking solemn, and took their positions in the council chairs. The lead clerk introduced herself as Greta Popplewell and shuffled papers nervously, clearly not expecting this number of people. Ethan soaked up the faces around him, trying to see what Greta saw. She couldn't have been terribly encouraged. No one was smiling. Everyone around the Tuttles had a look on their faces like they were expecting a pronouncement of a jail sentence.

Emily grabbed his arm and leaned over. "We better win," she whispered. Ethan squeezed her hand and reached out for Shannon. She gripped his hand as if dangling from the side of a building. Emily had Ethan's arm on one side and a white-knuckled grip on Xavier's hand on the other.

"We've finished our count," Greta said, face a little drawn but voice steady. She nodded to Haley, who stood by the whiteboard on the left-hand wall. Haley uncapped a marker and wrote "Referendum #1" at the top, and "For" on one side, with "Against" on the other. Ethan thought he'd never seen anyone write quite so slowly.

Haley wrote "571" under "For."

"Is that a lot?" Ethan heard Emily whisper to Xavier. He could feel the shrug without having to look.

She wrote "589" under "Against."

It was some while before anyone on that row could hear properly again.

"Somehow, the sunset is so much more colorful tonight than it ever has been before." Xavier dangled his feet in the water at the edge of the dock and brushed Emily's hair back from her face. She smiled.

"You're not looking at the sunset," she said.

"Well, I'm sure it is. It would have to be. It's the last one before you go home. And besides, I will have a lot more sunsets to look at, but your face won't be resting on my shoulder after tonight."

Next to them, Shannon flicked her wrist and cast a fishing lure deep into the dark water. Ethan slowly reeled in his own line, watching her more than his fishing.

"You know this isn't over," Shannon said. "The referendum might not have passed, but the city council isn't going to let that money go forever. It's too much incentive."

"You can stop them," Ethan said. "And if you can't, we did our best. How's the business at Thusnelda's?" he asked Xavier.

"Not bad. Better than it has been. We don't have long dead patches in the day any more. But I'm thinking the blast of enthusiasm will probably die off a bit and we'll be back to where we were."

"Not all the way back," Emily said. "And anyway, marketing is like that. You have to keep working at it. We'll help you think of stuff. It's not like we're going to be dead."

Xavier shook his head. "I don't know. From all the way out there, I'm not sure what you can do. You might need to visit a lot more than just once a year. Just, you know, to help out the town."

"The town needs help," Ethan said. "But the most important part of the town is right here."

"Right here, as in, Grandma's house? Or right here as in the people who are at Grandma's house at the moment?" Emily said.

Ethan glanced at Shannon, who reeled her line in with a little edge of tongue sticking out between her lips.

"You can decide that for yourself," he said.

Shannon jerked hard, and her pole bent. "Got one," she said, and smiled.

THE END

The computer opened wide and showed him all its secrets. At first, that didn't mean much. He had to decipher the directory style, figure out where the most pertinent files were kept, and then figure out what it was he was after. He was looking for anything relating to the building of the factory on the riverside. But there had to be other things, other information, other communication with organizations other than the chemical company that would give a hint as to what was going on behind the scenes.

He reminded himself that he wasn't looking just for information of an interesting or even unethical nature, but for anything incriminating that would allow him to make the government either unable to achieve its plans or less likely to win the referendum. If it was newsworthy, that would be helpful. If it was illegal, that would be even better.

"What did you find?" Uncle Brock said, looming over his shoulder.

"Nothing in the mayor's office?" Ethan said.

"Nothing so far," he said. "You look like you're having more success than anyone else."

"I'm not quite sure what I have here," Ethan said. "There's a chance that there is nothing on the machine. Who keeps that kind of information on an office computer?"

"Nearly everyone," Shannon said, from over by the file cabinets. "People keep everything on their computers: bank records, passwords, pictures of their children. Remember that guy who kept records of the money he was stealing from his boss? People keep all sorts of things on computers."

Ethan opened up the directories and found all sorts of files, most of them devoted to city council business, but a lot of them having to do with city administration, too. "Here's one that gives the salaries of every member of the city government. Do we want that?" Ethan said.

"I do," Uncle Brock said.

"Stay on target," Shannon said. "We're looking for things having to do with this referendum. I'm sure there's a whole lot of other dirt in here, too, but we don't have time to get all of it. We need to be out of here as soon as we can."

"We have all night," Uncle Brock said. "Here, click on that one," he said, pointing to the screen.

Not really having any sense for what exactly he was looking for, Ethan clicked on the file. It was a file of city council deliberations from a few years back. It had to do with establishing the salary for the new mayor.

"There was a huge fight over that," Uncle Brock said. "I'd love to know what was going on behind closed doors." When the file was opened, however, it was just a lot of work files with agendas on them. All of it looked like public information.

"That's not going to do me any good," Uncle Brock said, sounding disappointed. "Try something else."

Ethan was already doing that, but then he had a better idea. "I'm going to look at the emails," he said. "People say things in emails that they would never put in any other kind of document."

There were several email accounts attached to the computer, but the main one went through the city clerk. He opened up her Outlook file and started going through the unread emails. Fortunately, this was someone who believed in inbox zero, so she had cleaned out her inbox regularly and assigned folders to most of her emails.

Ethan was impressed. It was the best kind of e-mail organization system he had ever seen.

"What am I looking for?" he said. He cast a glance back over his shoulder. "You should go back in the mayor's office. Doesn't he have a computer on his desk in there?"

"He does," Brock said, "But I don't think he's careless enough to leave his password written on his desk."

"That doesn't mean he doesn't have one in there somewhere. Go see what you can find out. That computer is a lot more likely to have incriminating stuff on it than this one."

Still, Ethan went folder by folder through the information. There were emails about city administration, everything from watering the city's plants to plowing snow, when they got any. There was a whole lot of discussion back and forth about what time to hold city council meetings, whether those needed to be recorded, and on what system. He ran a search for any emails having to do with Jaxton and chemical, and found 1100 hits. They had obviously been discussing Jaxton quite a lot.

"This could be something," he said.

"I've got something here," Shannon said. "It looks pretty juicy."

Ethan started to get up and come over, but she waved him back down. "It's fine," she said. "I'm taking pictures of everything. You keep working on yours."

Ethan went through the emails one at a time. Sadly, there was no email helpfully titled "Our plan for taking over the city government and throwing people out of their houses." But there were, increasingly, emails about the properties along the riverfront and how the residents of those properties were unwilling to sell. There was a heated email from a member of the city council to the city staff, asking if there wasn't some way to speed up the process of getting rid of these people. *That wouldn't play very well*, Ethan thought. He hit print on that particular email. He heard the ticking of the clock on the wall. Relentless. Never pausing. Sooner or later, someone would come.

Besides, although some of this stuff was juicy, none of it was exactly illegal. It wouldn't really surprise anyone to know that the city council people hated each other, or that they didn't always get along with the mayor, or that they really wanted the people who lived on the riverfront to move out of their houses so they could build a chemical factory. Ethan was about to close down the e-mail and recommend that everybody get out of the building, when he found the thing he was looking for.

Turn to page 413.

The man, disconcertingly, kept his shotgun cocked and in the crook of his arm. At least he wasn't pointing it directly at them anymore.

"My face may not be much, but there's nothing wrong with my ears. You said something, sonny, about some kind of golf course. What were you talking about?"

"It's just something I overheard, I'm sure it isn't important."

"Anything that touches me and mine, or that touches this property, that's important."

Ethan thought that as long as he was holding a shotgun, whatever was important to him was going to be important to them too.

"I don't know what to tell you," Emily said. "We heard that the city was going to be building a golf course up in this area. But it doesn't look to me like you have anything to worry about, since you live here."

"Unless they're doing the same thing to you that they're doing to my grandmother," Ethan said.

At this, the man arched an eyebrow. Just the left one, as if the right side of his face were frozen. "Your grandmother?"

"Yes," Emily said. "Patricia Tuttle. She lives in the—"

"Little pink house," the man finished. He nodded heavily. "I know the one. It's been a very long time, but once we used to get cookies from her."

"Who is we?" Ethan said.

The man waved his shotgun as if dismissing the question. "Never mind that. What are they doing to your grandmother? And by 'they,' I mean the city."

"They're trying to force her off her land so they can build a factory there."

The man scratched his chin; every wobble of the shotgun made Emily wonder if that was going to be the last moment of their lives.

"Nothing like that happening here," the man said. "Except, I'm not sure we would know if it were."

"Why wouldn't you know? I mean, the bulldozers are just to the other side of your little road here, and there's dirt being moved around already."

"Saw that," the man said. Now he dropped the butt of the shotgun to the ground and kept it propped against his side, close enough for him to use it in case he needed to, but clearly thinking that these two were probably no major threat. "I thought that was just a subdivision. They're always building new houses or some fool thing."

Ethan shook his head. "It's not a subdivision, at least not like any subdivision I ever saw. It's wide and flat and there are hills and pits that looked to me like they're going to fill them with sand. I'm pretty sure it's a golf course."

"And is it coming up this far?"

"Hasn't crossed the road yet." Emily shrugged.

"We don't know. It's just something we overheard, and we thought we would check it out. We didn't mean to interfere."

The man's face softened a little bit.

"Don'tcha worry about that. You're not interfering, not with you being the grandchildren of Patty Tuttle. But just because this golf course, if it is a golf course, hasn't come up this far yet, doesn't mean it won't. Golf courses take out almighty tracts of land."

Ethan pointed at the house. "But with that house there, I'm sure you would be able to fight them off, at least for a little while. They would have to buy this house before they could take over the land to build the golf course."

The man put a cigarette to his lips and lit a match. He puffed a couple of times, dropped the match to the ground, and stepped on it. A wreath of smoke ascended around his head. "Ain't my house. Ain't never going to be my house."

Emily thought he might elaborate, make some sort of a comment about whose house it was, or where his house was, if this wasn't his own. But he just puffed on the cigarette, making an orange glow on the end of the stick, and regarded them with that same half-suspicious expression on his face. One eye halfway open and the other one staring.

"We might want to have a palaver on this situation," the man said eventually. "You two up for a conversation?"

"I would be happy to have a chat with you," Ethan said. "Is there any way we could do it with that gun someplace else?"

The man looked surprised. His face did not give the impression that he spent a great deal of time in that condition. "This thing?" He shook his head. "Hardly ever go anywhere without it. But I wouldn't worry about it if I were you."

"Yeah, it probably isn't even loaded," Emily said.

Without a word, the man whipped it up with his right hand, shifted it to his shoulder, and pulled the trigger.

One barrel emptied itself into a tree trunk. The tree was huge and sturdy, and the shotgun did little more than chip away at the bark, but the twins were confident that it would do a lot more damage to them.

The man didn't seem to think this called for comment. He just let the gun drop back to his side, into exactly the same position as before, and went on smoking a cigarette. "Still coming?" the man said.

Emily and Ethan exchanged glances.

"I guess," Emily said. "It's not that we don't like guns, you understand. We're just not big fans of being on the business end of them."

The man's chest spasmed and Emily concluded that must be what passed for a laugh.

He slung the weapon over his shoulder, gave a small wave of his left hand, and said, "Come along, then." He turned and began to walk toward the house. Just before he would have mounted the porch stairs, he took a right turn and followed a thin path around the right side, following the line of the porch, and back into the brush behind the place.

Turn to page 451.

Ethan chose to interpret her comment in the best possible way. Maybe she wasn't totally disgusted with him. Maybe she genuinely wasn't surprised.

"Are you not surprised, because the book isn't very old?" he tried.

Shannon nodded. "It's not a series most people have heard of. The author is young and new, and she's written a lot of good stuff, I think, but most people haven't heard of it."

"But it's a young adult novel, right? What's it about?"

Shannon took a deep breath and muttered something to herself. Ethan thought for sure she was going to refuse to talk to him, but then she appeared to come to a decision and laid the book open on the reference desk. She kept her voice low, so as not to disturb the other people in the library, but there was pretty much no way she was going to do that, there being hardly anybody in the place anyway.

"It's about magic, but a different kind of magic, where people have the ability to make living things out of man-made materials." She ducked her head a little, in case he thought that was dumb.

"Man-made materials? So, not like air and water, but paper... and, I don't know... plastic?"

Shannon gave a small laugh of relief. "Yes. Exactly. And glass, too, and other things. Anyway, in this book,

the protagonist doesn't really want to be a paper magician, but she ends up being brilliant at it and falling in
love with the master magician, who has a checkered
past and a deadly enemy coming for him. In this part
of the book, there's this paper heart and it holds the
memories of what happened to the master. She's being
chased through it, trying to stay alive."

"That sounds extremely cool," Ethan said, meaning
it. "I think I would like to read that book."

"It's not a boys' book," she said, nervousness reap-
pearing. "I mean, there's action and stuff, but there's a
lot of, like... kissing and things."

Ethan felt himself begin to blush. He knew he
shouldn't. Didn't even really know why he was doing it,
and especially didn't want Shannon to see it. But she
was two feet away from him, and her eyes were fixed on
his face. There was no way she was going to miss it. He
felt his ears burn.

"I'm okay with kissing," he said. He checked her face,
and then added hurriedly, "I mean, not that I do a lot
of it. I mean, I do some, you know. But, like, I think I'm
going to stop talking right now."

Shannon laughed and covered her mouth. It was
the most human sound she had yet made. "I did kind of
warn you," she said. "But it's a book I think you might
like. I'm surprised you would be into reading fantasy."

"I love fantasy," Ethan said. "Especially the classics."

Shannon was guarded, as if she were afraid she'd
wake up from a good dream. "I have the boxed set of

Lord of the Rings at home. Pretty much no one in this town thinks that's good reading material."

"Well, I do," Ethan said. "Those are some of my favorite books. But I still think *The Hobbit* is the best one."

What followed was the most enjoyable half an hour Ethan had spent the entire time he'd been in town. All of a sudden, it was as if the two of them couldn't say words fast enough. She had read practically everything he had, and a bunch of things he hadn't, which made sense because she worked in a library and she could read almost as much as she wanted, because the place was, let's face it, not particularly busy. Five minutes before the hour, Shannon rang a little bell, and the man reading the novel slid his bookmark in place, stepped back into his shoes, sketched a little wave and left. The mother came from over in the children's section, dragging two young children who looked to be twins.

"Good night, Mrs. Greene," Shannon said.

"Thank you, Shannon," Mrs Greene said. "We'll be back on Monday. I feel like sometimes it's the only break I ever get, coming here."

Shannon made a circuit of the place, Ethan trailing along behind her, double checking doors and windows to make sure they were all locked. They chattered on about dwarves and elves, about books like *The Hunger Games*, and about what they were hoping Brandon Sanderson would write next. The place secure, Shannon produced a key and locked the front door behind them.

There was still plenty of light in the sky, the sun not quite having reached the horizon. Long summer days were on their side.

"I walked here," Shannon said.

"I rode a bike," Ethan said. "I'm pretty sure it will hold both of us, if you want to try that."

Shannon shaded her eyes and looked off to the east-northeast. "That might be best," she said. "He lives on the edge of town; it would take us quite a while to walk there."

Children played all over the streets as they passed by. They found the sight of Shannon perched precariously on the front of the handlebars of Ethan's bike to be hilarious, and they ran alongside on their tricycles or their bicycles for a block or two before turning back for home. It was a merry little procession, a kind of relay parade, where Ethan and Shannon led and the rest followed along behind in a noisy rotation.

The weather could hardly have been better. It was not too hot, the humidity having dropped a little bit throughout the day. The breeze always seemed to be behind them. The land was green and fresh and filled with flowers, and yet Ethan found himself spending nearly as much time looking at the girl in front of him as he did at the scenery.

Headed toward this part of town, the abandoned houses disappeared. Every home was decorated for the Fourth of July, people reluctant to take down their flags and bunting, extending the holiday through the weekend. It being Saturday night, the smell of barbecuing meat floated through the neighborhood as well, and Ethan's stomach growled.

Shannon heard and laughed without turning her head back. "You hungry?" she said. "Maybe when we're done we can head for Thusnelda's."

If it allowed him to spend additional time with this weird, wonderful girl—now that they were talking—Ethan couldn't think of anything he wanted more. She seemed to add a new attractive quality every moment. Her loose red hair blew in his face as he pedaled along, and it smelled of strawberries.

The houses, which had been getting larger, began shrinking in size again, until they were reduced to one- and two-room homes on simple foundations. Their yards were large, however, and everyone seemed to have a swing set, garden gnomes, or some other decoration.

"It's really pretty here. Everyone seems to have decorated their property. That's not true in my neighborhood."

Shannon said, "Really? That's a big thing here. What do the properties look like where you are?"

"Well, most of the houses are similar, and we all have about the same size lot. There are restrictive covenants for the neighborhood, so things like garden gnomes—"

"Or painting your house bright pink?" she said with a laugh. She seemed to laugh at everything now. It was as if a weight had lifted off her heart, and her true personality was bursting forth like the buds in springtime.

"Um, yeah. I don't think that would go over too well in our neighborhood."

Shannon pointed a slim arm out to the right. The bike wobbled a little, but Ethan kept control of it. "We're going that way," she said.

Ethan took the right at a sedate speed, not wanting to spill his passenger. This street had only the one house on it, a low-slung affair, a little larger than some of the others in the neighborhood, but also quite a bit older, clearly having been expanded. The original house was none too large, much the same size as many of the other properties in this section of town, but additions like tumorous growths had been tacked on the back and sides, until the house sort of appeared to have a main building, with wings to the north and south, and another one sticking out the back like a tail.

Jutting up above the rooftop, Ethan saw four poles in a reverse pyramidal stack. Canvas surrounded them up to the apex of their connection.

"Is that…?" Ethan said.

"It is," Shannon said. "He's probably out back in it."

Ethan pulled his bike down the gravel driveway and flipped down the kickstand. Shannon vaulted off the front of the bike like a gymnast, jogged straight ahead through a grapevine-covered archway and into the backyard. Curious about what was clearly a tepee in the backyard, Ethan followed.

It was a tent, but larger than any Native tent he had ever seen. Sitting out front, a man in buckskin pants and a T-shirt sat smoking on a long, ornately-carved pipe.

Shannon crouched on her haunches in front of him, having a low-voiced conversation. She waved to Ethan when she saw him come into the backyard, and he walked over through the thick grass, liberally laced with dandelions. This man could probably use someone to help take care of his yard.

A thick, full voice as deep as the river rolled across the lawn toward him. "Don't mind the dandelions; that's what I call food storage."

Ethan's head came up to see if he was being made fun of. The man was indeed laughing, but it didn't seem he was laughing at him.

"Oh yes," the man said. "Dandelions are good eating. That is, if you get them young and tender. If you wait until they get old, they get pretty bitter. That also has its uses, but not for salad."

From a distance, the man looked quite a bit like Ethan's image of a Native American. But up close, it was easy to see that he was very tan, but entirely Caucasian. His britches were buckskin, complete with the fringes down the side, but his T-shirt was all Pittsburgh Steelers. He sported a bushy beard, again much more mountain man than Native American, but his hair descended in a braid flipped over one shoulder. He rocked forward in his chair and extended his hand without coming all the way out of it. "My name is Jackson St. Lawrence," he said.

"Ethan Tuttle."

"And you've been paddling around with this street urchin?" He meant Shannon, of course.

"Do street urchins usually work at the public library?"

St. Lawrence broke into a laugh. It boomed across the yard like a cannon. "I suppose not," he said, "But she hasn't always worked behind the reference desk. You should ask her some time about what she used to do and how we became such good friends."

And they were, clearly, good friends. Shannon sat like a baseball catcher on her haunches a couple of feet away from St. Lawrence, who lounged in a decaying lawn chair. Behind him was the finest example of a Native American teepee Ethan had ever seen.

He admired it for a moment, and St. Lawrence, his eyes ever roving and quick to perceive, said, "Yes, I built her myself. I had some help from some locals who are friends of mine, but the work they made me do myself. I know how to put it up, air it out and take it down, and I prefer sleeping in it to sleeping in most houses. Including," he said, ruefully rubbing his beard, "my own."

Ethan glanced down at Shannon. Her face was tranquil, peaceful in a way Ethan had never seen. Clearly, this was like coming home for her. And, he thought in a flash, how did he know this was *not* her home? Perhaps the red hair was a clue? St. Laurence's was a ruddy brown, but there was a hint of rust in it.

"Have you told him about our problem?" Ethan said.

Shannon shook her head. "Haven't really had time."

"We were getting reacquainted," St. Lawrence said. He shifted the pipe to his other hand, put it to his mouth, and drew in the smoke. The bowl of the pipe flared up red. "She hasn't been to see me in a little while."

He looked expectantly back and forth between their faces. It was Shannon who began to speak. "We need to stop Jaxton Chemical from bulldozing his grandmother's house," she said simply.

St. Lawrence took a long look at Ethan. "So, your grandmother is Patty Tuttle."

"Yes, sir," Ethan said.

This brought another booming laugh from St. Lawrence. "'Sir,' is it?" he said. "No one has called me sir since the Air Force." He made a come-on gesture in Ethan's direction. "But you just keep right on doing that, if it makes you feel better, son. I like it; it shows respect. Not like I get from this little one here."

Ethan expected Shannon to bristle, but it was more like purring. Apparently he was allowed to tease her as much as he wanted.

"All right," he said. "That's work enough for any day. What do I have to do with it?"

Turn to page 50.

"You say something?" the man said behind them.

"No offense," Ethan said, turning back just for a second, "but I'm not excited about having conversations at gunpoint. Besides, we don't really know all that much. It's just something we overheard. It's none of our business."

If he was disappointed by Ethan's pronouncement, it was impossible to tell from his face. It sat like weathered granite on top of his shoulders and just regarded them with the same baleful look. "All right, then," he said. "Be off with you." He whipped the shotgun up, rolled it onto his shoulder, and headed off around the side of the house. His leather boots made no sound at all on the hard-packed ground. Faster than the twins would have thought possible for a man of such obviously advanced age, he disappeared.

Ethan blew out a long breath. "Well, that was certainly the weirdest thing that's happened to us in the last decade or two."

"I think we'll both feel a lot better if we put this place in the rear view as fast as possible." Emily said. Ethan agreed with that sentiment wholeheartedly and the two of them turned and jogged back up the road toward their bikes. The twins saw with relief that they were still there. They untangled them with manic speed, threw themselves onto their seats, and whipped themselves out onto the main road headed back into town.

When they had ridden four or five blocks, straight down Main Street in the direction of traffic, Ethan began to slow. Emily matched him until they were riding along companionably and smiling a little to themselves.

"That was a close one," he said.

Emily wiped her brow. "Just because there's weird people on that land, doesn't mean we shouldn't keep trying to find out what's going to happen with it. Dad would probably want us to at least make another inquiry."

"Inquiry where? If you're thinking of going back and talking to the fellow again—"

"No, no, no," Emily said. "Absolutely not. I wouldn't go back there on a dare. But there's probably some kind of a map at city hall that we could look at, something that might tell us at least a little bit about what the plans for that area are."

"Or for Grandma's house. Remember we're trying to save that, too. I think that one might be more important."

"Okay. Maybe the city planner will be there and he can talk to us about it. You know, as concerned citizens."

"We aren't citizens of this town," Ethan said. He rose to stand on his pedals, coasting slowly down Main Street.

"I know that," Emily said. "But everywhere we go, Grandma's name seems to get a positive reaction. Maybe we could use that here, too."

"She *has* lived in town a long time," Ethan said, pulling his bike up a ramp on the corner and onto the sidewalk to get out of the street. This section of town, the six to eight blocks down the center of Main Street, had curbs and gutters, with wide sidewalks for strolling along. From the lampposts, baskets of flowers in red, white, and blue decorated the street. Every business seemed to be decked with a flag, or festive bunting, or some other decoration for the coming holiday. It looked like something right out of the movies.

"This is something our town really misses," Emily said. "We don't have a main street like this."

"The buildings are awfully old," Ethan said. "I'm sure they must cost a mint to keep up." He put his hand on the red brick facing of a tailor's shop. With a fingernail he plucked at the brick and a piece crumbled out, dropping to the pavement. "See? These things are falling down. They have to be unsafe to work in."

"Why would anyone work in a building that was unsafe?" Emily said. "It must be safe enough to satisfy the people who work there. What if it's better than not having a job at all?"

Ethan thought about that for a second. "If the government said the building wasn't safe, what would happen?"

"The business would have to move."

"And what if there wasn't any place close that they could move to?" He scanned the street. In every building a shop was open for business. "It's not like this is a big town. There aren't, like, big office spaces anyplace."

Emily shrugged. "They'd have to close, I guess. All the workers would lose their jobs."

"And that wouldn't be good for anybody," Ethan said. "But what if the place really is unsafe?"

Emily made a face. "You work there. Are you going to let the government tell you it's safe, or would you take the time to do your own research? Is the government going to send Atlas over to hold up the roof, if it turns out they're wrong?"

"Trust people to act like adults. I get it. City hall is down there, past the library." He got back on his bike and pedaled away.

Turn to page 36.

"We're licked," Ethan said. He slumped at the table, an untouched sandwich and a glass of milk warming in front of him. "I thought it was such a good idea to try getting the Native preservation people involved. I didn't think much about the fraud part."

"At least you didn't actually try it. Then we'd be having this lovely conversation from a prison visiting area," Emily said.

"It wouldn't have worked. The guy was very clear about that. The investigators aren't geniuses, but they'd be able to tell I was making it up before I could even start the paperwork. So that's it. I got nothing. We tried, and we failed."

"You don't know that. We might still win."

"We already know that even if we win tonight, we'll lose eventually. These people are relentless."

"You going into town for the referendum announcement?" Emily said, leaning on the counter. "I think the others will be there."

"No."

"Suit yourself. I'm going."

"Have a lovely time. No snogging."

"As if," Emily said, blushing furiously.

Grandma wandered in, putting on gloves. She gathered her handbag from its perch by the phone. "I take it sad sack here isn't coming?"

"He says not," Emily said. "Hey, you haven't even showed me the stuff you got out at the Native dude's teepee."

"Didn't I?" Ethan said. This at least got him to raise his head. "They're in on my nightstand."

Emily went out and came back a moment later with the potsherds. She turned them over in her hands, spending a moment on each. When she came to the ornately-carved one, she held it up. "Wow. This one is gorgeous. He really let you have these? For nothing?"

"Nothing at all. He was pretty great, I admit. At least I'll have souvenirs to remind me about this place once we never come here anymore."

Grandma stuck her head back in. "Coming, Em? Oh, how pretty. Where did you get that?"

"Ethan got it from this fellow over on the east side. Big artifact hunter."

"He should come dig in my garden," Grandma said. "Come on, Em. We'll be late."

Ethan narrowed his eyes. "What do you mean, 'He should come dig in your garden'?"

Grandma looked disgusted. "When your Grandfather and I put the garden in, we had all kinds of trouble with these things. Worse than rocks. Dozens of them, cutting into our gloves, balking our shovels. It took us weeks to get the soil ready. Still have a pile of them, someplace back there. Probably buried in weeds, by now."

Slowly, as if filled with helium, Ethan rose from his chair. "Grandma, would it be too much trouble to ask you to show me where you put that pile?"

"Darndest thing," St. Lawrence said. "I haven't seen a find like this since, well, since ever."

"It's really good, then?" Ethan said, knee-deep in a hole in the back corner of Grandma's garden, where she had been growing rhubarb. Shannon stood up on ground level, hands on her knees.

"It's good, all right," he said. "I'd say it's good enough for a few years' work. I might even get to do some of it."

Ethan said, "I didn't plant this stuff, honest."

St. Lawrence let the booming laugh go, and it echoed across the water and off the hills on the far side. "I know, son. I know. This site hasn't seen daylight in three or four hundred years. And see? No fraud necessary. All's well that ends well."

Shannon crouched down next to Ethan. "It's Lord of the Rings," she said.

"How so?"

"Frodo gets to Mt. Doom, but he won't throw in the ring. The whole seven hundred pages have led us to this, and now the good guys are going to lose because after all their work the hero won't do his job. And then Gollum bites off his finger and falls in, and they win anyway."

Ethan squinted up at her. "That's either the dumbest or the most brilliant literary analogy I've ever heard."

"It's brilliant," Shannon said. "You'll come to appreciate it shortly." She put her hand on his shoulder. Ethan began to appreciate the analogy immediately.

Emily and Xavier wandered over from the dock. Xavier picked up a sherd and turned it over and over in his hand. "You'd think I'd be frustrated, after all the work we did, and it's these little things that saved us."

"Come on," Emily said. "We only lost by twenty votes. We even had a couple people come and tell us that they voted just because we told them to."

"We would have lost anyway. But I'm glad we didn't. I mean, we did, but then we didn't."

"I think that means we'll be coming back here next year," Emily said.

"That's why I'm glad," Xavier said.

Grandma came out with a tray of lemonade. "Anyone thirsty?"

Everyone took one.

"A toast," St. Lawrence said. "To the lovely people who once lived here, whose garbage dump has saved the prettiest house on the prettiest spot on the Monongahela."

THE END

The great thing about summer vacation is that it comes in the summer. Days are long, and hot, which makes playing in the water a lot more fun. Even when the sun goes down, the land stays warm. In the middle of everything comes the biggest fireworks party on earth. In the right part of the country, you can even get fireworks from Mother Nature some afternoons, as thundershowers roll in to cool things off.

In the middle of one of those thundershowers, as Ethan was just settling into his favorite chair to read *The Dangerous Book For Boys*, Brock's head went by the window, headed out toward the dock.

"Would you ordinarily expect someone to go out boating on the river in the middle of a thundershower?" Ethan said.

Emily sat on the floor, bouncing a ball off the carpet, the wall, and back to her hand. "I would not," she said. "Why, are you planning to do that?"

"Not me," Ethan said. "But Uncle Brock seems keen. He's heading down the dock right now."

Emily got up and came over to the window. "That's odd."

"That's Uncle Brock. Odd is his middle name."

"Actually, it's Charles."

Ethan rolled his eyes. "I know that. Everyone knows that. Every Tuttle for a million generations is named Charles in one place or other."

"Oh! You were making a joke. I get it," she said. "No fishing gear. He's just getting on the boat and going."

"Upriver or down?"

"Which way is which?"

"Upriver is against the current; downriver is with it. So north is downriver, toward Pittsburgh. Upriver is south, into the mountains."

"Rivers should not be allowed to flow north," Emily said. "It confuses me."

"You'll need to repeal the law of gravity, because that's what's making this one do that. West Virginia is higher than Pennsylvania."

"Fine. He's going downstream. What's downstream?"

"Pittsburgh, like I said. Three Rivers Stadium. Remember when we went to watch a Pirates game there?"

"Of course I do. What else?"

"Pittsburgh's industrial suburbs. You go down the river a few miles, you start picking up some big river traffic. Big ships and all. The river's really just a highway, only wetter."

"It's not much wetter than the highway right now," Emily said, as a crack of thunder shook the house. "It's coming down out there like Noah."

"What time is it?" Ethan said.

"About 1:00pm. On a Thursday. It should not be thunderstorming. It should be sunny. We should be out there on the rope swing. I should be working on my tan."

"Thus far a rather uninspiring thing."

"Thank you, Zazu. Why did you need the time? You have a date?"

"No, I just want to know how long it takes Brock to do whatever he's going to do."

It took, as it happened, four hours and sixteen minutes, by Emily's watch. The rain had stopped and the sun was hot again making the air extra humid.

"How far can a guy get that boat in that amount of time?" Ethan said, pulling a weed from Grandma's garden.

"I have no idea. I don't know anything about boating." Emily chopped the hoe down on a couple of scraggly dandelions. "It would depend some on which direction you were going, too. It would be easier to go downstream than upstream."

"Round trip, it all works out, though, doesn't it? Average time is all that matters."

"Suppose he can go thirty knots. Whatever a knot is."

"It's a unit of measure," Ethan said. "It comes from when sailing ships would toss a log overboard with a line attached to it. The line had knots tied in it, and however many knots went by in however long, that's how fast you were going."

"Is that faster than miles per hour?"

"Just a little." Ethan wiped sweat off his brow with the back of his arm. Where was the downpour now, when he really needed it?

"Could that boat go that fast?"

"I don't think so," Ethan said, looking back over his shoulder at the craft. "But maybe twenty."

"So in an hour, he could go twenty miles or so. A little more. Would that reach the industrial district?"

"I think so. We can check the map."

But it didn't. No more than halfway.

"Weird," Ethan said. "Twenty miles down, there's, like, nothing at all. Maybe some houses, but nothing that would be a destination." He scrolled on the map, up and down. "Are you sure he went downstream?"

"I can tell my left from right," Emily said.

"Hmm. Well, okay. That didn't tell us anything."

"Maybe we should just *ask*."

"You really want to ask him about that? You know the rumors about him. He could be up to anything out there. Kidnapping. Smuggling. Gun running. You name it. You know what kind of guy he is."

Emily frowned. "Actually, if you want to get technical, I *don't* know what kind of guy he is. You don't, either. Dad and he are not really on speaking terms. All we know is he got into some trouble a while ago."

Emily said, "There's one more thing we can try, and maybe it will give us a clue. We'll have to wait until dark, though."

That night, she went into the kitchen and came back with a roll of duct tape.

Ethan was unimpressed. "Duct tape? You're going to duct tape yourself to the boat, so you can find out what he's doing."

"Silly boy. Of course not. If you want to know what it's for, come out to the dock with me."

But when they got there, the boat was gone.

"Maybe you should have taped yourself to the boat," Ethan said.

"It's the middle of the night. What's he doing out there in the middle of the night?" Emily said. A waxing crescent showed itself above the mountains on the far side of the river.

"It's only ten."

"Still."

The boat was there in the morning, and Emily put her plan into motion. She took the roll out to the boat and tore off a three-inch strip. She climbed onto the boat, went over to the starboard side, the side away from the dock, and reached down to the waterline. When the boat rolled on the swell, she stuck the piece of tape to the hull. "There," she said.

"Where?" Ethan said. "What will that do?"

"It will tell us if the boat is loaded or empty. You'll see."

"He won't go out tonight—it's the Fourth. There will be fireworks over the river."

The Fourth already, and the twins knew nothing about how to save Grandma's house. It looked a lot better than it had—the twins had put in a ton of work around the place: planting new flowers, painting the front porch, weeding the garden. They'd cleaned up and moved a pile of old pottery that Grandma hadn't gotten rid of. And there had been plenty of rope swinging. But Brock had occupied all their efforts otherwise.

"We're not being a great help, are we?" Ethan said.

"We didn't come here to be that kind of help. That's for grownups. We were sent here to vacation. And do chores. We've done a fine job of both."

"I still think we should try to do more, if we want Grandma to keep living in this house. Investigate Jaxton Chemical, or something. You know there's a big vote coming up on Tuesday. What if we could find some dirt on the company that would make them lose the vote?"

But on a holiday, what was there to do? Stuff themselves full of free hot dogs in the park, was what. Games, horsing around, and a good time was in order. And then came the fireworks, one of the best shows ever, right over the river. Emily sat with her head against Grandma and hoped it would not be the last time.

They were getting ready for bed when Ethan sat bolt upright, tossing off the covers.

"What?" Emily said, wandering in with her toothbrush.

"I heard a motor."

Emily's eyes went wide. "Brock!" she said.

They ran to the kitchen window and looked out toward the dock. No boat. He had gone out after all.

"I want to be awake when he comes in," Emily said.

They were. He had only been gone a little over two hours. Ethan nodded off a couple times, but Emily shook him awake and put a finger to her lips. Outside their bedroom door, the floor creaked. Then creaked again.

Ethan nodded. Brock headed downstairs to his room.

They threw on clothes and sneaked out the back door. They ran to the dock.

The boat sat in the same place as earlier, but there was fresh water on the bows. Emily climbed aboard and checked her tape.

"Wait... that's weird," she said.

Ethan leaned over the gunwale. "What?" he said. "The tape's gone?"

"No, it's still there, but it's not where it should be. Someone moved it."

"Why?"

"Because it's six inches above the waterline now. If the boat were loaded, it should be below the water."

Ethan shook his head. "No, don't you see? It's telling us just what it should. It's telling us that the boat was loaded when you put the tape *on*."

Emily slapped her forehead. "Oh, I thought I was so clever. He'd go out, and he'd come back, and the boat would be loaded with something, and we could find it and see what he's doing. But the time to search was last time. He's unloaded whatever he had."

"We're running out of time," Ethan said. "Maybe we can kill two birds with one stone."

"How so?" Emily sniffed. There was a campfire nearby, and the air was tinged with woodsmoke.

"Well, we want to know what's up with the chemical company, right? They have their headquarters just up the river. Maybe we can get Brock to take us out there, see what we can see."

"What, you think we're going to cruise by and there will be a big sign that says, 'We're scheming to take over Gnarled Oak and throw Patricia Tuttle out of her home?'"

"It would be nice. But you never know. People usually only guard themselves in one direction. All their security might be facing the road, not the river. And it will give us a chance to see how Brock handles the boat. Maybe he'll let something slip."

Emily clambered off the boat and headed back toward the house, slapping at a mosquito. "I have nothing better, so why not? Oh, dang!" she said, running back toward the boat.

"What?" Ethan said, spinning in place.

"Forgot my tape!" she said. "I'd hate for Brock to find out we were snooping."

Turn to page 62.

The email was titled simply enough. It just said "Thoughts?" But the body of the email was electrifying.

It was a forwarded email from an executive at Jaxton Chemical to a city council member who used to work at the chemical company. It outlined the terms under which the chemical company was prepared to make a sizable donation to the city, in return for the city changing the zoning of the property to allow the chemical factory to be built. It named names. It gave numbers. It mentioned Patricia Tuttle, and the little pink house.

It was, in short, a smoking gun. In broad strokes, the plan from the chemical company was to offer the city as a donation, to one fund or another, the exact sum of money the city would have to lay out to buy the properties from the people who lived along the river. This donation would be made at the point that the city rezoned the properties to allow the chemical company to be built instead of houses. The number was huge, well into the millions.

It also mentioned another source of funds that Ethan hadn't considered before.

"Anyone know what a block grant is?" he said.

Shannon said, "Doesn't sound familiar."

Uncle Brock yelled from the other room, "And no, I'm not having any success in here, either."

Ethan pulled the thumb drive out of his pocket and stuck it into the machine. He downloaded the e-mail, along with its chain and attachments. It was as close to an outright bribe as he could imagine. He could only imagine what his Uncle Ben would do with this information, or how that would play in the city newspaper, or what people would say when they saw the actual email. This was more than just stopping the referendum. It would bring down the entire city government.

"I've got everything we need right here," Ethan said. "We can pack up and go."

Shannon's voice rose with interest, "Are you sure? What I've got here is pretty good stuff. It's receipts for payments from Jaxton Chemical to the city for buying up property on the north side of town."

"Wait, the *north* side of town?" Ethan said.

Shannon slammed the filing cabinet door shut. "I don't know," she said, "there was too much for me to read, but I took photographs of all of it. We can read it at our leisure. Then we can decide what to do with it."

"Works for me," Ethan said. "I'm closing down. I don't want to stay here another moment."

A thunderous crash rolled out from the mayor's office. Ethan jumped up from his chair, his eyes wide, staring at Shannon, whose face was drawn and staring. They dashed into the mayor's office and found Uncle Brock, lying on his back, with the mayor's chair lying on top of him, and one of the mayor's framed photographs surrounded by shards of glass on the floor next to him. Uncle Brock groaned.

"What happened?" Ethan said.

"I tripped," Uncle Brock said. "Help me up."

The chair was heavy, but worse, the wall into which Uncle Brock had fallen was the one that was shared with the police station behind them. "We have to get out of here right now," Ethan said. Together they hauled on the chair and managed to lever it back into its sitting position.

One of the wheels was missing from the bottom, and Shannon crawled underneath the desk on her hands and knees to try to find it. "I can't find the wheel," she said.

Uncle Brock groaned. "It's lying under my back," he said. The side of his head was scraped, but he wasn't bleeding very much. There was nothing they could do about the picture, though. The glass was everywhere, and the picture itself had been scarred by pieces of the frame.

They would just have to leave it and hope. But what was there to hope for? They would know someone had been in the office. The moment somebody walked through the door, they were going to see the glass and know that someone had broken in.

When the information came out, there wouldn't be any way for them to hide what they had done. "All this information is useless if people know it was us," Ethan said.

"We'll have to send it somewhere anonymously," Shannon said, tugging on Uncle Brock's arm. "Let's get him up and get out of here."

And then the lights turned on.

"Hold it right there!" the voice said. It was accompanied by the unmistakable click of a weapon being cocked. Ethan's back was to the door, and he couldn't see who it was, but it didn't make any difference, really. He raised his hands, and in the process dropped Uncle Brock back on the floor and onto the broken chair caster. He cried out and grabbed his back.

After that, it was mostly chaos. Shannon tried to bolt out the door, but the policeman grabbed her by the waist, and threw her back into the office. Shannon flew back and crashed into Ethan, who barely managed to keep his feet while clutching at her to keep her from falling. She gasped and struggled as if he was the one who had caught her breaking in.

"Lie down on the floor! Face down!" the policeman said.

Ethan hesitated, all his worst nightmares coming true.

Then the policeman was screaming, pointing a gun at him, and ordering everyone to lie down on the floor right now.

Brock kept trying to get up, to try to move the caster from under his back, but this just made the policeman more angry, and he kicked him in the side. Brock cried out again, and clutched at his back.

"Don't hurt him," Ethan said. "He's just trying to get something from underneath his back."

"Don't touch anything, and don't move," the policeman kept screaming.

Finally, Brock just lay there whimpering. Ethan lay face down on one side of the desk, half his arm resting on Shannon's back.

It was white hot, like the flame of an oven.

Turn to page 24.

Morning chores completed, the twins were fed a lunch so large it could have been enough for six. But Grandma kept saying, "Any more?" and holding out, well, more. It would have been rude to refuse. They were finally released to go where they would, as long as they were back for dinner.

Seated on their bikes, the twins sat at the end of the driveway, looking right and left, up and down the road. "So what do we do?" Emily said. "You want to do some research. But how do we do that?"

"The first place to go when you want to do research is the library," Ethan said. "That's in the center of town, not too far from other places we might want to visit."

"Like city hall. I like that idea."

"Race you there," Ethan said, his pedals already in motion. It had been a long time since the twins had raced each other on their bicycles, but some things you never forget how to do. They flew down the street. Emily loved this old bicycle, with its long, 1970s handlebars, fluttering plastic streamers behind her as she blazed along. It made her feel like a little kid again. And although a lot of people still treated her like a little kid, which somewhat annoyed her, the truth was, every day she felt like she was entering a new world, where the rules weren't as easy to follow, because no one knew what they were.

When she and her brother had been nine or ten years old, when they had begun having the first of their adventures, there was only so much trouble they could get into. Even the taco truck fiasco had been more of a lark than anything else. This seemed to be another level. It was Grandma's house, for crying out loud. An adult thing.

Still, Emily knew she had to do something. Whatever was going on here, and she was sure she didn't understand all of it, it felt wrong to her. And hey, hadn't she and her brother come through some pretty tough scrapes in the past? Who better to start mucking around in the dark water of the town than two kids on summer holiday?

Ahead of her, Ethan whizzed around a corner, his back tire sliding momentarily on some loose gravel. Emily shot ahead. There it was, just down the street— an old brick building, built way back in the 1960s, that housed the library. Libraries had information. Information was good.

Emily thought that it might be worthwhile to go to city hall as well. There would surely be people there who would be able to give them information about what was going on with the town and with the Jaxton Chemical corporation and what they were attempting to do.

Ethan caught up. "Do you think we should go to the library first?"

Emily shrugged. "I don't know. I wonder if we might get more information from city hall than we get out of the library. I also think we might be able to have a better idea of what it is we are researching if we talk to some people at city hall first."

If you think they should go to city hall, turn to page 36.

If you think they should go to the library, turn to page 17.

Ethan hopped on his bike and raced toward the library.

It was Saturday and he had no idea how long the library would be open.

The likelihood was that it would close sometime in the middle of the afternoon, as he couldn't imagine a lot of people wanted to be in the library doing historical research on a Saturday night.

But all he could do was his best. For a Saturday, especially a holiday Saturday, the streets were fairly empty. That had something to do with the fact that no one lived in these houses anymore, of course, but Ethan would have expected to see more people—kids outside riding bikes, things like that. Still too light to be firing off fireworks, so that activity wasn't happening, although the remnants of the fireworks from the last couple of days were everywhere: burnt spots on the pavement, spent firework shells in the gutter, sparklers sticking out of trash cans. He got a little smile thinking about it. The fireworks show had been pretty cool, after all.

The library was practically empty, or at least the parking lot made it look like it was, when he arrived. For a minute he thought the place would be closed, but when he reached the front door the sign on the window said they still had a couple of hours before closing time.

He put his hand on the door handle and squared his shoulders before he pulled the door open. Part of him did not want Shannon to be working today. It was going to be an awkward conversation if she was. But part of him wanted to see her again, and he couldn't account for that. Shannon had done nothing except sneer at him and run him down ever since their first meeting. He tugged, and the door came open reluctantly.

The cool and quiet of the library rushed out thick enough that he felt like he could see it. Shannon was not at the front desk. That was good and bad.

But neither was anyone else, which meant she could still be in the building somewhere.

Off to the left of the reference desk was the bank of computers. One younger woman sat at a terminal, clacking away on the keys. Ethan selected the farthest monitor from her and wiggled the mouse. A login screen came up with the library's name in the username field. Underneath, the cursor blinked in a password entry block.

He tried a couple of things, just to see if they would work: password, ABC, 1 2 3. None of them worked. Shoot. He would have to get a password from the desk. He turned around to walk back to do that, and there was Shannon's red hair. Her back was to him. She hadn't seen him yet. For a crazy moment, he contemplated sprinting out of the library so he wouldn't have to say anything to her, but that was silly. He marched over to the desk, rapped twice on the wooden surface, and had to smile when, without turning around, Shannon reached back and held up a finger to tell him to wait.

"Hi," Ethan said, lamely.

Shannon still did not turn around, but moved her hand to give him a thumbs down.

Ethan laughed in spite of himself.

That seemed to be the appropriate thing to do, as Shannon turned around with a small smirk of her own.

"That's not very nice to do to someone who is trying to help you," he said.

"Oh, so you're trying to help me now?" Shannon said, but there was no heat in it. She didn't really want to start a fight, apparently. "So, when are we going to engage in the activity we discussed a little earlier," she said.

"We're not," Ethan said. "You know as well as I do it's a stupid idea. First of all, there's the whole moral question about whether the ends justify the means. But even worse, we're both incompetent and we'll get caught. And then where will our cause be?"

"*You* might be incompetent, but I feel like it's something I should be able to handle pretty easily."

"Where you come from, maybe that's a skill you need. But for me, I'm out. At least, I'm out on that. Emily and I, however, had another idea."

Shannon sighed and closed the book she was reading, carefully marking her place with someone's lost library card. "And you're here to ask me if I want to help you?"

"Kind of," Ethan said. "I'm actually standing here at the moment, asking you to tell me what the password is so that I can log into the machine so that I can use the Internet."

"And what will you be searching for once you have said password?" she said. She laid a finger across her lips, as if thinking about whether his answer was good enough for her to actually cough up the password.

"I intend to look for times when one branch of a city's government blocked another branch of the city's government from doing something. Or, since that seems a little far-fetched even for me, when some other government, say the state of Pennsylvania, stepped in to stop the city, or some other city, from building something it desperately wanted to build. Alternatively," he said, looking at her face and seeing that she was anything but sold on this idea, "I'm looking for any time any government anywhere stopped anyone from build-ing something, and what the reason would be for them having done that."

Shannon's face spoke eloquently about whether she thought this idea was going to be successful. "Governments mostly build things. They don't stop other things from being built."

"So I understand, but that doesn't mean that it never happens. If it's ever happened, and I'm sure it has, then I need to know when and how, to see if that's something that we can use. And by the way, I'm leaving in a few days."

Shannon walked over to the gate of the reference desk and lifted the drawbridge counter. She sashayed through the hole created, and set the drawbridge down gently behind her. "You have two days," she said, "Since this one is nearly gone. Still, if you're not going to help me break into the city office, and your next comment is that you'll turn me in if I do, I suppose I'd better help you do the search correctly."

Shannon, as it turned out, didn't trust Ethan with the password. She typed it in herself, keeping a close eye over her shoulder to make sure Ethan wasn't watching. Not that he would have been able to decipher the password anyway from her flying fingers.

She whacked the key and the computer came to life. She moved over and Ethan sat down. Then she plopped into the chair next to him. She typed the password in there as well and opened a web browser on her screen. "So you're going to help me after all?" Ethan said.

"No, *you* are helping *me*," she said.

Ethan snorted. That was just like her.

His first search didn't turn up much information. It appeared that the governments in the local area had not done a great deal of obstructing the building of things. Rather, they had gone out of their way to encourage it. But in the state of Pennsylvania, he found more information, some of it very interesting.

"I've got something," Shannon said. She pointed at her screen. "Have you ever heard of a fish called a snail darter?"

Ethan laughed. "That sounds like something out of a Dr. Seuss book."

Shannon smiled. Ethan thought she didn't do that enough. "But it isn't. It's apparently a real thing. When they were getting ready to build a dam in the West, some environmental groups complained because it would destroy the habitat for this little fish. It's called a snail darter. It says it's the Environmental Protection Agency that stopped the dam from being built."

"That's a federal agency. I'm pretty sure we wouldn't be able to get their attention in time. Besides which, do you know about any endangered creatures that live along the bank of the river?"

"You mean other than your grandmother?" Shannon said.

Ethan scowled and shook his head, turning back to his computer. That one wasn't going to work. But it was something. Maybe there was something else here.

Something like this.

The Pennsylvania Agency for the Protection of Heritage had blocked several construction projects because they interfered with archaeological digs for Native American sites. "Maybe we could use this," Ethan said. He tapped the screen with his fingernail.

"Native artifacts?"

"This organization is really aggressive in protecting Native sites from being despoiled by greedy corporations or clueless, ham-fisted governments trying to build things on the top of these priceless sites. Apparently they can move pretty fast, too."

"Sure they're not open on Saturday, though," Shannon said. "It'll be at least Monday before we could even get a hold of somebody. I wonder if they can work fast enough to make it happen."

Ethan swiveled his chair to face Shannon. She kept her eyes locked on her screen, clicking through various menus, searching news sites. He had to admit, she was pretty fast. She'd probably done a lot of this kind of research, working here in the library.

"But think about it," Ethan said. "We don't actually have to make it work before the referendum. The referendum is just a vote. The city will not have bought the house yet. If there's a chance of a reprieve, we can stall a day or two. Maybe we can get these people involved before there's any actual building going on."

Shannon didn't look over at him, but she was thinking about it. "Okay," she said eventually, "That's probably true."

She sounded as if she were a little embarrassed for not having thought of it herself. "We could probably get the state to stop the city from building, especially if we could find some ancient artifacts on the site of your grandmother's property."

It was Ethan's turn to sound dubious. "I'm not confident we can do that. I mean, after all, she's been living in that house now for sixty years or so. I'm sure if there were any artifacts like that she would know about them.

This will have to be on one of the adjacent properties. Preferably one of the empty ones."

That earned a glance from Shannon. In exasperation, she turned all the way toward him. "OK, let's say for the sake of argument we would be able to pull something like this off. There are lots of properties over there, and most of them don't have people living in them. That would allow us to build something that we could 'discover.' So far, so good. One problem: why are we over in this yard in the first place?"

Ethan frowned. "We're playing around. We're cruising derelict properties because that's a fun thing for teenagers to do."

"We're vandals. Not a position of strength in presenting our findings," Shannon said.

"Have it your way," Ethan said, swiveling back toward his computer. "Seemed to me that you were talking about something a lot nastier than vandalism, last I saw you. All we need to do is buy time. We just need enough time to let some of these ideas we're kicking around work."

"After the referendum, how quickly can they buy your grandmother's property and start digging?"

Ethan shrugged. "I have no idea. But they can push through the condemnation of the property very quickly, from my understanding. Then, once the property is condemned, Grandma has to take their money. Once she takes it, they own the property, and then sure as you're born, they're going to find something to do with it. Down goes the house."

"Is that the only thing you care about?"

Ethan looked over at her and saw that she was still facing him, her hands pursed in her lap.

"It's not the *only* thing I care about. But it's the most important thing. At least to me." He glanced back over, and added with a sigh, "I can totally understand if that's not true for you."

In the glare of the computer screen, he could see her nod, as if glad that he understood something, and then she went back to doing research.

Ethan's article was interesting. It appeared that this Agency for the Preservation of Native Historical Sites (APNHS) had blocked a football stadium from being built in the Pittsburgh area. That was just a few dozen miles up the river. So they were active in this town, and active in the local area. Also, the idea that there were Native artifacts in the Pittsburgh area gave him some comfort and confidence that perhaps there would be some in this area as well.

A new problem reared its ugly head. What would he show these people? Undoubtedly, they would be experts. These would be people who knew what a genuine artifact looked like. They would be able to spot a phony pretty easily.

He was going to have to think fast and act even faster. The referendum was Tuesday and by the end of the week, he would be gone.

Frustrated at having what he thought was a really good idea mostly ignored, Ethan clicked to close the browser and stepped back from his chair. "I think this is an idea that has some real possibilities. I'm going to try it. Are you going to help me, or not?"

"Oh, now you're the one who needs help, and you want me to come along?" She clicked the mouse over and over, pointlessly. "Fine, I don't have anything better on the hook. So I'm in," she said. She also clicked her browser closed. She hit two buttons and behind Ethan he heard a machine warming up.

"As I see it," she said, "we have two things we need to do. We need to 'discover' the artifacts, which means we need to have artifacts to discover, and then we need to call the historical agency and ask them to come and take a look."

"The artifacts are kind of the problem," Ethan said. "I don't really think I will be able to manufacture Native American artifacts that will fool anyone at all in the next couple of days."

Shannon smiled widely. *There* was a look Ethan hadn't seen before, and it caught him off guard.

"There I can help you. At last, I can do something useful."

"You can? Do you have experience in forging Native American artifacts?"

"No, silly, I have a friend. He happens to be an expert in Native American archaeology. I guarantee you he not only knows where they are in this area, but he also has some that he would be perfectly happy to lend us. And if he wouldn't, he has other pieces I'm sure he'd be happy to *give* us."

Way better than forging, Ethan thought. But it wasn't enough to just have stuff. Wouldn't local artifacts, even real ones, have to be placed in such a way that it would fool an expert, someone who is used to looking at these kinds of sites and figuring out where the artifacts might be? If they got this wrong... "And is that fellow you know local? And possibly into something that is a little bit sketchy and possibly illegal?"

"I don't think he would go in for outright fraud," she said, "But it doesn't have to be straight fraud. It could be a mistake. It could be an accident. It could be almost anything." Her voice betrayed excitement. "You keep saying we don't have to pass a miracle here, right? All we have to do is get an authentic artifact, discover it, then we'll let the wheels of government do the rest. All we need, as you say, is a delay. All we need is time." She looked up into his face. Her eyes really were very blue.

"I have no better ideas," Ethan said. He smiled back at her, a genuine smile. His first in forever, it felt like. "Let's go meet this friend of yours."

"I'm not off work for almost an hour," she said.

"That's OK, " Ethan said. "I haven't anything to do right this moment anyway."

Shannon went around behind the reference desk again. "You're just going to wait for me, then?" she said. "I'm not sure this guy is even going to be home."

Ethan shrugged. "As I said, I don't have a lot going on right now. I might as well stay here. It's a library, right? You have books."

"We have books," Shannon said. "If you're very quiet, I might even be able to get some reading done." She scanned the rest of the library. "There doesn't really seem to be a lot of work I desperately need to do."

Ethan heard a couple of kids over in the juvenile section, and there was one fellow sitting in a comfy chair, reading a novel. Other than that, the place was empty.

"Or you can talk to me," Ethan said. He leaned on the reference desk to catch sight of the book that Shannon was reading. It was *The Paper Magician*.

"I haven't heard of that book," Ethan said.

"I'm not surprised," Shannon said. Ethan frowned. That was just like her. He was trying to be friendly, get to know her more, develop a relationship that might allow them to work well together, and all she did was resist. She was the hardest person to get to know, the hardest person to be friends with, that Ethan had ever met.

If you think Ethan should stay and talk to Shannon, turn to page 388.

If you think Ethan should keep to himself, go to page 298.

"I think I'll get a cookie, since that seems to be the thing to do," she said, managing a smile.

"Do as you like," Brock said. "I hope while you're here, we'll have a chance to talk a bit, get to know each other. It's been a long time."

Emily was already headed for the kitchen. She shouldered her way through her gabbing family and grabbed a cookie off the cooling rack on the kitchen table.

Ethan had one in each fist, with a bite out of each. "Maybe it's something in the air," he said, "But no one makes a cookie like Grandma."

Emily bit into hers. It was so chocolatey, there was hardly any cookie to hold the chips together.

"Did you see the neighborhood?" Emily said.

Ethan nodded. He swallowed his cookie, and picked up another. "I've never seen it so empty," he said.

"It's like half the neighborhood has disappeared." Emily sat heavily into a chair. "I think it's something to do with what Xavier told me at the restaurant," she said.

"Xavier?" Ethan said, pronouncing the X like he was clearing his throat.

"Not chh-avier," she said. "Ex-avier. Like the dude in the wheelchair that has the school for mutants."

Ethan stared. "Huh. OK."

"Anyway, he said there's a big chemical corporation, Jaxton Chemical, that's buying up all the houses around here."

"Wait, Jacks-ton, not Jackson?"

"That's what he told me."

Ethan shook his head, chuckling to himself. "Okay. This town does have some weirdness to its nomenclature, is all."

Emily grinned. "Remember when we learned about Jekyll Island? Is there a Hyde Island over a few miles?"

"Well, no matter what they call themselves, there's no way they're getting their hands on this place." Ethan took another bite of cookie. "Grandma always says she wants to die in this house. Unless they plan to kill her, and that's a little dark even for a chemical corporation, there's no way they're going to get her to give this place up."

"I'm not so sure," Emily said. "Sometimes these corporations can be awfully persuasive. You remember what happened with the road out to Surfdom Beach. Sometimes they don't play fair."

Ethan stopped chewing. "What do you mean they don't play fair?" he said. "They offer her money. She says no. End of story."

"That's what I told Xavier, as well," Emily said, "And that was when he stopped talking about it. But clearly there's something else going on here other than a market transaction."

Turn to page 242.

Uncle Brock's eyes turned on Emily. Truth be told, Brock scared her. It was something about the new way he sat, the way he carried himself. He'd always been as unable to sit still as a kitten with string. The jitteriness had been replaced by a kind of eerie stillness. Except for his leg that continued to bounce, bounce, bounce, bounce, the rest of him was entirely still. The old Uncle Brock could never have held still for so long.

Emily heard Ethan bang out the back door toward the river. She started after him.

"Just a second," Brock said. "You're named after Great-Grandma Emily Tuttle, I'm assuming."

"That's what mom tells me," Emily said.

Brock slowly rose from his chair. He was not a large man, and his head was barely taller than Emily's. But there was a kind of muscular intensity to him. Emily felt, somehow, that he was a dangerous person to be around. Then, without warning, his face broke into a huge smile.

"You know," he said, "I can remember Great-Grandma Emily. Not very well of course, she was getting very old by the time I came around, but I remember playing on her kitchen floor, running little matchbox cars back and forth as if her kitchen was a race track. She was one of the kindest, best people I ever knew. I wonder, now that I'm in a mental state to be able to appreciate you, if you'll turn out to be the same kind of person."

When he smiled, an amazing transformation came over his face. It was as if the sun broke through the clouds. It was like watching a firework explode. Inadvertently, almost against her will, Emily found herself smiling back.

"I'm pretty sure Ethan would say that I'm nothing like as nice as Great-Grandma Emily," Emily said.

"That's a brother talking," Brock said, but the smile remained on his face. "They love to tease us, don't they? But deep down, I think they would miss us desperately if we were gone."

Emily thought so, too. It was something of a shock to her to find that she and Uncle Brock thought alike about things. "I better get going," Emily said.

Brock waved his hand toward the back door. "I've done some work on the dock," he said. "You'll probably find that it's in a little better condition than it was the last time you were here. And there's a little motor skiff out there as well. Maybe we can go out in it sometime."

"Thanks a lot," Emily said, and she raced to join her brother.

Ethan looked back toward the house. What could be keeping Emily?

Then he saw her coming through the back door, a small smile playing on her face as she shaded her eyes against the going down of the sun.

"What took you so long?" he said.

"I was talking with Uncle Brock," she said.

"Uncle Brock? I'm sorry. That must have been pretty harsh."

"No, actually, it was kind of nice. He had some nice things to say," she said. "It really seems like he has turned his life around."

Ethan scoffed at this. "I'll believe that when I see the sun rise in the west."

"So you don't believe that people can change?" Emily said. She sat down at the end of the pier, and began to unlace her shoes.

Ethan sat down next to her. "I believe people can change," he said. "I also believe that they almost never do. He's been lurking around that house for a long time now. As far as we've heard he's never done anything of value and never amounted to much. I'm not sure why he would start now."

Ethan could see Emily was thinking about this for a second.

But then she said, "I'm not sure either. I just get the sense that he's made some changes, and those changes all seem to have led him somewhere better."

The river drifted lazily by. Every so often, a bird would swoop down from the trees at the edge of the water, snatch something from the surface, and head back to the trees with its catch. The river gurgled through the posts of the pier and murmured its way south. Emily unlaced her shoes and dunked her feet in the water up to the ankles. She couldn't be sure, but it appeared as if the river was a little clearer than it had been the last time they were here.

All in all, it was a pretty good beginning to their summer vacation. If it weren't for the question about whether Grandma would be able to keep her house, Emily thought she would be as content as she had ever been. And it was a good thing, too, because big decisions were coming.

Ethan and Emily went down to the end of the dock. Brock had definitely been at work.

Several places had new boards riveted on and all of the broken slats that had been there the year before had been replaced. That wasn't the only new thing.

At the end of the dock there were two metal cleats for tying up boats. This year a new boat sat, tied up, bobbing in the water.

It was much larger than the little rowboat they used to have. This one had a much more powerful engine and even a small cabin. It was about fifteen feet long, brown. It was not a sleek boat, but a capable river craft. Ethan ran his hand along the gunwale.

"Wow," he said. "This sure is sweet. "

"I'll say," Emily said, rubbing the bow of the ship. "It must be Uncle Brock's."

It lay on the upstream side, with plastic buoys to keep it from rubbing against the dock.

Ethan walked back to the stern of the boat. There was a little cabin in the front, and toward the rear, a captain's wheel.

But there were electronic gizmos there too, compasses, depth meters, and other things. "It's pretty well tricked out," he said. "I'd love to go for a ride in her. Maybe we can ask Uncle Brock to take us out this afternoon."

"I'm going to climb aboard," Emily said.

"I don't think we should do that," Ethan said. "You know what Uncle Brock is like when people mess around with his stuff."

"What he doesn't know won't hurt him."

Emily was already clambering aboard.

Ethan stood back a moment, imagining what it would be like to pull the sleek boat out into the river. From there, you could go anywhere.

A couple of extra tanks of fuel sat at the stern of the boat next to the engine.

There was also a small hatch there, something wide enough for a body to slither down into, but not much wider. It was cinched down with a simple lock, but also something more sturdy, a padlock latch with a thick and brand new padlock clasped to keep it closed. The lock might have been the only new thing on the boat.

"That's curious," he said.

Emily stood at the captain's wheel, swinging back and forth as if she were piloting the boat. "What?" she said.

"This lock. It's brand new. Everything else on the boat looks like it's been there for quite a while."

Emily turned and saw what he was talking about. She tramped back down the floorboards, reached down, and rattled the lock on its hasp. "Not coming off though, is it?"

About halfway along the length of the boat the cabin raised up, and there was a small door leading to the interior. The cabin couldn't have been very large, judging by its position, but it would have been big enough for someone to sleep in, if that were a necessity. The cabin also sported a brand new lock. "I think Uncle Brock must have just recently acquired the boat," Ethan said.

"Bought used," Emily said. "This thing has to be at least twenty years old, and he didn't have it the last time we were here. I wonder where he got the money. He's never really had much."

"Mom says he hasn't kept a job for more than a few weeks ever since she can remember," Ethan said, and drummed his fingers on the gunwale. "He's certainly been working for more than a few weeks now, if he could afford this thing. I mean even if it's used, and this thing has obviously been out here on the water for a while, it certainly cost thousands of dollars. No one's going to *give* you a boat like this, not one that's seaworthy."

Emily had gone back to the wheel. "So whatever he's doing pays pretty well," she said.

"I wonder if what he's doing even has something to do with the river," Ethan said.

"Maybe he's carrying things out on the river. Or, maybe it's fishing or something like that."

"Do you see a lot of fishing gear on board?" Ethan said. "I mean, look at the deck. There's no stains or anything. No, whatever he's doing, he's not a fisherman. If you remember he never liked to go out fishing with us on the river anyway. Dad always had to take us."

Ethan looked back up toward the house. It had lost a couple of shingles off the back. It seemed as if the house were struggling against forces too large for it.

Everything in their neighborhood seemed to be in a state of decay.

Except this particular boat. It was as if the boat were going upstream against the tide of circumstance. It just didn't fit. "We should watch and see what Uncle Brock does with this boat. We should see when he takes it out, and when he comes back."

Emily climbed back onto the dock. "Hey," she said. "We could stow away." She pointed at the small door to the cabin. "Getting inside there, we could hide and then when he takes the boat out we could see what he does with it."

"Or we could just ask him," Ethan said. "It's not like he doesn't speak English."

"Yeah," Emily said, jogging toward the house. "But where's the fun in that?"

"This isn't what we're here for," Ethan said. "It's not important why Brock is plying the river. What's important is Grandma's house, like Dad was talking about in the car. We should be exploring that instead."

But that night was for a big dinner and some of Grandma's peach pie, and the next day began bright and early with chores.

And what chores!

Although Grandma's house looked pretty well taken care of, there were a hundred little things that needed doing—scraping paint, cleaning baseboards and ceiling molding, weeding the garden—and it wasn't long before Emily's enthusiasm for the "vacation" started to wilt a little.

She wiped sweat from her brow and chipped some more paint off one of the posts on the porch. "I thought there would be more rope swing than paint flecks on this trip," she said.

"You said it," Ethan said, pounding in a loose nail.

"You two look like you could use a break," said a voice behind them. Uncle Brock stood there with a pair of tall lemonades in his hand.

"Oh, wow. Lemonade!" Emily said, and rose stiffly to take one from her uncle. "Thanks!"

"I know the chores never seem to end around here, but we're all lucky to get to do them for this old place. If certain people had their way, this house wouldn't even be here any more."

Ethan took the other lemonade and drained half of it. "What's the story with that?"

Uncle Brock took off his cap and rubbed his head. "That depends on who you ask. If you ask the city, it's blighted properties along the road here, making the town look bad. There's a referendum coming up on Tuesday, a vote on whether the town can take over the rest of the block. They want to buy everyone out and sell the land."

"Sell to whom?" Emily said.

"That's party number two in our little play. Jaxton Chemical has made it no secret they'll buy any property they can along this river. They're talking—unofficially, of course—about building a factory here."

"I heard that from Xavier at Thusnelda's," Emily said. "That would make this referendum pretty important to them, I bet."

"Who's the other player?" Ethan said.

"Ah," Uncle Brock said. "That's a secret." He sketched a bow, like a butler, and went back into the house.

Ethan dropped his voice. "A secret, huh? Well, I have a hunch I know."

"Doesn't matter," Emily said. "The big players are the ones we should care about. Maybe we can push the scales back in our favor by doing some snooping."

Ethan drained the last of his lemonade. "Not today, though. We still have to tame the jungle in the backyard, and then if I don't get a swing on the rope I'm going to dry into dust and blow away."

"Tomorrow, then," Emily said.

If you think they should spy on Brock, turn to page 405.

If you think they should concentrate on saving the house, turn to page 167.

Ethan thought about Shannon's question for a long time back at Grandma's house, and finally decided he and Emily had to talk about it.

Ethan said, "We can't give up. Grandma's house means too much to us."

"I'm with you," Emily said. "I just don't know what else we can do. We've really done everything that I can think of. We've put out flyers, we've tried to call Uncle Ben, we went around the park and tried to get people to register to vote and to come and vote against the referendum, but I don't think those things are going to work."

"There are a couple of other things we can still try."

Emily sat back in the chair and propped her feet up on the coffee table. "I don't see what."

"Well," Ethan said, "Shannon and I were talking. She doesn't want to lose this thing any more than we do, maybe even less. After all, she lives here, and this town is really important to her."

"Granted," Emily said. "I don't see that that has anything to do with whether we still have options. It doesn't make any difference how bad you want something to happen. If it's out of your control, it's out of your control."

"What do you think it would take for us to stop this from happening?" Ethan said.

Emily pursed her lips and blew out a breath. "I think it would take a miracle. It would take, I don't know, divine intervention, or catching the mayor or half the city council doing something totally illegal. Even then, I'm not quite sure how we would get notice to everybody in town in time to stop the referendum from happening. I mean, it's only a couple of days away. I suppose there's always the newspaper. The local paper usually comes out once a week, but I guess they could print a special edition, maybe get it out in time on Monday night to get it to everybody in time for the vote on Tuesday. It's going to be close, anything we could do to push it in that direction might work."

Ethan stood up and began to pace back and forth across the room. "That's what we were thinking," he said. "It would take something miraculous, some real clear evidence that what the city council was doing was wrong, that they were being bribed or something."

"But are they?" Emily said. "We hate them, and what they're doing is obviously wrong, but do we know that it's actually illegal?"

"No, we don't," Ethan said. "But I *think* they are doing something illegal. And Shannon thinks they are, too. So we're going to try to prove it."

Emily laughed, but not as if it was funny. "What, you think you're going to just go talk to the city councilman, and they're going to say, 'Oh yes, We're doing all kinds of illegal things. Look at all this money the chemical company is funneling into our pockets.'" She stared at Ethan as if he had lost his mind.

But Ethan was unruffled. A slow smile crept across his face. "No, I don't think they're going to voluntarily give us that information. But I think if that information exists, there will be records of it. There will be minutes, things the city council has kept in order to make sure that the chemical company comes through with their part of the deal."

"OK, even allowing for the sake of argument that these documents might exist, it's not like they're just lying around. Do you expect them to mail them to us or something?"

"Of course not," Ethan said. "They would never be so considerate. We're going to have to go and get them."

"Get them from where?" Emily said. She sat up and leaned her arms on her knees, staring at Ethan as if trying to bore a hole in his face. "You have something up your sleeve," she said. "I just wish you'd come right out and tell me what it was."

"We're going to break into city hall."

Emily leaped to her feet. "You're going to what?"

"Now, I know what you're thinking," Ethan said, holding his hands out in front of him, asking Emily to hang on a minute until he finished. "I know it sounds crazy, and I know there'll probably be security there. I know the officers won't really be inviting us to break in and get stuff, but think about it for a minute, what can we possibly do other than what we have done? We break in there and find that they haven't done anything wrong, or that they've covered their tracks too well? We leave, and that's it. We just do the best we can on election day and not worry about it. But what if something illegal really is going on? Wouldn't it be wrong to allow them to get away with it?"

"Are you sure you really want to try turning two wrongs into a right?" Emily said. She stood up, facing off with Ethan a few feet away. "This is a pretty big decision," she said. "You better be sure you know why you're making it."

Ethan met her eyes with a set jaw and a solemn face. "I have thought about it. I thought about it all night. I'm sure I want to do this."

"Wow," Emily said. She looked for some place to sit down, finally choosing a chair in Grandma's front room, surrounded by the family photos.

"Look around you," Ethan said. "If we don't do something, this will all be gone. You *know* that's wrong. We promised each other that we wouldn't let that happen. I intend to keep that promise."

Emily took a good long look at the photos before she blew out a breath and nodded. "If we're going to do this—and I'm not saying it's a good idea to, or even that there's any chance we're going to be successful—we're going to need some help. Personally, I've never broken into anything before."

Ethan waved his finger in Emily's direction. "That's not quite true," he said. "Remember when Mom made those fantastic orange drop cookies? You know, the ones with the frosting?"

Emily looked wary. "Yeah. What about them?"

"You're not seriously going to tell me that you didn't break into the freezer and steal a bunch of those before mom could take them to the funeral, are you?"

Emily burst out laughing. "I totally forgot about that. That isn't at all the same sort of thing."

"Perhaps not legally, but morally, you can't tell me that breaking into the freezer to steal mom's cookies and breaking into city hall to steal secret information to save Grandma's house is terribly different. To me, it feels like almost the same thing."

"To you, it might feel the same, but to me, it feels quite different. Breaking into the freezer was a lark. Breaking into city hall is five to life. And that kind of breaking and entering I've never done." Emily flopped back down in her chair. "Still, how hard can it be? You pick up a rock. You heave it through the glass door. It smashes, and in you go. "

Ethan snorted and stared at her. "You can't seriously be suggesting that. The idea is not to do something loud enough that it would raise the entire neighborhood."

"OK, what's your idea? You're going to become an expert with lock picks in next fifteen minutes?"

Ethan shook his head. "Not likely," he said. "There just has to be some way to do it. I think it's my job to figure out what it is."

Footsteps sounded in the kitchen, and a scruffy head peered around the corner. "Did somebody mention lockpicks?" Uncle Brock said. "It's a subject I'm quite interested in, actually."

The corners of Ethan's mouth turned up a little. "You have experience with lockpicks?"

"Not terribly recent experience, but in the past, yes. Actually, at one point, I was quite good with them."

"When was that?" Emily said.

"After I got out of jail the first time. I met a guy there. He had certain skills. We became friends, shared meals, that sort of thing. He was a nice guy. He just had a really hard time keeping his hands to himself. It seemed like a useful skill, since I seemed to always have a need for things that were on the other side of locked doors, or was getting locked into things myself. So when we would get together afterward, you know just for a drink or a meal or whatever, he would pull out his set of tools and show me a few things. It's just a matter of practice. He went away a while ago but when he did he left me his picks. Let's just say, they haven't been gathering dust."

Turn to page 305.

It was hard to believe what was back there.

Small houses—RVs, actually—a huge oval of them probably a quarter-mile long, stood like circled wagons. In the center was a big common area, at least fifty yards wide down the whole quarter mile. And it was packed with people.

At first, the glances that came their way were wary, guarded. But within five minutes after Zoltan had worked his way around the gathering, they were far more cordial. And fifteen minutes later, after word had gotten around that they were Patricia Tuttle's grand-children, they were practically family. It made Ethan feel a little bad to be the bearer of unpleasant news with regard to the golf course. But he considered: What did he actually know? What could he actually tell them about what was going to happen?

He didn't really know anything, if it came right down to it. He could of course embellish, but that seemed ungentlemanly after such a cordial welcome. The best he could say was that there was certainly something going on just across the road, and it didn't have anything to do with the subdivision. A mouthwa-tering barbecue smell came from an open pit, on which a number of beef and chicken kebabs had been laid. It seemed, from the cooler placed next to it, that these were always cooking.

One kebab would come off, be handed to a hungry child, and a new one would go on. A few minutes later, that one would come off, and the rotation continued. It was a fascinating and efficient system. Two older ladies, their hair starkly grey and tied back in buns, stood guard over this procedure, making sure that the kebabs kept up their steady rotation and that nobody who wanted one went away hungry.

Hiking had given him a sharp appetite, Ethan was only too glad to accept one of the kebabs from one of the ladies tending them. She smiled at him, a gap-tooth grin that showed several places where her teeth had fallen out, but the grin was welcoming and warm for all of that. Her eyes twinkled as she handed him the stick. The stick itself was some kind of wet bamboo with large, neatly cut hunks of meat, spaced by onions, garlic, and soft vegetables. The whole thing had been dunked in some kind of marinade, brown and spicy and delicious.

Ethan pulled a hunk of meat off and popped it in his mouth. It burned his fingers, but the juiciness of it spread throughout his whole mouth and ran down his throat. He couldn't remember having tasted anything quite so good. Emily saw the look on his face and grabbed a piece for herself.

She had roughly the same reaction. The woman cackled, watching them. She waved her hand at the apparatus over the fire, asking if they wanted another one.

Ethan felt a little weird about it and said no, and Emily thanked her for her generosity but said she would wait a little while before she had one. The woman didn't seem to understand the words they used, but the sense of it came right through. She smiled and nodded, as if to say "come on back any time, children."

Zoltan held court at one of the picnic tables farther back toward the house. Ethan and Emily traversed the playground, dodging children playing tag and some other kind of complicated playground game that seemed to require an enormous amount of screaming. Emily smiled, but Ethan wondered if his ear drums might burst before he got back to the old gentleman. He had propped his leg up on the bench and patiently waited for them to take a seat opposite him.

"Now," Zoltan said, snuffing his cigarette out on the table and tossing it into a bucket underneath, "What's this about a golf course?"

"The truth is," Ethan said, "we don't really know very much about it. All I can really tell you is that there were a couple of guys in Thusnelda's burger joint having a shake and discussing it. They seemed to know quite a bit about it and were even talking about moving equipment and moving dirt down toward the river, where they couldn't wait to get the course up and running so that they could start having lunch in the clubhouse. That's really all I heard."

Zoltan considered this, his slate eyes boring into Ethan's face, as if looking for any sign that he might not be on the square. Apparently satisfied, he blew out a breath and said, "They've been talking about doing something like this for a long time. We don't pay much attention, because this is kind of a sleepy little burg, and despite the big talk, nothing much happens. But the truth is I always wonder if this time might be the time they get their act together."

"It seems like from the equipment and all the digging going on across the road that this might be one of those times," Emily said. "Plus, we heard something from our parents about the city and some corporation trying to buy her land for a building project. They could just as easily do something with this part of town as well."

"You don't know if the homeowner has received any letters or anything from the city, do you?" Ethan said.

"Not as far as I know, and I get most of his mail."

"That doesn't make sense, then," Ethan said. "They would have to communicate with the homeowner if they wanted to use his land for something. That's basic property rights. When you own a property, you decide what happens to it."

"Do you know if he owns the parcel of land across the road?" Emily said.

"He does, meaning the landlord," the man said, heavily. "That means there is definitely something happening. He would surely not have sold to those ugly buzzards at city hall. Something else must be going on, and we better figure out what it is."

"You're talking about eminent domain," Ethan said.

Zoltan stared at him. "How do you know about that?"

"We had a chance to see it up close, when they built a freeway that bypassed La Playa, our favorite beach. If they condemned the property, or something like that, the city could just give the owner whatever the city decides is market value and take the property. Maybe that's what they did."

"That's what we need to find out," he said. "Time for me to make a call."

The twins made sure they each had another kebab, savoring the delicious marinated meat and vegetables as they gazed around the curious little courtyard.

In the end there wasn't much more to say. They had told the people all they knew. They shook hands with the old man, astonished by the strength of his grip. "Proud to meet any of Patricia Tuttle's people."

The twins were doted on by the old ladies guarding the kebab pit and shouted at by the children, asking them if they would come back one day and play tag. Emily said she would. Then, as if wandering out of a dream, they headed back up the grassy lane toward their bikes, which were untouched in the brush next to the main road.

Emily stood for a moment, gazing back the way they had come. "It's like something out of a fairy tale," she said. "I can hardly believe I didn't dream the whole thing."

"You didn't dream it, all right," Ethan said. "My ears are still ringing from that shotgun blast that blew part of that tree off."

They mounted their bikes, checked the traffic, and rode slowly back down Main Street, turning right to head toward Grandma's house. They kept a close look to their right as they did so, hearing the diesel construction equipment, the motors grumbling back in the brush, and an occasional shout from one of the workers.

"Whatever it is they're building in there," Ethan said, "they seem to be in an almighty hurry about it."

They headed west. The sun was full down on top of them at high noon. In front of them, the river sparkled and danced in the noonday sun.

"What do you want to bet the plans for whatever is going on in this construction zone are at city hall?" Ethan said.

"What do you want to bet that there's no one at city hall that will be happy to see a couple of teenagers come rolling up asking questions about it?" Emily said.

But Ethan was already checking back over his shoulder, as if getting ready to make a turn. Emily knew that look all too well, and flipped a u-turn on her bike as quickly as she could.

City hall lay just to the east of Main Street, behind another building that turned out to be the library. It occupied half of a long wide block, with a grassy sort of courtyard in between the library and the city hall building. The twins took a slow cruise around the block, surveying the grass and the property. City hall turned out to be a dual purpose building, with half of it being the city hall part, and the other half being the police department and what looked like a small court.

"Executive, legislative, and judicial, all in the same building. How convenient," Emily said.

"There's no way *that* could go wrong," Ethan said. The buildings themselves were not impressive—squat, single story, with red brick facades and recessed windows. In the ten-stall parking lot next to city hall, only two cars rested: one a beat up pickup truck and the other a fairly new Honda Accord. At the police station, a small car sat with its nose pointed toward the street, engine on and air conditioning going full blast.

"Our tax dollars at work," Emily said.

"Or at least Grandma's," Ethan said.

They rode clockwise around the block until they reached the southside, where there was a concrete ramp that led into the middle of the block, between the library and city hall. Next to the library, bolted to the concrete, was a bike rack, the sturdy metal kind, and the twins racked their bikes on it.

Emily said, pointing to the library, "We might find out something from newspaper clippings that will tell us what we're dealing with, before we go and start making trouble."

If you think they should go into the library, turn to page 17.

If you think they should take city hall, turn to page 36.

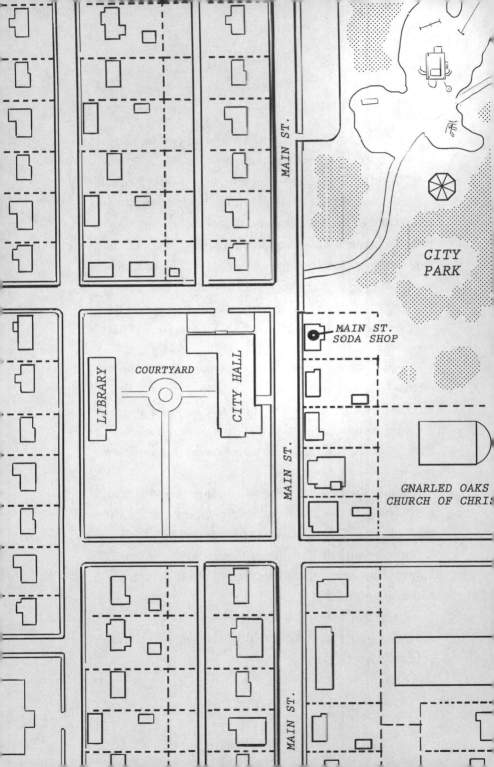

MAIN ST.

CITY
PARK

MAIN ST. SODA SHOP

LIBRARY

COURTYARD

CITY HALL

MAIN ST.

GNARLED OAKS
CHURCH OF CHRIS

MAIN ST.

Nobody had a car. Even Xavier, who said he had access to a car, did not have one now.

"I don't get to drive it just whenever I want," he said.

So it was double-riding on bikes back down the main road to the opposite end of town, then left and into the bushes. This time they took their bikes all the way to the house, and around behind it. They had to carry them part of the way, but they didn't lose a tire.

They had been told to come singing, so they did.

Standing in front of the house, Ethan said, "What's a song we all know?"

"I don't know. How about 'Summer Lovin' from Grease?" Xavier said.

Emily stared at him. "You can't be serious," she said.

In the end, they settled on "Row, Row, Row Your Boat." At least they all knew it and could sing it with a certain amount of volume.

When they rounded the house, they found lunch in full swing. Children were running about madly, and their old friend, Zoltán, was standing there with his shotgun resting diagonally across his chest, the very faintest hint of a smile on his face. "I did tell you to come singing, didn't I?"

Ethan flashed back a wide smile of his own. "You did. We wanted to make sure it was a song you could definitely hear."

"That's the only reason I let you get this far," he said. He let the shotgun slide to his side. "Come on," he said, waving. "Lunch is almost served. I'm assuming you're bringing me back news. If not, turn around right now and go away."

Emily laughed. "Hello again, to you, too."

This finally broke through his reserve and his laugh thundered through the campground like an earthquake. Children stopped running about playing tag and let their jaws fall open in amazement.

"I guess you don't laugh very much," Emily said.

All he did was shake his head. Lunch proved to be long strips of marinated steak, grilled over the open fire, with fresh vegetables obviously pulled from the nearby garden. It was one of the most delicious meals they had ever eaten. That they ate it in a line of tables twenty-five yards long, packed on both sides with children and adults jabbering away at the top of their lungs, some of them in a language the twins had never heard before, just made it all the more surreal and amazing.

When the meal was finished, the twins and their friends sat still while they were surrounded by interested parties.

"Now," Zoltán said, "Suppose you tell us why you're here."

The four friends looked at each other back and forth, until Ethan finally shrugged and began to relate the story of the golf course. "We think that the referendum paves the way for the golf course to get built. There's no question that they'll come after this piece of land as well, and given their reluctance to even talk with you about it so far, I wouldn't be surprised if they just rolled the bulldozers in here and knocked everything down."

"I'd like to see them try," Zoltán said, but his eyes gave away that he knew what would happen in such an event. Sooner or later, you couldn't fight them.

They would come and they would get what they came for, and no amount of gunfire was going to make any difference, except that he might end up in jail while they knocked the camp down. They could see that he knew this. The only hope was to find a way to stop this legally.

"What can we do?" their friend said.

Emily took up this part of the thread. "We know it's difficult, but we need to get everyone registered to vote. You can do it at the polls tomorrow, as the referendum vote is being taken. They should have materials there. Then all the votes you cast will count, and that might be enough to turn the tide."

"How many adults do you actually have here in the camp?" Ethan said.

Without hesitation, Zoltán said, "Forty-seven, but we have eighteen more who are away working, and we can get a hold of them. They might be willing to come back tomorrow just to cast a vote."

Shannon punched Ethan in the shoulder. "You told me seventy. That's only sixty-five."

Ethan turned to her. "Does that mean you won't be reassessing your opinion after all?"

"No, I've been reassessing it for quite a while now."

Ethan didn't know exactly how to take that, but there was no time to discuss it now.

Zoltán stood up and bellowed for attention. All the adults came and took their places on the long table. He told them what it was they needed to do, and although there was a great deal of moaning and complaining about it, it seemed that everyone understood the importance.

At the end he sat back down across from Ethan and nodded. "We will come. We will cast our votes, although for most of these people this will be the first time they have even been into the centre of town. I can only imagine what sort of reception we will get."

Xavier laughed. "I personally *cannot* imagine the reception you will get. That's why I'm going to make sure I'm there to see it for myself. This is going to be something I'm going to want to talk about for a long time."

Turn to page 186.

Instinctively, Emily put her hand on her brother's shoulder. "OK," she said, "I guess nothing bad can happen to us if we just come and listen."

Grayson smiled. It reminded Emily of Shark Week on the Discovery Channel. "That's great! Come on inside for a few minutes. It won't take long. There really isn't that much to tell." At the foot of the steps of city hall, he spent a moment chatting with another policeman, then turned back to the twins. "Come with me," he said.

He marched up the stairs, the twins trailing in his wake. He fished a key ring out of his pocket and unlocked the door, holding it wide for the twins to go ahead of him. They stepped into the dark and silent building. The city councilman flipped a switch, turning on the hallway lights. "Come along inside here," he said.

He selected a different key, unlocked the city council chambers, and stepped inside. The room was not large, Emily thought, not for a major government building. Though it was comfortable, with fifty or sixty chairs for the audience to sit in, and the city council's five seats arrayed in a semicircle in front. In between sat the lectern where people stood to speak when addressing the city council.

It was warm in there, stuffy even. Emily wiped her brow where she had begun to sweat a little bit.

The man noticed and said, "Sorry. We keep the air conditioning off in here to save money. We really are trying to be fiscally responsible for the city. As you may know, things haven't been too great here economically for the last little while."

"A lot of people say that's because of the chemical company hiring mostly people from out of town," Emily said. She didn't know if that was true, but it was a fair guess from what she'd heard that evening.

The man sighed ostentatiously. "I know a lot of people say that. I don't understand it. We've done a lot of things for this town." He corrected himself quickly. "I mean, Jaxton Chemical has done a lot of things for this town. I don't work for them anymore, but sometimes it just slips out."

Behind her back, Emily felt her brother squeeze her shoulder blade. He didn't really need to do that; she wasn't any more convinced by that explanation than he was.

The man indicated a couple of padded chairs toward the front. "Why don't we sit down?" Grayson said.

The overhead lights were harsh and left shadows on his face. Emily thought he looked like someone from an old-time melodrama. "Now, before we go any farther, why don't the two of you tell me who you are. I couldn't hear you very well outside."

"My name is Emily and this is my brother Ethan. We are the grandchildren of the woman in the pink house by the river."

The man smiled. "I know that house very well. I've always liked it. Whenever I drive through town, I like to go down the road where I can see it."

"Then why are you trying to bulldoze it?" Emily said.

The man looked shocked. "I'm not trying to bulldoze anything. What we're trying to do, though, is to acquire enough land to be able to build a new factory, and the best place to do that is next to the river. There are lots of technical reasons for that, most of them having to do with various chemical processes and the need for access to water. Regardless, there's no better place, and we've acquired a significant fraction of the land we need, I mean the company needs, already. There are only a couple of holdouts, and your grandmother is one of them."

He could see he wasn't making the right impression and tried a new tack. "I never introduced myself," he said. "My name is Dick Grayson."

"Seriously?" Ethan said, raising his eyebrows.

The man nodded. "Yeah, I get that a lot. And no, there isn't a Bruce Wayne in town, if you're wondering."

"We weren't," Emily said.

He shifted in his chair. "Anyway, it's a simple thing really. The town could use a major new construction project. We can provide that. I mean the company can provide that. That section of the town is an eyesore, and we will be able to build something there that will actually be quite stylish."

"Stylish for a chemical factory, or *stylish* stylish?" Emily said. Skepticism dripped out of every word.

"Well, it won't look like Apple's new computer campus, but it will be, I think, actually fairly attractive. Our chemical processes don't really use the same kinds of smoke-belching architecture as it used to. Most of our work is very clean. There will be a lot of solar panels, renewable energy, that kind of thing. And a lot of the people who work at this plant will be people from this town."

"So this town has a lot of chemical engineers, all of a sudden?" Ethan said. "I think when you make a sales pitch for this, you should probably tone that part down."

Grayson seemed to resent being interrupted. Ethan noticed that, but since he was going to keep on interrupting, he didn't care. Grayson went on.

"The land we need is almost all purchased, as I said. The zoning change is a simple one, and something that the town needs. The city council has the authority to make the change. It's been recommended by the planning commission. All we need now is a simple vote."

"What about the referendum?" Emily said, shifting forward in her chair like a leopard getting ready to pounce. "Aren't you forgetting the referendum? What if the people vote it down?"

"Well, that will be annoying. But first, they won't vote it down. And second, even if they do, the votes are there on the city council to pass the zoning change. We strongly prefer that the referendum pass. It's much more popular that way. But make no mistake, we can pass it ourselves if we need to."

Ethan's eyes grew wide. "Imagine my shock!"

"What if the people on the riverside still don't want to sell?" Emily said. "I'm pretty confident that my grandmother will say no, no matter what sum of money you offer her."

"Well, the property values are declining all the time because of the neighborhood blight, so the amount of money she's likely to get from the city council is also declining. Now would be the best time for her to sell."

"Best time for you," Ethan said, "but the best time for her to sell is never. I know how markets work. You need a willing buyer and a willing seller. In this case, you have a willing buyer, but not a willing seller."

"Not at the price we've offered so far," Grayson said.

"Not at any price. There will be no sum of money you can offer her that will get her to sell. And what will you do then?"

Grayson sighed. He looked as if he were genuinely distressed. "In that case, the city may have no choice but to condemn the properties and just seize them in the name of the city."

Emily was horror-struck. "You can do that? You can just condemn the property and take it away from someone?"

The man nodded. "The city has the power to take the property from anybody that it wishes. It's not something we want to do, you understand. In fact, we have gone long past the point when most other cities would have already done so. We're trying everything we can to make sure that everyone comes out of this a winner. We really aren't being bad guys about this."

"But why do you have to do it in the first place?" Emily said. She shifted forward another inch. "What is it about this particular project that means you have to do it? Why couldn't you just leave these people alone."

"Well," Grayson said, shifting a little in his seat and crossing his legs, "It's important to the town—"

Ethan cut him off. "You said that already."

Grayson scowled. "And it's important to the chemical company."

"You said that, too, although you didn't need to," Emily said.

"And it's a project that matters to enough people that we're going to go ahead with it. That's all."

"Even if the referendum shows you that there are a lot more people who are opposed to it?"

"You have to understand, there's a lot of money riding on this. Even people who think that it won't be good for the town, those people are wrong. We have to do the right thing for everyone, even if that means doing something that people think they're not going to like. We know better than they do what will improve the town. We can see things they can't. Sometimes, government has to force people to accept things that are in their best interests, because—"

"Because they're too stupid to know what is really the best thing for them," Emily finished. "I've heard that before. I didn't like it the first time."

Abruptly, Grayson stood up. "Well, thank you for taking the time to pretend to listen to me. It's clear you're not interested in actually understanding what I have to say, or what the position of the chemical company is in this matter. But I assure you, we're doing nothing illegal, and we intend to accomplish this project for the good of the city, no matter what the people of the city think."

Emily looked at Ethan. "Come on," she said. "We've taken up enough of this gentleman's valuable time."

"I agree," Ethan said. "It seems to me like he could use the remainder of the evening to figure out some better talking points."

The bike ride home that night was not a cheerful one.

Turn to page 167.

"And I can't?" Ethan said. Then he heard what that sounded like and shook his head. He rubbed his hands over his face and stood up. "You know what? I'm sorry. I apologize. I've been a grade-A jerk since I walked into this town, acting like I knew how to do things that I don't know how to do, and generally bossing everybody around or acting like they didn't have any good ideas. It's really stupid of me to do that, and I know better. I'm sorry. This is your town, and as bad as I'm feeling right now, you must be feeling a hundred times worse. So whatever you want to do, I'm ready to help you." He paused, feeling around in the dark for the next thing to say. "I don't know if you have any genius ideas, but if anybody does, it would be someone like you."

For a moment, Shannon didn't react to this. She just sat there picking at her corner of the float and doing nothing, as far as he could tell. Then he saw her shoulders were shaking. At first he thought she was crying, which was about the least possible thing he'd ever expect Shannon to do. But then he realized the sound he was hearing from her wasn't crying at all. She was laughing. Probably laughing at him.

"Well, if you're just going to laugh at me—" he began.

"No, no," she said. "Don't say anything else. That was either the most ridiculously insincere apology I ever heard, or you really mean it, but you just are terrible at being convincing when you make a speech. The truth is, I've been a jerk too, and I did it on purpose because you were so insufferably smug about everything. This *is* my town," she said, "and I always thought that it was going to go on in the way that made me always wanted to live here. But now it isn't, and I guess that means I'm going to have to change, too." She stood up and kicked at the pile of crepe at her feet. All of a sudden she whirled on him and said, "Did you mean what you said about helping me? I mean, whatever I want to do?"

Too late, Ethan saw the trap. "Whatever she wanted to do" left a lot open to the imagination, and he had little doubt that her imagination was terrific But now, with the offer hanging there, and her eyes glowing fire in the late afternoon, he thought he could be up for whatever. Maybe it would be a little risky. But what was a little risk?

So he nodded. "I meant it," he said.

She was wary. She shuffled away from the float, her back to city hall and her face to the sun. "Even if it was dangerous? How much do you want to win this thing?"

"Bad."

"Real bad?"

"As much as I've ever wanted anything," he said, and as he said it, it was true.

She decided to believe him, because she turned abruptly to face the city hall building. "There," she said.

"Everything we need is in there. All we have to do is go in and get it."

"During office hours? I don't think they're going to hand over incriminating documentation to us."

"Of course not during office hours. After hours. We're not going to ask. We're going to sneak in and take what we need," Shannon said. "Up for a little breaking and entering? For a good cause, of course."

If you think they should break in, turn to page 445.

If you think they shouldn't, turn to page 136.

"This is the strangest council of war I can imagine," Shannon said. Four of them sat in uneasy partnership around Grandma's kitchen table, half curious, half mistrustful.

"We use the soldiers we have," Ethan said.

"I don't think very many generals would be excited to have you as a part of the army," Shannon said. She was in the mistrustful half.

"That's not what I meant." Ethan said, and sat back and folded his arms

"What *did* you mean, then? You talk awfully big for somebody who's only been in town a couple of days."

Xavier leaned forward and slapped his hand on the table. "Hey! We aren't the enemy here. The enemies are out there," he said, pointing out the door toward the street and city hall. "We'll either work together, in which case we have a chance, or we will fight with each other, in which case we have no chance at all. "

"I'm not sure we have much of a chance anyway," Emily said, "But I'm not ready to give up. Are any of you?" The four looked at each other, but no one was willing to say that they thought it was hopeless. "OK, then stop arguing," Emily said. She flipped her notebook open and clicked her pen. "What is it we need to do?"

Xavier was the first to speak. "Isn't it obvious?"

"It's probably not obvious to *them*," Shannon said. The scowl never left her face.

Ethan rolled his eyes. "It's obvious to us what we want to do," he said. "We want to save our grandmother's house. That's our number one priority."

"That's pretty selfish of you," Shannon said.

"It's not the *only* thing we want to do. It's just our number one priority. I would think that would be the thing that was most obvious," Emily said.

Xavier kept making peace. "Yes, it's obvious that's the first thing you want to do. That's entirely understandable. And we want that too, because if you get it, that means we've gotten most of the things that we want as well."

"Which are?" Ethan said.

"We want our town back," Shannon said.

"That's lovely and charming," Ethan said, swiveling his chair so he could face her a little more, "But it's pretty vague. 'Taking our town back' could mean all kinds of things."

Shannon opened her mouth, ready to retort, but Xavier held his hand. "You know he's right," he said. "I'm not even sure what it is you mean when you say that. If I were the one saying it, I would know what it meant, but I don't know that I know what it means when you say it."

Shannon rounded on Xavier. "It means I want the chemical corporation's people off the city council. I want the people to have control over their town again.

I wanted the decisions to be made by the people that live here, the people that have always lived here, not the people who moved in just because they saw an opportunity to make some money."

"That makes much more sense," Xavier said. "I'll be interested to see how Ethan and Emily react to that, though."

Ethan reacted by snorting, and reached for a can of soda. He took a loud slurp out of it. "I don't think much of it," he said. "I think making money sounds awesome. I intend to do as much of it as I possibly can. I suspect most of the people at this table would."

"Not me," Shannon said, and pulled her baseball cap slightly lower over her face.

"You seriously don't want to make any money?" Ethan said.

"Money is the root of all evil," Shannon said.

"*Love* of money is the root of all evil," Ethan said. "That's not quite the same thing."

"Then what are you doing here? What is it that you would like to see happen? If you're all about the money, why aren't you on the side of the chemical corporation? Or, maybe you are," Shannon said, color coming into her cheeks.

Ethan started to respond angrily, but then realized that she might actually be asking a good question. "I'm not on the side of the chemical corporation, because they're not using the market to get the things that they want. They're using the government to force people to give them what they want, and they don't care if they crush individuals in the process. That one of those private individuals happens to be my grandmother is not terribly relevant."

"Oh, I suppose you'd be all angry about this if it was a complete stranger."

"As a matter of fact, yes. We've done this kind of thing before, and we don't always do it for people who are related to us. Injustice is injustice."

"The market makes injustice; it's the government that fixes it," Shannon said.

Emily said, quietly, "Like right now?"

Shannon turned to her as if she had never seen her before.

Emily leaned across the table, her eyes locked on Shannon's face. "Think about it," she said. "If the chemical corporation could just use the market to get what they wanted, don't you think they would have done that? It's not like they have a shortage of cash. But the market actually protects our grandmother. She doesn't want to sell. The chemical corporation can't force her to. The only way they can get the property from her is to use the government to make her do what they want."

Xavier frowned. "That makes a kind of sense," he said. "But isn't the chemical corporation making a business offer to your grandmother?"

"Yes, they are. But when that offer is rejected, what do they do? They go to the government. They buy up seats on the city council. They spend their money to get people to use the power of government to force the people on the riverfront to sell. That's not the market; that's government force. That's the thing we're opposed to."

Shannon scoffed and waved her hand as if this were all irrelevant. But on her face was a look they hadn't seen before. She was seriously considering what they were discussing. She was no dummy. That they already knew. The question was, would she listen? It appeared she was. At least, she was as long as she didn't have to hear it from Ethan.

"Well," Xavier said, "That leads us to what it is that *we* want, and whether our goals are incompatible. I know what you want to do, but what I want is transparency. I want to know what it is that's going on, and who it is that is pulling the strings. I want to have the information to be able to make good decisions. I don't mind the power of government. What I mind is people manipulating that power without the people affected being able to tell who they are."

Emily jotted down some notes on her pad. "So we want to save our grandmother's house. You want to know what it is that's going on in government in a way that will allow you to make better decisions," she said, pointing at Xavier. "And you," she said, pointing at Shannon, "want to take the government over yourself."

"I want to return the government to the people," Shannon said, correcting.

Emily scratched something out on her pad and wrote something new in its place. "CK, to return the government to the people. I don't know that all of our goals necessarily sync up. But it doesn't sound to me like they're mutually exclusive. I think all of us can get what we want, and a lot of the activities we would do to go about getting what we want would result in success for all of us. Does everyone see that?"

"We can stay here and argue about this for another couple of hours, or we can do something useful to try and turn this thing around," Ethan said.

"I'm not the one arguing," Shannon said. But she didn't say anything more.

Xavier took a moment and looked around the table. "We all want to win this thing. None of us wants to see this house get bulldozed, and all of us want to stop bad people from doing bad things. We don't have to like each other to work together."

Ethan muttered under his breath, "Darn good thing." It was quiet enough that only his sister could hear him.

"As I see it, we have a couple of options. The referendum is coming up four days after the Fourth of July. We have a number of Fourth of July activities for the town that we can use to get our message out. We have some volunteers, the people who were at the protest. By ourselves, it might not be enough to do the job, but we have other opportunities as well. I think you guys have some media you can bring into play."

"Our Uncle Ben is a media guy. We've worked with him on protests before," Emily said. "He can give us some good publicity. That might help."

Shannon blew out a long breath. "I'm not so sure," she said. "He may be really big on YouTube and stuff, but I don't know how much of this town is going to be focusing on that. I don't know how much attention his channel will be able to bring to the problem in such a short amount of time."

That was a good point, and the mood turned somber.

"Still," Ethan said, "it's better than nothing. I suspect this referendum is going to turn on a very few votes. Do we know how many votes were cast the last time there was this kind of referendum in the city?"

Everyone looked at Shannon. This was the kind of thing she could be expected to know. "The last time there was a referendum was six years ago. In that referendum, about eleven hundred people cast votes. And before you ask," she said, swiveling her eyes on Ethan, "That represents a little over twenty percent of the town."

"Twenty percent?" Ethan said. "So twenty percent of the town gets to make decisions for everyone else?"

"That's how it works," Shannon said.

She didn't sound happy about it, but she also didn't sound like she had an alternative.

"That doesn't frost your garters?" Ethan said. "Twenty percent of the people in town making decisions for everyone else?"

"It's even worse than that," Xavier said. "If twenty percent of the town comes out to vote, and the vote is close, you really have eleven percent, or just over ten percent of the town making the rules for everyone else. So a little less than ten percent of the town decides what the other ninety percent will do."

"That is how referendums work," Emily said. "I read about an alternative way that I liked a lot better. I don't know any town that uses it today, but it used to be that there was a thing called a constitutional majority."

Shannon shook her head. "I've never heard of that," she said.

"It's where you have to get a majority of all of the eligible people in a pool in order to be able to make a decision."

Xavier's mouth curled upward in a smile. "So, let me get this straight. If there are two thousand registered voters in a town, you have to get a thousand and one votes to pass a measure, is that right?"

Emily nodded.

Xavier laughed. "I can certainly see why no town would go for that. Heck, we can't get that many people to come out and vote when there's a contentious mayor's race. On a referendum, something like this, twenty percent seems like a pretty big turnout."

"If we had a constitutional majority provision," Shannon said, "Nothing would ever get done."

"Sometimes that's not a bad thing," Ethan said. He pitched his voice low, the way he did when he was explaining something that was important to get across. "Measures that can't get fifty percent of the population to come out and vote for them, are they really important enough that they should be enacted? Is it right that six hundred people will be able to decide the fate of everyone else in town? How much more thoughtful and beneficial would legislation be if you had to get four thousand people to vote for it or you couldn't do it? Anyway, cities don't adopt that provision. They want to be able to do things without having to rally that much support. But there are measures in some places that can get that sort of backing. And those are the kinds of things that the city should really be doing, the kinds that are important enough that more than half of the registered voters in the city are willing to vote in favor of it."

"Well, we don't have that to defend us this time," Xavier said. "It's going to be five or six hundred votes, maybe a little bit more this time, and that's what it will take to win."

"In that case, we need every vote we can get. Picking up some of the younger voters using YouTube and other media is probably not a bad idea."

"What we really need," Ethan said, "is some kind of scandal, a smoking gun, some way of incriminating the chemical company and making it so that the whole town would be opposed to it and not just the people who live in the affected zone." He cleared his throat a little as if he were apologizing, without saying so. "Shannon, you've been in the center of this for a long time. Is there anything like that in your files?"

"Nope. There isn't a lot of proof about any of this. A lot of people talk about the underhanded tactics of the chemical company and how they're buying the city council, but they're not stupid enough to leave that kind of evidence lying around."

"Maybe not lying around," Ethan said, "But I'll bet we can find it somewhere. Maybe we can find someone who can hack into the computers at city hall."

Xavier licked his lips and his eyes went back and forth from corner to corner as if he were checking to see if he were being overheard.

"That's kind of underhanded," he said, "But I won't tell you we haven't tried it. No one's been able to do it."

"I'll bet that information isn't even on a computer disk, anyway," Emily said.

From behind her a voice came floating out from the kitchen. "You're right about that," the voice said. "If any of that information exists, it's on paper. Someone is going to have to go and get it."

Strolling out of the kitchen came Uncle Brock. "Sorry," he said. "I couldn't help but overhear. I've lived in this town all my life. I can tell you that that information is written down somewhere, and probably at city hall. Either that, or it's out at the chemical company. Tough to choose between them. Neither one has what you would call tight security. Not out on the river, anyway."

"Hmmm. The chemical company." Shannon said. "What if we could catch them doing something wrong? I mean, something like dumping chemicals illegally into the river?" She looked around the table. Everyone nodded.

"That's exactly the kind of thing we need," Ethan said. "But again, I doubt that they're going to be doing it on some kind of a schedule that they'll be publishing in the local newspaper."

"They aren't dumping," Uncle Brock said. "I've been out there enough to know."

"Doing what?" Shannon said.

Brock just looked at her, his face blank.

"Okay," Ethan said. "That's an option, anyway. Unless it's too dangerous or complicated."

Uncle Brock rubbed his chin. "Not all that complicated," he said. "I have a boat, and I have some equipment. Just let me know."

The mood in the room brightened considerably. "We could also go door to door with flyers, or could we pass them out during the Fourth of July events tomorrow?" Xavier said.

"There's a thousand things we could do," Ethan said. "The only problem is, we're running out of time. And we don't have a whole lot of resources. We're going to have to concentrate our fire on one or two things at the most."

If you think they should make flyers to hand out, turn to page 110.

If you think they should investigate Jaxton Chemical by boat, turn to page 62.

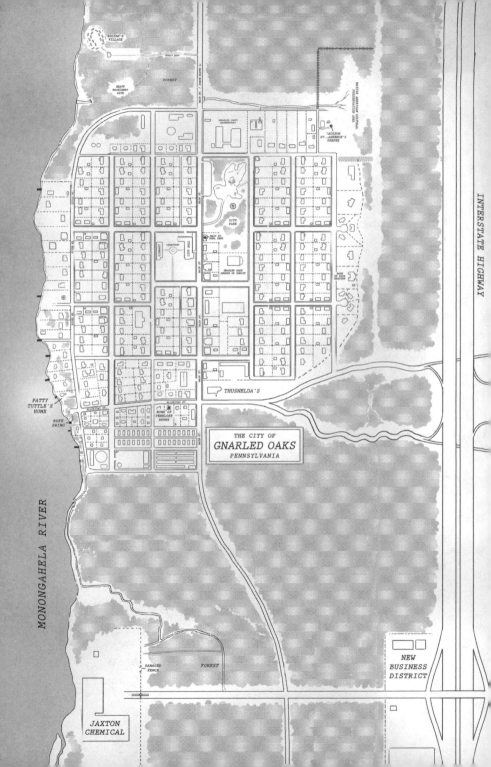

While Emily made what seemed like a thousand copies, Ethan went back to the computer and called up the map program again. He played around with some of the filters and overlays and found one that would superimpose the street lines and names on the satellite map. He hit print. Scrolling with the mouse, he zoomed out a little and selected that as well. Conveniently, Jaxton Chemical was labeled on the map, along with Thusnelda's Malt Shoppe and a couple other buildings. To the north of town, a forest thinned down to rolling hills as Main Street ran north through the hills and off the edge of the map. To the south, though, the forest was heavy right from the edge of town—only three blocks south of Grandma's, it appeared—down to a cleared patch of land where several buildings stood clustered on the riverbank. Jaxton headquarters. A road led from the southern edge of town out to what must be the main gate of the plant, a thick, new-looking road, wider than most in the area.

They must have got some special permission for that, Ethan thought. They'd need it, to ship material in and out. But why here? Why in Gnarled Oak? Cheap land? Surely there was cheap land anywhere. And why expand onto that particular part of the waterfront? If they could get permission to build the big, multi-build-ing factory there in the middle of the forest, nothing could stop them from expanding it however they liked. They didn't need the little pink house, or any of the other pieces of the town.

It made no sense.

He nearly left the map up on the monitor as he left, with the satellite image centered on Jaxton Chemical, but at the last moment, before he headed out to the printer to collect his maps, he wiped the page and put it back to the home page. For fun, he checked the browser and found that he could wipe the history as well. He did. Nothing made him feel more like he was engaged in a secret mission like covering his tracks. In the monitor's reflection, he could see a small smile on his face.

Emily met him at the door, a sheaf of paper in her hands. "I found some interesting stuff," she said. "You got the maps?"

"I got them," Ethan said, holding up his own sheaf. "I don't know how they're going to help us, and there are some things about them that don't make any sense."

"A lot of things don't make sense," Emily said. "But I'm pretty sure there are things going on in this town that aren't common knowledge." She took one of the maps from Ethan and scanned it. "There's Klickitat," she said. "It's only a few blocks away. You up for a ride?"

"Always," Ethan said. "But there's another kind of map I couldn't get from the computer that I think we need."

"What's that?" Emily said, pushing the front door open and stepping into the evening air.

"A zoning map."

"Zoning? You mean, like, the map the city puts together that says what goes where? What you can build on this lot, and what on that?"

"That's the one," Ethan said. "I'm sure they'll have one over in city hall. I want to see how the area is zoned. I'd also like to know who owns what around here."

"You're thinking of something," Emily said, folding the papers and stuffing them into the back pocket of her jeans. "What got you thinking about this?"

"Something I saw on the map—or rather, what the map shows. There are loose ends with this building project. It doesn't make any sense. There's no reason for the chemical company to build on that particular piece of land. You know, the one Grandma lives on? They have all the land they need. Or, I think they do. I can't tell because I don't know who owns the forest. I don't know who owns the other properties along the river, either. Grandma says the city bought them up, but if they did, and they're still zoned residential, there's nothing they can do about it. They have to keep those houses there—or some houses, anyway. They can't build the chemical plant unless the zoning changes."

"How hard is that to change?"

Ethan shrugged. "I have no idea. It's not real hard in our city—the city council can do whatever it wants. It's probably the same here. I'm not even sure we'd know about it if they did. They might have already done it."

"Grandma would know."

"Would she?"

"They'd have to notify her," Emily said, scowling and reaching for the papers in her back pocket. "There would be a public meeting."

Ethan saw the look in her eyes. "What? You remember something?"

"The paper has minutes from the city council meetings, but I have no way to know if they're complete. Not without talking to the editor."

"Let's go do that," Ethan said. "She's probably at home. Unless she left for the holiday."

"We need that zoning map, though," Emily said.

"So. We headed for the editor, or are we going to get the zoning maps and such like?" Ethan said.

"We could do both. We should do both."

"Which first, then?"

If you think they should head for the editor, turn to page 88.

If you think they should get the zoning maps, turn to page 148.

The twins watched as Xavier ran across the green toward the knot of people in front of city hall. It was hard to make out what anyone was saying, because the noise and confusion was so great, but Emily thought she heard someone say, "Referendum won't mean a thing. Only the same fifty people will go to the polls, and they'll just tell the rest of us what to do." Xavier reached the outskirts of the group of about sixty people, but couldn't push his way in.

A couple of them had their hands in fists, as if they were tired of talking with their mouths and wanted to do some talking in a different way. One of them lurched sideways and bumped into Xavier, knocking him to the ground. Without thinking, Emily leaped down off the porch of the library and went running across to help.

The grass was spongy under her feet, soft from recent rain. Xavier had fallen over on his backside and sat on the ground, looking up at the man who had knocked him over.

He was back on his feet before Emily could get there and was struggling to push his way into the group.

Emily grabbed his arm and tugged him back a pace. "What's going on here?" she said. "This is a lot of anger over a referendum."

Xavier wiped his sleeve across his mouth. He kept his eyes locked on the group in front of him and the two policemen trying to keep them back from city hall. The man on the steps of the government building hadn't moved, nor was his voice any more audible over the hubbub than it had been from farther away.

"If you don't want to get involved, this would be a good time to bug out of here," Xavier said.

"I do want to get involved," Emily said, "But I'm not going to go charging into a mob unless I know what the deal is. Tell me what this is all about, and don't talk to me about zoning. That might be why you all came here tonight, but it's not why everyone is so angry."

"The problem is," Xavier said, his arm swinging up and pointing, "that guy there used to work for Jaxton Chemical. A couple of years ago, he moved into town, bought a house on the outskirts of the East Side, back in the woods a little, and got himself elected to the City Council, mostly by buying the votes of the people in town with big parties and lots of campaign swag. Pretty much everyone looks at him as a symbol of why this thing is wrong, and also why we can't stop it."

Emily dragged Xavier's head down to where she could yell in his ear. "We know something about this kind of battle," she said. "We can help you. But we can't do it if people start a fight. You've got to find a way to get this under control."

Xavier shrugged her off his arm, spotted a hole in the crowd, and slithered inside. Emily started after him, but a heavy hand dropped onto her shoulder.

"Don't do this," Ethan said. "You know it won't end well. If you really want to help him, and heaven knows why you would, you've got to let him go and keep us out of it."

If you think they should get involved, turn to page 266.

If you think they shouldn't, turn to page 158.

"Sorry," Emily said, as if she really was, "but we have to go home now. We were supposed to be back long before now."

"That's disappointing," the man said. "I was really hoping we could have a chat about this."

"Don't worry," Ethan said. "You'll see us around, for sure. Maybe we could talk then."

The man—Xavier later told them his name was Grayson—stared at them very hard, as if trying to make a decision. "Maybe," he said, and threw a threatening glance at Xavier, who stood about ten feet away, arms folded across his chest and a devil-may-care grin on his face.

"Don't mind me," he said. "I'm just here for the cotton candy."

Without a word, Grayson let a scowl slip through the pleasant exterior, turned on his heel, and retreated to city hall.

"That went well," Ethan said.

Emily looked over to Xavier. "How about a shake to celebrate?"

"That could be arranged," Xavier said. "But I thought you were supposed to be home by now."

"We were," Ethan said. "But now that we're late, what's another hour? We can't get home on time anyway."

"This is excellent thinking." He checked his watch. "It's time for the library to close. Would you mind if we invited Shannon to come with us?"

"Not at all," Ethan said. "I think that's a splendid idea."

Fortuitously, Shannon chose that moment to exit the library, a bunch of keys in her hand. She turned and locked the door. Noticing the clot of people watching her, she stuffed the keys into a pocket of her jeans and sauntered over.

"Anyone arrested?" she said.

"Not this time, largely thanks to these two," Xavier said, beaming mostly at Emily.

"They buy the cops?"

Ethan said, "Nothing so crude. Anyway, we were headed to Thusnelda's for shakes to celebrate not being locked up. You want to come with us?"

Shannon looked dubious.

Xavier said, "If you come, maybe we could talk about that other thing, too. These guys are pretty handy when it comes to political stuff."

"That's not a political thing," she said, but shrugged and said, "Okay. I'll come. I don't see the good it will do, but I'll come along. At least I'll get a shake out of it."

"Don't let Shannon fool you," Xavier said, heading out across the lawn. "She's one of the five that have conquered El Diablo. She doesn't brag about it, but her name is in the Hall of Insanity." He tossed a thumb at

Ethan. "Ethan tried it earlier, but he couldn't quite get it down."

Shannon looked more closely at him. "You actually tried that thing?"

"You actually *finished* it?"

She nodded, but the look on her face was telling. "I did it for the t-shirt. But it wasn't worth it. Not that day or for two days afterward."

"I told you when you came in: the Diablo is not food," Xavier said. "We going or not?"

Turn to page 340.

The Author

Connor Boyack is founder and president of Libertas Institute, a free market think tank in Utah. In that capacity he has changed dozens of laws in favor of personal freedom and free markets, and has launched a variety of educational projects, including The Tuttle Twins children's book series. Connor is the author of over a dozen books.

A California native and Brigham Young University graduate, Connor currently resides in Lehi, Utah, with his wife and two children.

The Illustrator

Elijah Stanfield is owner of Red House Motion Imaging, a media production company in Washington.

A longtime student of Austrian economics, history, and the classical liberal philosophy, Elijah has dedicated much of his time and energy to promoting the ideas of free markets and individual liberty. Some of his more notable works include producing eight videos in support of Ron Paul's 2012 presidential candidacy. He currently resides in Richland, Washington, with his wife April and their six children.

NATIVE AMERICAN CULTURAL
PRESERVATION AREA

JACKSON
ST. LAWRENCE'S
TEEPEE

GNARLED OAKS ELEMENTARY

CITY PARK

MAIN ST.
SODA SHOP

MAIN ST. / STATE ROUTE 41

MAIN ST.

FOREST

GRASSY ROAD

CITY HALL

TOWN
CENTER

LIBRARY

ZOLTAN'S
VILLAGE

HEAVY
MACHINERY
SITE

RIVER RD.

RIVER RD.

LA RIVER

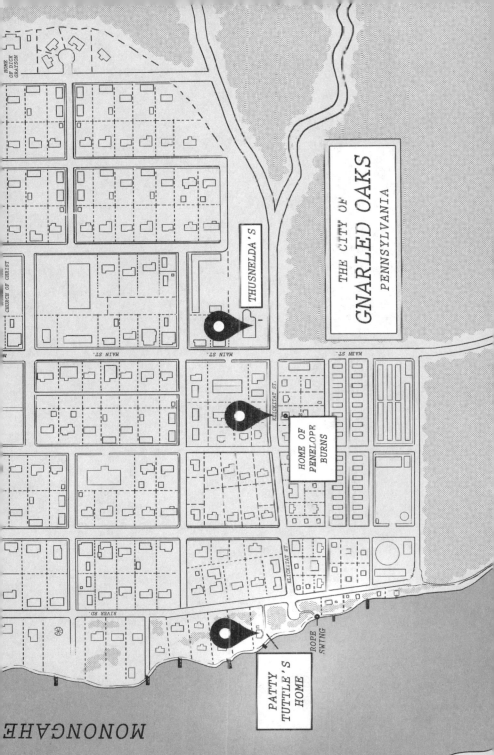